What Your Colleagues Are Saying . . .

This book is a gold mine for both longtime picture book lovers as well as those just beginning to build a classroom library! It is a comprehensive resource jam-packed with some of the best, most recent titles accompanied by learning strategies sure to make reading aloud a joyful experience for all. Her fresh ideas helped me see familiar, well-loved books in a new way as well as discover new titles to get the most out of a read aloud session! Her recommendations are thoughtful and purposefully chosen to engage, delight, and ignite a sense of wonder in even the most reluctant readers.

As you read, be sure to have your highlighter, sticky notes, and "books to read" list ready! I've already used many of these read aloud experiences with great success and know this will be an invaluable resource I will return to again and again to inspire readers! It is the perfect read aloud companion every teacher needs to invite students to read, think, and talk about books.

—Kristen Mullikin, First-Grade Reading Coach
Elk Grove, California

Maria Walther has become one of my most trusted resources for quality book recommendations for use in the classroom. Maria has a keen eye for identifying books that pair well together, matching books with effective lessons, and noticing details within books to enhance lesson plans. In this new book, Maria demonstrates how educators can squeeze every drop out of a read aloud experience, while providing an abundance of tips, resources, and ideas to maximize these sacred times in classrooms. Maria's book not only educates us on strategies for making the most of read aloud experiences; she also introduces us to a plethora of high-quality children's literature titles essential for classrooms.

—Dylan C. Teut, MEd, Executive Director,
Plum Creek Children's Literacy Festival

If you were even the slightest bit trepid about selecting and reading picture books . . . this book will thoroughly erase that feeling, forever! Get ready to be "ramped up" so you can spark a fire and get your students to love diving into picture books! Dr. Maria Walther has done most of the work for you in this easy-to-read guide to just about everything picture book–related! All you have to do is implement, implement, implement, and then read, read, read!

—Rhonda Jenkins, Library Media Center Director
Kendall Elementary School, Naperville, Illinois

This book is filled to the brim with practical and inspirational advice about the importance of read-alouds! Maria offers every teacher a way into this vital literacy practice. Her energy and love of children and books—as well as her imagination and creativity and love of learning—are evident on every page. From why to how—Maria has it covered. She writes from a place of knowing with a voice that's authentic and powerful. And Maria's book choices are brilliant and fresh (which, of course, caused me to buy way too many of her recommendations right away!). *The Ramped-Up Read Aloud* is an important book to energize your literacy classroom now and into the future.

—Ruth Culham, Author of *Teach Writing Well:*
How to Assess Writing, Invigorate
Instruction, and Rethink Revision

The Ramped-Up Read Aloud by Maria Walther is one of the most important books of our time! Read it and rededicate yourself to the importance of reading aloud to primary-grade children as well as to students in Grades 4 through 12. Reading aloud simultaneously nurtures positive relationships with students, builds community and vocabulary, and shows children how to think deeply about books. Equally important, read alouds expose children to beautiful, literary language, to visual literacy, and to stories that touch their hearts and feed their minds. Walther starts with 10 proven reasons for reading aloud, in case you or your principal doubts the learning power of this daily practice. Then, skillfully and passionately, Maria takes you through ways to develop successful read alouds, how to network to find new books, and how to use the ideas in this book to make the read aloud "a joyful celebration for all." If there's one book you read this year, put Walther's at the top of your list. It will change your life and your students' lives forever!

—Laura Robb, Author of *Read, Talk, Write*
and *Vocabulary Is Comprehension*

In the *Ramped-Up Read Aloud,* Maria Walther writes, "I've selected the texts in this book to help you nurture an intellectually and emotionally healthy classroom." What a beautiful rationale for book selection and read aloud support! The book lists that so richly texture this resource are organized to facilitate teaching points and showcase lesson supports designed to elevate student engagement through teacher think aloud, comprehension conversations, vocabulary building, and open-ended questions. This one is a must-have!

—Linda Hoyt, Author of *Make It Real:*
Strategies for Success With Informational Texts

Dr. Walther breaks down the methods and science of reading picture books aloud without losing sight of the fact that, at some level, a good read-aloud experience is just plain magic. This book makes me want to read to kids.

—Tom Lichtenheld, Author/Illustrator

THE RAMPED-UP
READ ALOUD

In memory of my parents, Bob and Kay Tausch, who filled my life with experiences that broadened my horizons and fostered my sense of wonder about our world.

THE RAMPED-UP
READ ALOUD

WHAT TO NOTICE AS YOU TURN THE PAGE

101 PICTURE BOOK CONVERSATIONS

MARIA WALTHER

CORWIN LITERACY

FOR INFORMATION:

Corwin

A SAGE Company

2455 Teller Road

Thousand Oaks, California 91320

(800) 233-9936

www.corwin.com

SAGE Publications Ltd.

1 Oliver's Yard

55 City Road

London EC1Y 1SP

United Kingdom

SAGE Publications India Pvt. Ltd.

B 1/I 1 Mohan Cooperative Industrial Area

Mathura Road, New Delhi 110 044

India

SAGE Publications Asia-Pacific Pte. Ltd.

3 Church Street

#10-04 Samsung Hub

Singapore 049483

Director and Publisher, Corwin Classroom: Lisa Luedeke

Acquisitions Editors: Wendy Murray and Tori Bachman

Editorial Development Manager: Julie Nemer

Senior Editorial Assistant: Sharon Wu

Production Editors: Amy Schroller and Laureen Gleason

Copy Editor: Ashley Horne

Typesetter: C&M Digitals (P) Ltd.

Proofreader: Rae-Ann Goodwin

Indexer: Karen Wiley

Cover and Interior Designer: Gail Buschman

Marketing Manager: Rebecca Eaton

Printed in the United States of America

ISBN 978-1-5063-8004-9

This book is printed on acid-free paper.

21 22 12

Contents

Chapter 1: Create a Joyful Classroom Community   27

Chapter 4: Converse About Comprehension— Informational and Narrative Nonfiction   133

Chapter 5: Build Foundational and Language Skills

Chapter 6: Inspire Writers   207

Acknowledgments

When you are writing a professional resource about reading aloud, you surround yourself with fellow readers who lovingly put books in your hands and engage in text-related conversations.

- Lenny, my husband, and first reader of many of the picture books that flow through and are strewn about our home. Thanks for helping me stay happy, fed, fit, and in clean clothes! Without your love and support, I couldn't balance the worlds of mother, wife, teacher, writer, presenter, and friend. Where do you want to go to celebrate?!

- Katie, our daughter, who has approached her teaching career with a wise sense of balance. I appreciate you pulling me away from my computer to enjoy experiences together.

- First graders at Gwendolyn Brooks Elementary School. Every time we read a book together, you gave me brilliant ideas to share with teachers. Like me, the readers of this book are so fortunate to learn from you.

- Nadia Ji, who spent a year in my classroom and lived this book with me every school day. Your insightful comments and skilled noticing captured the small moves I make when reading aloud to first graders along with many of the beautiful photographs that grace the pages of this book.

- Katherine Phillips-Toms, my longtime teaching teammate, and the rest of the Tuesday Night Team. I'm so fortunate to work with teachers who are willing to reinvent the wheel, read new books, and stand up for what is best for kids.

- Sarah Cooley, former first-grade teammate and newly minted L.M.C. director who has transformed our school library into a student-focused place of wonder.

- Karen Biggs-Tucker and Brian Tucker, my writing buddies, friends, and frequent Turf Room tablemates. Your expertise in the world of children's literature is unmatched.

- The following publishers who provided me with many of the titles that I included in this book: Albert Whitman, Candlewick, Chronicle, Disney/Hyperion, Macmillan Publishing Group, and Scholastic.

- Joanna Davis-Swing, my longtime editor. You've worked by my side through many huge projects. I am in awe of your ability to see patterns in a random collection of ideas and guide me to create an organized and cohesive resource for teachers.

- Wendy Murray for inviting me to write about my greatest passion—reading aloud to children.

- Lisa Luedeke, Tori Bachman, and the rest of the Corwin team for supporting me in creating the book of my dreams and getting it into the hands of teachers.

About the Author

Maria Walther is a first-grade teacher in Aurora, Illinois. She's been spending her days with children since 1986. Along with teaching young learners, Maria inspires other professionals by sharing her knowledge at local, state, and national conferences. The ideas she shares reflect her continued commitment to teaching, researching, writing, and collaborating with her colleagues. Maria earned a doctorate at Northern Illinois University in 1998 and was recently named The Outstanding Literacy Alumni by the Department of Literacy Education for professionalism, service, and career success. Maria has been a long-time advocate for reading aloud. She was honored as Illinois Reading Educator of the Year and earned the ICARE for Reading Award for fostering the love of reading in children. Before partnering with the Corwin team, she coauthored five professional books and the *Next Step Guided Reading Assessment* with Scholastic. Learn more about her books at mariawalther.com and follow her on Twitter @mariapwalther.

Photo by Nadia Ji.

*A read aloud should be a **joyful celebration for all**.*

For you, for your students, and indirectly, for the author and

illustrator who toiled over each word and every image

that lies on and between the covers of the book.

READ ALOUD = JOY!

I have to confess. I've had a career-long love affair with children's literature. Long before the dawn of Amazon and Twitter, I spent hours sitting on dusty bookstore floors turning pages. To discover the latest publications, I listened to experts at my local independent bookstore (Anderson's Bookshop in Naperville, Illinois), read professional journals, attended conferences, and researched my favorite authors. Slowly and thoughtfully, I added to my collection. After many years of teaching, I began writing professionally to help myself and teachers, like you, use the work of talented authors and illustrators to enhance literacy learning for students. All the while, I shared the books with my first graders—the most honest critics. As a result, my *library classroom*—where books fill every empty nook and cranny, surrounding the students with endless reading opportunities—is stocked with kid-appealing texts that illuminate just about any strategy, topic, or theme.

When you love books as much as I do, you're compelled to share them with anyone who will listen. Luckily, for me, I have a captive audience in my classroom every day. Over the years, I've observed the positive effects of read-aloud experiences on children's attitudes and achievement. In fact, the kids and I have kept a read-aloud tally for the past ten years. See the results of one year of tallies in the photo to the right.

So, before you read another word in this book, I want to make sure that you clearly understand my stance on the read-aloud experience. First and foremost, a read aloud should be a *joyful celebration for all.* For you, for your students, and indirectly, for the author and illustrator who toiled over each word and every image that lies on and between the covers of the book. In my mind, a picture book is a piece of art created to be cherished and applauded. Right from the start, I give you permission to simply READ ALOUD—no questions, no stopping, no after-reading conversations. When your students are having a bad day—read aloud. If you need a break from a tough topic in math—read aloud. When you just want to have fun with your kids—read aloud. Enjoy the book and the experience!

At the same time, I'm well aware of the demands of our overscheduled days. Certainly, it makes sense to take advantage of the instructional opportunities that a read aloud presents. In my classroom, I streamline instruction by intentionally selecting books to enhance student learning and expand their horizons beyond our classroom walls. Before reading that book, I consider student learning

Tally read-aloud experiences

(Text continues on page 5)

Read-Aloud Experiences at a Glance

Read-Aloud Experience Title

To assist you in making strategic book selections, I've categorized the picture books by strategy and learning targets. This is reflected in the title of each read-aloud experience and also appears on the Learning Target Chart located on the companion website. I recognize that, like your students, picture books don't fit neatly into categories. Because books are nuanced and readers bring their unique backgrounds and perspectives to the text, each of the picture books that I've featured in Chapters 1–6 could easily fit into multiple categories. Use your professional judgment as you select experiences. I'm sure that once you begin reading, your learners will notice and bring up topics that you (or I) never considered.

Book Title:
The 101 titles I've featured in this book are my most-recently-published selections based on over three decades of reading aloud and studying children's literature. That does not mean you will like them or that they will become your students' favorites. I give you permission to say to yourself, "Maria Walther likes this picture book, but my kids do not!" You can easily adapt the learning targets, questions, and extensions to accompany a different text that may better match your children's interests, their learning needs, and your learning targets.

About the Book:
The description provides a brief synopsis of the book along with any additional information that might be helpful when deciding whether or not this particular title will fit your learners' needs and preferences.

To find a book like this one, look for the following:

If you can't locate the featured book, look here to find my criteria for choosing this particular title and the characteristics I considered when searching for similar titles.

Learning Targets:
This section will help you zero in on what you are aiming for students to be able to know and do as a result of the experience.

Comprehension Conversation:

Before Reading

Notice the Cover Illustration: To save you time, I've researched a bit about the illustrators' media of choice and guided you in previewing the book with your students. The preview might include noticing artistic and design techniques used on the cover illustration and if applicable, the back cover, a discussion of the title, and other ideas to build excitement and invite wonder.

Set a Purpose: The purpose statement, written in a conversational manner, matches the learning targets and calls students' attention to what to notice and consider as you are reading aloud.

Bracketed Text

To differentiate conversation you will have with your students from teaching tips, I've placed the teaching tips in brackets.

During Reading

Because most picture books do not have page numbers, I used the first few words at the top of page to point you toward specific pages. You will notice that for each book, I have only included a handful of questions at critical key points in the book. *In my opinion, asking too many questions disrupts the flow of the story and distracts the listeners.* It is better to let the author and illustrator magic do the job!

Infer Characters' Feelings

Book Title: *A Dog Wearing Shoes* (Ko, 2015)

About the Book: Young Mini finds a lost dog wearing little yellow shoes and desperately wants to keep him. One day, while playing at the park, he runs away from her. When she finds him at the animal shelter, she empathizes with his owner and works to reunite the two. After the happy reunion, Mini adopts her own dog from the animal shelter.

To find a book like this one, look for the following:

- Illustrations that clearly reflect the characters' feelings
- Characters who have to make a difficult decision
- Stories about returning lost items

Comprehension Conversation:

Before Reading

Notice the Cover Illustration:
- What colors do you see on the cover? This author/illustrator chose to draw all the illustrations with a pencil and add these colors using the computer. I'm wondering if yellow and red are going to be the only colors in this book. . . . Hmmm.
- What does the back cover blurb say? Turn to a friend and make a prediction based on the blurb.

Set a Purpose: Put a finger on your nose if you have a pet at home. Whether you have a pet or not, let's think about how it would feel if you lost your pet. Turn and tell a neighbor. Keep those feelings in your mind as we read *A Dog Wearing Shoes* because thinking about your emotions can help you infer how the characters in the book are feeling.

During Reading
- [Without disrupting the flow of the story, pause, when appropriate, and invite students to use the illustrations and pose their own questions to help infer the characters varied emotions.]
- *Mini's mom looked everywhere for the dog's owner.* page: Why do you think Mini's mom says, "We'll have to take him home **for now**?"
- *And then he started barking.* page: What do you think Mini should do? Turn and talk with your thinking buddy about that. Look at the way Mini's mom is standing. Can you infer from her body language how mom is feeling? What do you think Mini's mom wants her to do?
- *Now Mini knew. . .* page: What happened to change Mini's mind? [If your students are familiar with the story *Horrible Bear!* (Dyckman, 2016; see read-aloud experience on page 32), you can compare and contrast the two stories.]

30 ● The Ramped-Up Read Aloud

Learning Targets:
- I can use illustrations and my schema to infer how a character is feeling.
- I can talk, write, or draw about how the characters felt in the story.

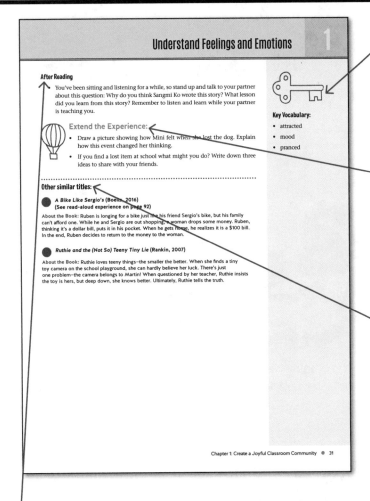

Understand Feelings and Emotions — 1

After Reading

You've been sitting and listening for a while, so stand up and talk to your partner about this question: Why do you think Sangmi Ko wrote this story? What lesson did you learn from this story? Remember to listen and learn while your partner is teaching you.

Extend the Experience:

- Draw a picture showing how Mini felt when she lost the dog. Explain how this event changed her thinking.
- If you find a lost item at school what might you do? Write down three ideas to share with your friends.

Other similar titles:

A Bike Like Sergio's (Boelts, 2016)
(See read-aloud experience on page 92)

About the Book: Ruben is longing for a bike just like his friend Sergio's bike, but his family can't afford one. While he and Sergio are out shopping, a woman drops some money. Ruben, thinking it's a dollar bill, puts it in his pocket. When he gets home, he realizes it is a $100 bill. In the end, Ruben decides to return to the money to the woman.

Ruthie and the (Not So) Teeny Tiny Lie (Rankin, 2007)

About the Book: Ruthie loves teeny things—the smaller the better. When she finds a tiny toy camera on the school playground, she can hardly believe her luck. There's just one problem—the camera belongs to Martin! When questioned by her teacher, Ruthie insists the toy is hers, but deep down, she knows better. Ultimately, Ruthie tells the truth.

Key Vocabulary:
- attracted
- mood
- pranced

Chapter 1: Create a Joyful Classroom Community ● 31

Key Vocabulary: The two or three key vocabulary words are listed in alphabetical order here. For a more detailed discussion on the selection criteria and strategies for highlighting vocabulary during the read-aloud experience, see page 10.

Extend the Experience: The first extension aligns with the learning targets and purpose statement. The second extension offers a different option. Since the read aloud and conversation are the main event, I would advise that you use these extension ideas sparingly and only when they make sense for your learners.

Other similar titles

I carefully selected the related titles to ensure that you could have a similar conversation surrounding the *bookalikes* as you did with the *featured* book. You might choose to read the similar titles to reinforce learning targets, compare and contrast, or continue the conversation with a small group of students. In addition, if multiple teachers in your school are using this resource, you have a wealth of titles from which to choose.

After Reading

The concluding questions and conversation starters draw students' attention back to the learning targets and help them apply what they've learned from this book to their lives, their learning, or the own writing.

Ten Compelling Reasons to Read Aloud

Promotes reading

Fosters a strong
sense of community

Celebrates the
written (and
illustrated) word

Builds a foundation
for future learning

Expands vocabulary

Showcases a proficient
reader's strategy use

Supports budding writers

Sparks collaborative conversations

Encourages perspective-taking
and empathy

Opens windows to other worlds

Source: istock.com/yelet, istock.com/pijama61, istock.com/Bezvershenko, istock.com/primulakat, istock.com/sonicken, istock.com/TopVectors, istock.com/eliflamra, istock.com/sabelskaya, istock.com/Dar_ria, and istock.com/DmitryMo.

targets. Then, as we read for enjoyment, I ask a few key questions (not 100!) that spark conversations and wondering. Through these authentic interactions, the targeted concepts and ideas bubble up. After reading, I may choose to extend the read-aloud experience by inviting the students to talk, write, draw, and/or explore the topic in a new way. The book you hold in your hands will guide you in having a similar experience with 101 different texts. On page 2, I've annotated a sample read-aloud experience with a brief explanation of each component.

In the pages that follow, I will outline the rationale that supports read aloud as a key instructional strategy. This is the section of the book to have handy when a parent or administrator questions your decision to spend instructional time on something he or she might view as *fun* or *extra*.

Ten Compelling Reasons to Read Aloud

As I work with colleagues across the country to strengthen our literacy instruction, I often hear teachers say, "I don't have time to read aloud" or "My administrator doesn't see the value of read-aloud experiences." In this section, I present 10 compelling reasons to carve out time to read aloud to your learners.

Promotes Reading

Passion and excitement are contagious. When you, as the teacher, are enthused about anything—whether it is the Cubs winning the World Series or the latest *Groovy Joe* book by Eric Litwin and Tom Lichtenheld—most children pick up on it. In fact, in 2016, when the Cubs pulled off their BIG win, my first graders witnessed my delight. The next day, a few kids who never really cared about sports, were wearing brand-new Cubs hats, Cubs shirts, and requesting to sing the "Go Cubs Go" song over and over again. Clearly, they were swept up in Cubs' fever.

I believe read aloud does for reading what the Cubs did for baseball in Chicago—ignite (or reignite) the passion. I've watched many a reluctant or vulnerable reader turn around

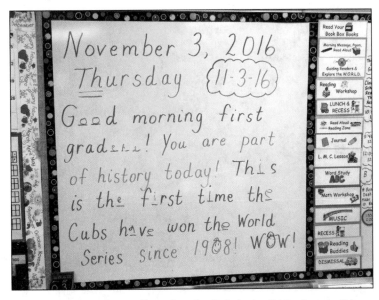

Read aloud does for reading what the Cubs' win did for baseball in Chicago—ignite passion!

after I strategically selected read-aloud books that I knew that particular child would enjoy. Because read aloud is a low-stress learning event, we welcome children to *the reading club* and show them all the possibilities. Students in classrooms where teachers read aloud are more likely to pick up books on their own and check them out from the library. Certainly, it is essential that we teach children HOW to read, but I would argue it is a necessity to teach them to LOVE reading.

Here's How This Book Will Help You Promote Reading

If this book helps you to squeeze one more read aloud into your day or discover an author that your students have never met, you will, undoubtedly, be changing readers' lives. With more than 300 titles at your fingertips, you are sure to find the ideal book to spark your students' interest. When we read aloud, we not only promote books, but we also bring a diverse group of individuals together to form a community of caring learners.

Fosters a Strong Sense of Community

Community. Our support system when life takes a turn. A place where we feel safe and protected. Sadly, not every child enters our classroom with a strong sense of belonging. Some of our little learners come to us from homes and neighborhoods shattered by violence and tainted with struggles. When they walk into our classrooms, it may be the first place they've felt truly secure. A positive classroom environment begins with our day-to-day interactions with individual children. When we smile and greet children as they walk in the door, we put them at ease by making them feel welcome. Then, our instructional decisions communicate what we value. When we place interactive read aloud center stage, it conveys that we value books and conversations. Read-aloud experiences create bonds through shared emotional moments and by discussing texts that promote positive social interactions.

Read aloud fosters a strong sense of community.

I believe a cohesive classroom is one of the natural by-products of the read-aloud experience. When kids are sitting shoulder-to-shoulder with tears in their eyes as Henry's family is sold away in *Henry's Freedom Box* (Levine, 2007) the shared sadness brings them together. On another day, sounds of laughter ring out as Penelope Rex, a little T. rex, can't stop eating the children in her class in *We Don't Eat Our Classmates* (Higgins, 2018). When a group of people laugh, cry, and wonder together their relationships grow stronger.

I've selected the texts in this book to help you nurture an intellectually and emotionally healthy classroom, an environment where students begin to understand that learning is challenging and that our brains grow when we take risks, think flexibly, ponder, and power through the hard parts. In addition, the books and conversations that surround them promote positive social decision making and develop children's social imagination. Social imagination is loosely defined as ability to read another's face to infer how he or she is feeling and to imagine another's actions, emotions, and beliefs from various perspectives. To learn more about developing social imagination, I highly recommend Peter Johnston's (2012) book *Opening Minds*. How do we highlight social decision making during a read-aloud experience? Johnston urges us to do this by "choosing books with emotional tensions and conflicts and inviting conversations about feelings, motives, and beliefs" (2012, p. 76). After these conversations, ask students, "How might you use what you've learned from this story in your own life?" I kept Johnston's wise words in mind as I selected books and crafted the conversations you find in this resource.

> ### Here's How This Book Will Help You Foster a Strong Sense of Community
>
> Chapter 1 is brimming with books and extension ideas to sample as you build relationships and community at the beginning of the year. Every moment you spend shaping your students' abilities to make appropriate choices and interact with others in a positive way will pay off throughout the year. This brings me to the next point, creating a classroom community that's brimming with joy and celebration!

Celebrates the Written (and Illustrated) Word

Think about the activities that make you happy. Surely, we focus more time and expend increased energy on preferred activities than on those we dread. Therefore, if we elevate the written word by enthusiastically celebrating all text-related events, whether small or large, we can catch some of those readers who are vulnerable or disengaged. For example, in my classroom we not only celebrate the kids' birthdays, but we also applaud book birthdays. This is just one simple way to elevate the written word.

To draw readers into the joyful read-aloud experience you want to begin with books that are fun, humorous, and engaging. My go-to series to launch our read aloud is Mo Williems's Elephant and Piggie series. With a total of 25 books, you can't go wrong when you read any of these on the first days of school. You can also rely on many of the Elephant and Piggie books to launch conversations about friendship and other social skills. (See page 8 for a few ideas). In addition to Elephant and Piggie books, I look for unique and engaging picture books that will catch my listeners' attention.

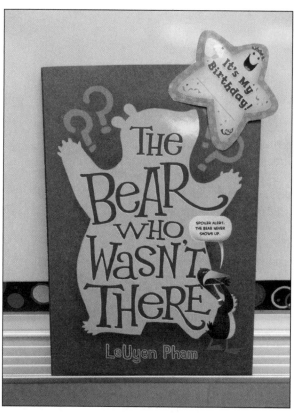

Celebrate book birthdays!

Launch your read-aloud experiences with a book from this hilarious series.

A sampling of social skills highlighted in Elephant and Piggie books by Mo Willems	
Elephant and Piggie Book	**Social Skill**
Can I Play Too? (Willems, 2010)	Friendship; Problem solving; Including others in play
Happy Pig Day! (Willems, 2012)	Feeling left out; Accepting differences; Including everyone
Listen to My Trumpet (Willems, 2012)	Using your social filter when sharing thoughts with friends; Being honest with friends
My Friend Is Sad (Willems, 2007)	Inferring friends' feelings
Should I Share My Ice Cream? (Willems, 2011)	Sharing and being generous with friends

Making the author and illustrator come alive for your students is another way to honor the hard work and dedication that goes into writing and/or illustrating a picture book. It is so much easier today than it was when I first started teaching. Checking out authors' websites, connecting via social media, and attending virtual or live book events are just a few ways you and your students can meet and connect with authors. In her book, *More About the Authors* (2016), Lisa Cleaveland provides another rationale for making authors come alive for our students. Through intentional author and illustrator studies, Lisa shows her students the possibilities they have as writers and illustrators. She suggests we shift our mindset away from focusing on mentor texts and instead consider introducing writers to mentor authors. In her words, "What it boils down to is this: a mentor text gives you lessons; a mentor author gives you a relationship" (p. 17). When you welcome authors and illustrators into your classroom, you can motivate readers and inspire writers.

View the book trailers and the author and illustrator Twitter handles at resources.corwin.com/rampedup-readaloud

Builds a Foundation for Future Learning

Unfortunately, some our students come to us unlucky in literacy. In other words, they have not been raised by adults who are able, for one reason or another, to provide the literacy-rich environment that is essential for future success in schools. We know that "parents who frequently engage in shared reading experiences and frequently teach about alphabetic knowledge have children with the most reading success after a few years of elementary school" (Cunningham & Zibulsky, 2014, p. 129). Consequently, we need to fill in the gaps one read-aloud experience at a time. Book by book, we build a foundation for future learning as children accumulate a bank of familiar books, stories, songs, and poems from which to draw when reading, writing, thinking, and talking about texts.

When read aloud becomes a priority, you gain endless opportunities to forge connections among all the learning your children experience throughout their day, week, and year. Former U.K. Literacy Associate President, Henrietta Dombey, posits that read-aloud experiences provide children "with a shared frame of reference—a path for taking their understanding forward in company with each other" (as cited in Layne, 2015, p. 46). For example, while I was reading aloud the book *Poppleton in Winter* (Rylant, 2001), I paused to explain what a *bust* was (Poppleton was sculpting a bust of his neighbor Cherry Sue). To help students understand, I referred back to the time the children made snowman sculptures in art class. This seems like a simple statement, but it carries great weight in helping children begin to consider the interconnectedness of their learning experiences.

Expands Vocabulary

If you've been teaching as long as I have, you may have noticed that your students' vocabulary knowledge is not as rich as it was in the past. Their bank of known words seems to be shrinking. In my opinion, it is because adults are not always taking the time to talk, discuss, and expand their children's vocabularies. In the grocery store, everyone is on their own electronic devices. So, children aren't hearing a conversation like the following that I use to have with my daughter in the grocery store, "Hey look! That's an apple. Apples grow on trees. People use apples to make the applesauce you like for breakfast. What colors of apples do you see?" and so on. As you'll see with the experiences in this book, you can have a similar kind of expanded-vocabulary conversation about the pictures, words, or ideas in a book.

Not only does read aloud open the floodgates of conversation, but it also helps all students, especially English Language Learners, expand their vocabulary and hear the nuances of the English language including intonation, pauses, rhythm, and pronunciation. I recently met two different Uber drivers who had taken that job specifically to improve their English. As a teacher, I was happy to help! They commented that unlike the textbooks they read or online programs they used, their passengers would explain the nuances of the English language. That is what read aloud–focused talk does for our students.

Book by book we build a foundation for future success.

> ### Here's How This Book Will Help You Expand Vocabulary
> For most of the read-aloud experiences, I've selected three vocabulary words to highlight as you come upon them in the text.

Demonstration of an effective instructional sequence for teaching vocabulary

1. Read the text.	"Soon Mini's dog had *attracted* quite a crowd."
2. Review the story context for the word.	See on this page how all the people are crowded around the dog. The dog *attracted* a crowd.
3. Provide a kid-friendly definition of the word.	*Attracted* means when people or animals want to be near someone or something.
4. Have the children say the word.	Say the word *attracted* with me.
5. Provide examples of the word used in contexts different from the story context.	Bees are *attracted* to flowers.
6. Engage children in activities to get them to interact with the words.	Tell your partner something that you are *attracted* to. Say, "I'm *attracted* to _____."

Source: Beck, McKeown, & Kucan, 2013, p. 62.

Highlight three words as you read aloud.

When I was making decisions about which words to pick, I revisited the work of Isabel Beck, Margaret McKeown, and Linda Kucan (2002). These researchers suggest focusing on *Tier Two* words or those that "are likely to appear frequently in a wide variety of texts and in the written and oral language of mature language users" (Beck, McKeown, & Kucan, 2002, p. 16). Children learn *Tier Two* words through interactions with books. To determine whether the word I was selecting was a *Tier Two* word, I used their tip that children should be able to explain a *Tier Two* word using basic, familiar words they already know. Those basic words are *Tier One* words or words found in oral language that don't usually require direct teaching.

Building a word base requires both direct teaching and plenty of reading on the part of the children. Beck, McKeown, and Kucan (2013) offer an effective instructional sequence when teaching meaningful vocabulary to our young readers. In the chart on page 10, I demonstrate what this might sound like with the word *attracted* from the book *A Dog Wearing Shoes* (Ko, 2015).

In addition to assisting you as you expand your students' word knowledge, Chapters 3 and 4 highlight proficient reader strategies, yet another compelling reason that read aloud is a key instructional component.

Showcases a Proficient Reader's Strategy Use

One good thing about being old, like me, is that I make a lot of mistakes while reading aloud. I'm not sure if it because my mind is elsewhere or if it is because my eyes are getting worse! I'm sure you, too, notice times when you've accidentally misread a word, line, or page in the book. Great news! You've got an instant lesson on metacognition. Stop and say, "Wait! That didn't make sense. I must have skipped a page. I need to go

Turn read-aloud miscues into teachable metacognitive moments.

back and reread. That's what readers do." In other words, when you catch yourself in the act of making a miscue or a situation where meaning is breaking down, turn it into a teachable moment.

Read aloud is the ideal venue to consistently showcase and reflect on the strategies proficient readers use. In this resource, you'll find conversations and extensions that target these strategies:

- Make meaningful connections
- Predict
- Ask questions
- Visualize
- Infer
- Determine Importance

If you make strategic reading and thinking about your thinking the norm, students will rise to the occasion. I've noticed that my learners are more engaged in the read alouds when they are challenged to process the text at a deeper level (or at least *attempt* to process it). The expectation that everyone can listen and dig into the text to try to elevate their understanding is communicated through the questions I ask and interactions I encourage the children to have with each other.

> ### Here's How This Book Will Help You Showcase a Proficient Reader's Strategy Use
>
> As you peruse the read-aloud experiences in this book, you will see that I've carefully crafted questions and metacognitive moments that will lead your students to better understand the complex thinking that goes on as we read. These moments occur in the *Before*, *During*, and *After* read sections of each experience. Along with growing thoughtful readers, the experiences in this book will introduce your young authors to mentor authors and illustrators.

Supports Budding Writers

Writing is a thinking and decision-making process. When you unpack the inner workings of a book for students by highlighting the decisions authors and illustrators make, you bring this thinking to light. As children listen to all the verbs Angela DiTerlizzi (2016) uses in *Some Pets* or pore over Tom Lichtenheld's (2011) visual details in *E-mergency*, they absorb some of these artists' brilliance. Soon you'll see shades of the published author's and illustrator's techniques appear in their writing. A speech bubble here, a visual joke there, and students begin crafting texts with their readers in mind. Ralph Fletcher sums this process up perfectly.

> The writing in a classroom can only be as good as the literature that supports and surrounds and buoys it up. Reading aloud is an essential way to build vision in your students for what strong writing looks like, sounds like, and feels like. (2017, p. 76)

I'm sure you've already discovered the power of mentor texts for helping young writers envision the possibilities. The books in Chapter 6 will help you continue the journey with your students.

Budding writers use what they've learned from mentors authors and texts.

Sparks Collaborative Conversations

Before we begin talking about collaborative conversations and questioning, it is important to reiterate loudly and clearly that there are many times I read aloud just for FUN! I don't stop to ask questions because it would interrupt the action in the story. Now that we have that out of the way, I'll begin with my definition of a collaborative conversation. In our book, Katherine Phillips and I (2012) defined a comprehension conversation as "an interactive discussion about a piece of text that is best sparked by posing higher-level questions and inviting students to listen to and respond to their peers' thoughts and ideas" (p. 21). To support you facilitating collaborative conversations, I'll break that definition into two parts. First, let's look at some effective questioning techniques (see page 14). Then, I'll share ways to help children listen to and respond to their peers (also on page 14).

Effective questioning techniques

- Notice and name the strategies and conversational norms students are displaying
  - I noticed you used clues to make that prediction. That's what readers do.
  - I heard you ask your partner, "Why do you think that?" That's how you both get even smarter.
  - You've got a lot of questions about this book! Asking questions helps you better understand the meaning.
- Ask open-ended thinking questions
  - What do you notice?
  - What do you think about that?
  - What do you predict might happen next? What clues support your prediction?
  - How do you infer the character is feeling right now? What clues helped you make that inference?
- Respond to answers with nonjudgmental comments
  - Hmmm! I didn't notice that!
  - Thank you for sharing your thinking with us today!
  - You just made a prediction—that's what readers do!
- Scaffold students who are having difficulty articulating their thinking
  - Tell me more about that.
  - If you thought you knew the answer, what would it be?
- Alert students to important events in the text.
  - Pay close attention—here's the BIG ending!

Tips for facilitating collaborative conversations

- Set expectations for kids' comments. For example, in my classroom the listeners know not to raise their hand when we're nearing *the big ending* of the book.
- Don't spoil an engaging read aloud by asking too many questions.
- If the read aloud warrants a lot of collaborative discussion, read it in two or three settings.
- Pay attention to your students' level of engagement.
- Provide ample opportunity for students to have peer-to-peer conversations.
- Post the language of a collaborative conversation somewhere near your read-aloud area

You may have noticed a common theme running through both charts: the focus on the *students*. As much as possible, I try to take myself out of the conversation equation by making sure students know that I am not the keeper of knowledge and that *their* thoughts and ideas are valued.

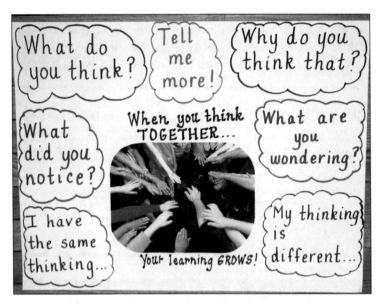

Collaborative conversations provide ample opportunities for students to have peer-to-peer discussions.

Encourages Perspective-Taking and Empathy

Cunningham and Zibulsky (2014) discuss the following reasons that fictional books offer optimal opportunities to develop perspective-taking and empathy by discussing characters' emotions, actions, and thoughts:

- Include some issue or conflict to be resolved

- Showcase interpersonal problems between two or more characters (whether they are people, animals, or aliens!)

- Contain emotion-focused statements

By conversing about the internal state of characters, we help children develop what Peter Johnston (2012) refers to as a social imagination or the "ability to make sense of social cues and to think through their implications" (p. 72). Children with stronger social imaginations are viewed favorably by peers and exhibit the following:

- Increased comprehension of narrative text

- Positive social skills

- Better social cooperation

- Larger social networks

- Stronger moral development
- Enhanced self-regulation
- Fewer angry responses during personal interactions
- Less misbehavior at home and school

(List paraphrased from personal notes taken during a presentation by Peter Johnston at the International Literacy Association Conference held on July 17, 2017.)

When we consider the characteristics of children with strong social imaginations, it is a gentle reminder of how important it is to intentionally cultivate this skill through read aloud. If all of our students displayed those traits, our classrooms (and our world) would be a much happier place. Isn't this what we want for our students?

Here's How This Book Will Help You Encourage Perspective-Taking and Empathy

At every turn, you will find questions that contain mental verbs (*imagine*, *feel*, *believe*, *wonder*, and so forth) as Peter Johnston (2012, p. 76) suggests, reminding you to focus on the thoughts and actions of the author and illustrator, the characters in the book, and your students. When you open these discussions and respond without judgment, you will begin to see the benefits. Moreover, you will notice that when this type of language is the norm during read-aloud experiences, it will seep into your other classroom conversations and eventually become the way you and your students converse all day long.

Books offer opportunities for students to develop empathy.

Opens Window to Other Worlds

Books have the power to transport readers to unfamiliar new locations, to immerse them in new cultures, and to turn back the clock in order to experience and learn from historical events. Therefore, we intentionally select read-aloud texts that will stretch our readers as they become familiar with a world outside their own. As we read and converse, we scaffold learners' beginning realizations that "the world is best if we all learn to respect, appreciate, and honor our mutual humanity—and strive to understand the different ways in which people and societies think and live" (Yokota & Teale, 2017, p. 633). As you add to your classroom library collection, search for stories peopled with diverse characters and settings that offer your students a glimpse into another world. Because, after all, "it's through a rich, technicolored collection of print and nonprint media that reflect the values and strengths of *every* culture that we learn about and come to understand provinces beyond our own" (Culham, 2016, p. 5).

Here's How This Book Will Help You Open Windows to Other Worlds

Throughout this professional book, I've made deliberate text choices that will help you to *begin* to introduce your students to new locations, cultures, and historical events. Whether it be riding on a bus with CJ and his grandma to *The Last Stop on Market Street* (de la Peña, 2015) or designing buildings alongside Zaha Hadid (Winter, 2017), it is my hope that the picture books found in this resource will lead you to many other *technicolored* texts and media to share with your learners.

Books open windows into the past.

Six Secrets to Successful Read-Aloud Experiences

Do you want to know my secrets? Here I will share everything I've learned so far from my three decades of sharing books with kids. Of course, there is always more to learn, and I can always count on my students to teach me what I need to think about next!

Secret #1: Strategic Book Selection

You might be wondering what I look for when I'm searching for books. First and foremost, I think about the children in my class during that particular year. As I'm sure you've noticed, just as every individual in your class is unique, every class, as a whole, has a distinct personality. Certain books are popular while others fall flat. From there I look carefully at the book and consider the criteria highlighted in the box on page 18. In the pages that follow, I will share the thinking behind my strategic book selections. I will talk to you a little bit about each criteria and share a few book titles that illuminate that particular aspect of children's literature.

Engaging, Diverse Characters

I'm always searching for books with characters that my students can call friends. I want them to be able to relate to the characters' emotions or actions and think about how it would feel to walk in that person's (or animal's) shoes. This not only helps my students comprehend stories, but it also nudges them toward understanding and expressing their own feelings. Together, we study how authors reveal insights into a character and make an anchor chart listing the following ways:

- Narration

- Conversation

- Illustrations

- Thoughts of the character

- Thoughts of other characters

- Actions

Then, we notice and discuss examples during our interactive read alouds. We meet characters like *Janine* by Maryann Cocca-Leffler (2015) who is excluded from a party because she is different, but instead of being upset, she throws her own party and invites EVERYONE! We converse about how Janine reacted to the actions of her peers. Then, to gain more insights into the characters, we read the back flap and learn that Maryann wrote this book about her daughter, Janine, who has bravely navigated her life with disabilities.

In addition, I try to ensure that the books I read to my students are peopled with characters that look like and have similar life events as my students. Fortunately, in recent years, there has been a call-to-action for children's book publishers to include more diverse characters in their books. The *We Need Diverse Books* ™ organization or WNDB ® advocates for "essential changes in the publishing industry to produce and promote literature that reflects and honors the lives of all young people." As educators, it is our responsibility to do the same in our educational communities. Look at the shelves in your classroom library; do the books mirror the children you teach? Work with your school librarian to critically examine the collection and make necessary adjustments so that students have the opportunity to check out books to which they can relate.

Rich Language

When children are immersed in texts with rich language, they begin to use that language in their conversations and, eventually, in their writing. In her position statement, Linda Gambrell reminds us that "book language is a second language" (as cited in Layne, 2015, p. 44). An example of such a text is the book *One Word From Sophia* (Averbeck, 2015). In this story, Sophia desperately wants a pet giraffe and presents her arguments (along with pie charts and graphs) to her family. As she's trying to persuade her family, she uses words like *effusive*, *loquacious*, and *verbose*. Fortunately, the author has included a humorous, and informative, glossary at the end of the book leading to further discussion about the wonderful world of words.

Fascinating Illustrations

At the Judson University Literacy in Motion Conference in June, 2015, I had the pleasure of listening to children's author and illustrator Tom Lichtenheld speak about why he loves creating books for kids. One of his many reasons is that kids are innately skilled at understanding visual storytelling. So, when he's working on his illustrations, he carefully crafts them to create interest, draw the reader into the story, color a mood, add magic, or simply make kids (and adults) laugh. In the book he illustrated called *Stick and Stone* by Beth Ferry (2015), you can find examples of each of the above-mentioned criteria to notice with your students and discuss how they might do the same in their own illustrations.

Thought-Provoking Themes

At the beginning of the year as we build our literacy community, I select texts that illuminate themes such as accepting differences, working together, or being kind. We discuss how the theme of a story quietly ties together the characters, setting, and plot and may reveal the author's purpose. Guiding students as they uncover the theme leads to a deeper understanding of the text. Kadir Nelson's (2015) book *If You Plant a Seed* is a perfect example (see page 96). In this story, Rabbit and Mouse plant seeds, but their selfishness leads to trouble. They discover that planting a seed of kindness is much sweeter. I pair this text with *Be Kind* by Pat Zietlow Miller (2018) as we bond with each other and learn how to use kind words and actions.

Kid-Appealing Content

When I look for kid-appealing content, I think about the three categories we use in our classroom when we consider the different reasons that we read (Walther & Phillips, 2012, pp. 44–46). Sometimes we read to laugh, other times we read to learn, and many times we read to ponder. In the *read to laugh* department, you can never go wrong with a *butt* book like *Chicken Cheeks* (Black, 2009) or an *underwear* book such as *Monster's New Undies* (Berger, 2017). In addition to *butt* and *underwear* books, a few others that have a rib-tickling effect include *This Is the Moose* (Morris, 2014) starring a moose who would rather rocket to the moon than be filmed for a nature show and *Bedhead* (Palatini, 2000) featuring Oliver's picture-day misadventures. Certainly, you can't beat any book by Mo Willems to raise the level of laughter in your classroom.

Knowing how important it is to read aloud nonfiction texts to my students, I'm always on the lookout for those that will draw them in. Selecting engaging nonfiction read alouds is the key to *reading to learn*. Not every nonfiction text makes a winning read aloud. Ted Kesler coined the term "poetic nonfiction picture book" to describe books that "blend poetry or poetic qualities and expository writing, expressing an artful level of craft, with provocative effects on readers" (2017, p. 691). Many of the books included in this resource fit into this category such as *All the Water in the World* (Lyon, 2011) and *Squirrels Leap, Squirrels Sleep* (Sayre, 2016). Another type of nonfiction book that works well as a read aloud are those that are structured in such a way that you can read a page or two a day. Books like *Creature Features: 25 Animals Explain Why They Look the Way They Do* (Jenkins & Page, 2014) or *Pink Is for Blobfish: Discovering the World's Perfectly Pink Animals* (Keating, 2016) are perfect for enjoying a bit at a time.

When I'm seeking out books that might cause children to ponder, I choose those that address thought-provoking topics and are told from a child's perspective. For example, we might march with Dr. King alongside Minnie and her sister in *A Sweet Smell of Roses* (Johnson, 2005) or dream of doing something out of the ordinary with Millo in *Drum Dream Girl: How One Girl's Courage Changed Music* (Engle, 2015). Even when you think you've selected a book your kids will love, you might find that you were mistaken. If so, don't be afraid to abandon a book if it is not going well. Say something to the effect of, "I'm noticing this book is not really holding your attention." Make it available for

Choose winning nonfiction read-aloud texts.

those who were interested to read on their own or check out to finish at home with a family member.

Original Premise

Over the years, I've read enough picture books to begin to see some repetition in ideas, and I can usually spot an instance where the author, illustrator, and/or book designer have decided to try something new and different. For example, when I first read aloud Hervé Tullet's (2011) interactive book *Press Here*, my kids couldn't get enough. The concept that the reader, in some way, had control over the happenings in the book was brilliant. As you've probably noticed, many interactive picture books have followed in *Press Here's* wake, some better than others. Therefore, part of my selection criteria is to look for distinctive examples that will not only engage my readers but also offer invitations to my writers and illustrators. I love introducing my listeners to stories like *This Book Just Ate My Dog* (Byrne, 2014) where all the characters in the book disappear into the gutter of the book or *Robo-sauce* (Rubin, 2015) which invites the reader to re-wrap the book jacket to make a *Robo-book*. As I'm writing these words, I'm sure that picture book creators have many more surprises in store for us. We just have to take the time to read the books and find them.

Unique Perspective

To help children better understand point of view and consider topics for a variety of perspectives, I include books in my read-aloud fare that are told using more than one character's voice in the text or those that approach a topic or an idea from a fresh perspective. A story like *You Will Be My Friend!* (Brown, 2011) is an example of a book told in more than one character's voice. What makes this text even better for drawing students' attention to point of view is that each characters' dialogue is marked in such a way that it differentiates among who is talking because the narrator's words are blue, Lucy's are orange, and Mom's are pink. The second type of book is exemplified by *School's First Day of School* (Rex, 2016). You probably have a handful of *first day of school* books, but this is the first one I've read where the author chose to tell the story from the perspective of the school. This shift in perspective offers readers the opportunity to view a familiar concept in a unique way. Helping children to see the world from perspectives other than their own not only will help them as readers, but it will also serve them well as citizens in a global community. Which leads to my last criteria—books that help broaden students' horizons.

Horizon-Broadening Subjects

Only you can select the books that will broaden your students' horizons because you know about your learners' backgrounds, interests, home life, and culture. With this information in mind, I choose these texts that will extend the learning beyond our classroom walls. If you live near the ocean, take a trek through the *Grand Canyon* (Chin, 2017). If your students have never visited a barbershop, join the young protagonist in *Crown: Ode to a Fresh Cut* (Barnes, 2017). Ride a *Rollercoaster* (Frazee, 2003) or a *Locomotive* (Floca, 2013). Looking for books that open windows to other places, situations, or cultures is just one way to broaden your students' horizons. Now that you know how I select books, let's peek into my classroom to see where we read aloud.

Secret #2: A Comfy Place to Read and Listen

If you haven't already created an area to read aloud to your children, here are a few ideas to consider. First, make enough room so that children can sit comfortably in their own space. If you have large class sizes, like I do, you might want to find someone handy to make you a little bench for those sitting in the back of the group.

We have the books, we have the space, next I'll share a few hints to make your delivery as engaging as possible.

Secret #3: Expressive Oral Reading

Each of us has our own read-aloud style, and that's okay. When I'm reading aloud, I think to myself, if I want these kids to love books, this performance has to rival the latest hit movie they are watching. After all, read aloud, like acting or storytelling, is a performance art. It takes time and intentional practice to get even better. The following are a few qualities of a read-aloud performance to consider that will make the experience for your students even richer.

At my fingertips in the read-aloud area

Whiteboard and Markers: Use to write down a vocabulary word you want children to see or draw quick images to define terms.

U. S. and World Map: Grab when you want to locate a setting or trace distances.

Tablet to Access Google Images: Google images are ideal for defining terms and showing learners pictures of people, places, animals, or objects.

Teacher Notebook: Record children's thinking to place on anchor charts or to refer back to in future conversations.

- **Match your tone of voice to the mood of the text:** When you think about the mood of the text, consider the author's purpose. How does the author want the reader to feel while experiencing the book? For example, I read Ryan Higgins's rollicking books about Bruce the grumpy bear in a humorous and silly tone of voice (except when Bruce is grouchy!). On the other hand, I read Jane Yolen's (1987) quiet book *Owl Moon* in a peaceful, childlike tone of voice.

- **Vary your pitch:** When reading like a small, weak character you might choose a high pitch. When reading like a big, strong character you could use a low pitch.

- **Use pacing, pauses, and volume for dramatic effect:** When suspense is building, slow your pace, quiet your voice, and insert long, drawn-out pauses. On the flip side, as excitement mounts or a chase ensues, raise the volume and pick up your pace.

- **Read rhyming texts and poetry with rhythm:** I often find myself tapping my toes to help me keep the rhythm going as I read rhyming books like *The Gruffalo* (Donaldson, 1999) or *Doris the Bookasaurus* (Murray, 2017).

Reading aloud is just like singing along to your favorite tunes. Some songs are uplifting, others make you cry, some are toe-tapping, and others make you sway back and forth. If you *sing* books to your students, you are sure to compete with the latest video game or box office hit! But sometimes even though you are performing your most expressive reading, kids still need a break, don't be afraid to give them one!

Secret #4: Frequent Brain Breaks

We know that young children can only sit and listen for short amounts of time. If you are reading and discussing a lengthy book you might consider pausing for a *brain break* or two. A brain break might be as simple as inviting the children to stand up and play a quick game of Simon Says or asking listeners to stand when they turn and share their thinking. One tip I've learned over the years is that after they've had a moment to stand, direct students to *shrink back down* by counting backward from a number less than twenty. Before shrinking, I always ask the kids, "What is half of 10?" That way, they will know when their bodies should be half way down. Shrinking down helps calm students before you begin reading again. Other ideas for quick brain breaks include the following:

- Walk around the room one time with your partner while you talk about _____.
- This character is grumpy [or another emotion]; stand up and show three people what your face and body look like when you are grumpy [or other emotion].
- Stand up and act out what just happened in the story.
- The word *joy* is an important word in this part of the book. Use your arms to spell the word *joy* (Y. M. C. A. style).

The next secret includes a few classroom management strategies that have served me well over the years.

Secret #5: Joyful and Purposeful Classroom Climate

Be Proactive!

Think about the events that interrupt your read-aloud experiences and develop some go-to responses. I've included a few that I've found helpful on the next page.

Use Strategic Seating—Places for Learning

In our classroom, I have set aside a read-aloud space for my students on the carpet dubbed our *place for learning*. To facilitate smooth transitions from their working spaces to read aloud, I assign each child a designated spot on the floor, so that when it is time to join in our *place for learning* they know exactly where to sit. To do this, I simply make a chart listing the students' names in order on a grid. Depending on how much space you have and the number of students in your class, you might have children sitting in five rows of five or six students. In addition, I strategically match children with a "think and share" partner. By thoughtfully pairing students with a supportive peer, I create situations where they can coach striving learners and those learning English. To build community and give children a chance to interact with a variety of classmates, I adjust their places for learning at least one time per month (Walther & Phillips, 2012). To adapt the expectations and spaces in our place for learning for students with special needs, I've made the following modifications:

- Purchased small plastic chairs (from toddler kitchen sets) for alternative seating
- Posted a photograph of the child exhibiting expected read-aloud behavior

Possible responses to common read-aloud interruptions	
The minute you hold up a book children are anxious to tell you, "I've read that book before!"	• Develop a silent signal so that students can show you they've read the book before. (In my classroom, the kids put their hands on top of their heads.) • Celebrate *rereading* by saying something similar to, "I'm so glad to see you've read this book before, because I have a challenge for you. See if you can notice something you didn't hear or see the first time you read this book. That's what learners do when they reread."
Children want to tell you that their uncle/aunt/grandma has the same name as the main character.	Say something like, "Sometimes as I read you might notice that you know a person that has the same name as a character in this book. That connection might help you remember the character's name, but it probably won't help your friends, so you can keep it in your head. What may help you even more as a reader is to think about someone who acts that same as the character in the book."
Students blurt out answers to questions.	Have a conversation about why it is essential to let their friends have thinking time by asking, "Why do you think it's important to wait to share your thinking?" Based on students' responses say something like, "When you shout out an answer, that takes away other people's thinking time, and we want to make sure everyone has enough time to think."

- Offered flexibility with conversational norms
- Provided a copy of the book I was reading to the child to hold and follow along
- Invited children to bring whiteboards and markers to draw on while I'm reading

Finally, I'll share some purposeful ways to use technology tools to enhance your read-aloud experiences.

Secret #6: Meaningful Technology Connections

I grew up as a teacher long before there were document cameras, interactive whiteboards, and the like. I would still argue that nothing beats the real thing—children gathered around you on the floor looking at the actual book. Interactive media can enhance and extend the read-aloud experiences in so many ways. For example, on the first page of the book *I Am George Washington* (Meltzer, 2016), readers see George standing in front of Mount Vernon. Children don't realize that Mount Vernon is now a museum of which you can take an online interactive tour. In addition, trade book publishers and authors are creating media that helps promote books and broaden the book experience.

Try these! Tech connections to broaden the read-aloud experience

- Author and Illustrator Websites
- Book Trailers
- Emily Arrow Picture Book Song Videos
- Google Images to Help Define Words or Concepts
- Connecting With Authors on Twitter

In the box on page 23, you will find few technology connections that students enjoy. In addition, I have included links to many of these connections in the companion website.

Four Ways to Network and Find New Books

When I present about read alouds, teachers often ask, "How do you find all of these books?" Here are the resources I consult when searching for the best books to read to my students.

Consult Your School or Public Librarian

Partner with your school or public librarian. Encourage your school's librarian to highlight what's new in the library by displaying or book talking his or her latest purchases. For example, our school librarian posts pictures of her new purchases above the drinking fountains. If your public library has a children's section, get to know the librarians. The librarians are typically the people who order the books, so they often have access to book review sources. Ask the librarians about their most-recent picture book purchases. Many public libraries display their new books in a certain area and offer teachers increased limits on the number of books they can check out and extended check out time.

Use Social Media

View author and illustrator Twitter handles at resources.corwin.com/ rampedup-readaloud

Although social media as a professional learning tool is fairly new to me, I've been active on Twitter since 2013. Having the opportunity to connect with book enthusiasts across the globe has added a whole new dimension to my read-aloud searches. If you haven't already, I would highly recommend joining a professional learning community on Twitter or Facebook. Follow authors, publishers, and other book fanatics. You'll be amazed what you can learn.

Visit Local Independent Book Stores

Unlike employees at chain bookstores, the experts working in the children's section at an independent bookstore have a working knowledge of children's literature and can assist you in locating the most recently published books to match your students' needs or curricular topics. To locate the closest independent bookstore go to Indiebound.org.

Attend Conferences, Edcamps, and Webinars

Join your local or state reading council. They often offer professional learning opportunities at a reasonable cost. Look for Edcamps in your area. National organizations like ILA (International Literacy Association), NCTE (National Council of Teachers of English), and ALA (American Library Associations) have robust websites, professional journals, conferences, and much more to offer. In addition to face-to-face meetings, seek out webinars and other virtual opportunities to connect and learn about books.

Four Ways You Might Use This Book

I designed this book with you, the hard-working teacher, in mind. Each two-page read-aloud experience has the same structure so you can easily find the components of the experience that help you the most. I read and studied each book so that, with a quick glance before or during, you have the insights you need to enrich the experience. Here are some other ways you can consider using this resource to enhance your literacy instruction.

Enjoy Books With Your Students!

I can't say this enough, so I'll repeat it one last time. I wrote this book so that I could sit by your side as you make read aloud an even more joyful time of your day. My goal was to introduce you to a book or two that you might have missed and send you off to your library or local bookstore with a list. As you share read-aloud experiences with your students and listen to their insightful discussions, share the stories with your colleagues and administrators so that they, too, will embrace the value of reading, thinking, and talking about books.

Energize Your Core Reading/Writing Program

If you already have a core reading or writing program, match the strategies and skills found in the program's scope and sequence to the skills and strategies that appear in the learning targets. You might find the *Learning Target Chart* (located on the companion website) helpful in this work. The Learning Target Chart lists all of the learning targets along with the books and target vocabulary in one at-a-glance document. Once you've matched the learning targets, you can either replace or extend the shared reading titles or writing mentor texts in your program with these books or the questions and extensions that accompany them.

View the Learning Target Chart at resources.corwin .com/rampedup-readaloud

Teach Specific Literacy Skills and Strategies

If you are looking for read-aloud experiences that highlight a specific literacy skill or strategy, start by reading the title of the experience. The titles showcase the big idea of the experience. To dig into the specifics, check out the learning targets. Then, the last bullet in each "Before Reading" section sets a purpose for reading and directly aligns with the learning targets you might choose to focus on with each book. Using these three features, you should be able to easily find the books and experiences that match your students' learning needs.

Assess Learners' Understanding by Extending the Experience

If you choose to use the ideas found in the "Extend the Experience" section of each read-aloud experience, the products that learners create could provide additional insights into your students' understanding of the learning target. You might use these responses as you and your colleagues gather in your professional learning communities to make decisions about students' learning and your next instructional steps. You could also use them to assist you as you decide what types of books to select for your upcoming read-aloud experiences.

Now that I've set the stage, it's your time to shine! I've created meaningful read-aloud experiences that I hope will restore your delight as you share your days with children, while at the same time help you meet the never-ending demands of your state and district initiatives. Once you've gathered the books, you'll have everything you need to keep your students at the edge of their seats as you bring to life the words and illustrations that are hiding between the covers. Wishing you joyful reading!

"People remembered and would quite often mention

that Sally had been paying super extra special attention.

And how the world could transform and a change could be made

by the smallest girl in the smallest grade."

—*The Smallest Girl in the Smallest Grade*
by Justin Roberts and Christian Robinson

Create a Joyful Classroom Community

Transforming the Classroom World

The children in our classrooms will have the power to change our world. To prepare learners for the future and help them navigate the present, we teach them much more than the content or the *what* of learning. We spend ample time modeling, practicing, and discussing the *how* and *why*. The purpose of the read-aloud experiences in this chapter is to build a foundation by sharing the *what*, *how*, and *why* of literacy learning in a joyful classroom community. As you layer experience upon experience you will do the following:

- Use and explain key comprehension strategies
- Teach literary language
- Develop students' social and emotional learning
- Foster a growth mindset

Wow! That seems like a lot to think about! Fortunately, I've done most of the work for you. In recent years, I've noticed that I was spending a lot more time on social-emotional learning. In an effort to be proactive rather than reactive, I searched for books that would open conversations about some of the issues that were bubbling up in my classroom. The chapter you hold in your hands is a result of that quest. We know that "helping children recognize that thoughts, feelings, and behaviors are interrelated is an early step toward self-awareness and empathy for others, the basic building blocks of social and emotional development" (Cunningham & Zibulsky, 2014, p. 332). The books in this chapter move children toward becoming more self-aware, while at the same time scaffolding their understanding of literary terms and developing their facility with key comprehension strategies. To start the year off on a positive note, the read-aloud experiences in Chapter 1 will guide your students to do the following:

- Understand Feelings and Emotions
- Develop Empathy and Social Imagination
- Embrace Differences and Include Others
- Become a Problem Solver and Resolve Conflicts
- Exhibit a Growth Mindset

On the next page, I detail the concepts you will introduce while reading aloud the books in this chapter. Additionally, I've written kid-friendly definitions for you to use on anchor charts or as you converse with your students. The beginning of the school year is such an exciting (and exhausting) time. Enjoy getting to know your learners and guiding them as, together, you create a joyful learning community.

Use and Explain Key Comprehension Strategies

Infer: When you infer, you use your schema along with the clues from the text and pictures to figure out what is happening in the story. Some people call inferring "reading between the lines," which means figuring out what the author didn't tell you with his or her words.

Predict: Use clues from the pictures and words to think ahead of your reading or to imagine what might happen next.

Schema: Your schema is everything you've experienced so far in your life. The places you've visited, the experiences you've had, and the stories you've heard. Thinking about what you already know, or using your schema, helps you better understand stories and situations.

Foster a Growth Mindset

Imagine: To picture yourself in real or make-believe places or situations.

Mindset: How your attitude shapes the way you think and act.

Notice: Pay attention to what is happening in the world around you or in the words and pictures in a book.

Persevere: To keep trying even when something is challenging. People who persevere don't give up when things are hard.

Ponder: Pausing and really thinking hard about something before raising your hand or sharing your ideas.

Problem Solve: Using common sense and your schema to figure out different ways to fix or do something.

Think Flexibly: Being able to change your thinking or actions when things don't go exactly as you thought they would.

Create a Joyful Classroom Community

Develop Students' Social and Emotional Learning

Embracing Differences: Understanding that we are all unique and that is what makes our classroom and world so special.

Empathy: Understanding or sharing another's feelings or situation.

Feelings/Emotions: The way our heart and brain react to different situations.

Including Others: Inviting others to join in your group, game, or conversation.

Kindness: Being nice to, helping, or thinking about others.

Resolving Conflicts: Talking with your friends and figuring out a way to agree or compromise so that everyone is happy.

Teach Literary Language

Characters: The people, animals, or other talking objects in a story.

Conflict/Problem: The struggle between the character and him or herself, a character and another character, a character and nature, or a character and their community/world.

Illustrations: The pictures the illustrator created.

Lesson, Moral, Big Idea: The messages that we get from a story and can use in our own lives.

Perspective: Looking at something in a different way.

Point of View: The author's choice of narrator(s) or who is telling you the story.

Resolution: When the conflict is over.

Text: The words the author wrote.

Text Clues: Hints that an author gives you about what is happening in the text using his or her words.

Chapter 1 Concepts, Terms, and Kid-Friendly Definitions

My Favorite Read Alouds for Creating Community

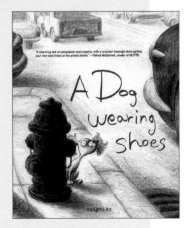

Learning Targets:

- I can use illustrations and my schema to infer how a character is feeling.
- I can talk, write, or draw about how the characters felt in the story.

Infer Characters' Feelings

Book Title: *A Dog Wearing Shoes* (Ko, 2015)

About the Book: Young Mini finds a lost dog wearing little yellow shoes and desperately wants to keep him. One day, while playing at the park, he runs away from her. When she finds him at the animal shelter, she empathizes with his owner and works to reunite the two. After the happy reunion, Mini adopts her own dog from the animal shelter.

To find a book like this one, look for the following:

- Illustrations that clearly reflect the characters' feelings
- Characters who have to make a difficult decision
- Stories about returning lost items

 ## Comprehension Conversation:

Before Reading

Notice the Cover Illustration:

- What colors do you see on the cover? This author/illustrator chose to draw all the illustrations with a pencil and add these colors using the computer. I'm wondering if yellow and red are going to be the only colors in this book. . . . Hmmm.
- What does the back cover blurb say? Turn to a friend and make a prediction based on the blurb.

Set a Purpose: Put a finger on your nose if you have a pet at home. Whether you have a pet or not, let's think about how it would feel if you lost your pet. Turn and tell a neighbor. Keep those feelings in your mind as we read *A Dog Wearing Shoes* because thinking about your emotions can help you infer how the characters in the book are feeling.

During Reading

- [Without disrupting the flow of the story, pause, when appropriate, and invite students to use the illustrations and pose their own questions to help infer the characters varied emotions.]
- *Mini's mom looked everywhere for the dog's owner.* page: Why do you think Mini's mom says, "We'll have to take him home **for now**?"
- *And then he started barking.* page: What do you think Mini should do? Turn and talk with your thinking buddy about that. Look at the way Mini's mom is standing. Can you infer from her body language how mom is feeling? What do you think Mini's mom wants her to do?
- *Now Mini knew. . .* page: What happened to change Mini's mind? [If your students are familiar with the story *Horrible Bear!* (Dyckman, 2016; see read-aloud experience on page 32), you can compare and contrast the two stories.]

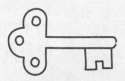
After Reading

- You've been sitting and listening for a while, so stand up and talk to your partner about this question: Why do you think Sangmi Ko wrote this story? What lesson did you learn from this story? Remember to listen and learn while your partner is teaching you.

Extend the Experience:

- Draw a picture showing how Mini felt when she lost the dog. Explain how this event changed her thinking.

- If you find a lost item at school what might you do? Write down three ideas to share with your friends.

Key Vocabulary:

- attracted
- mood
- pranced

. . . .

Other similar titles:

A Bike Like Sergio's (Boelts, 2016)
(See read-aloud experience on page 92)

About the Book: Ruben is longing for a bike just like his friend Sergio's bike, but his family can't afford one. While he and Sergio are out shopping, a woman drops some money. Ruben, thinking it's a dollar bill, puts it in his pocket. When he gets home, he realizes it is a $100 bill. In the end, Ruben decides to return to the money to the woman.

Ruthie and the (Not So) Teeny Tiny Lie (Rankin, 2007)

About the Book: Ruthie loves teeny things—the smaller the better. When she finds a tiny toy camera on the school playground, she can hardly believe her luck. There's just one problem—the camera belongs to Martin! When questioned by her teacher, Ruthie insists the toy is hers, but deep down, she knows better. Ultimately, Ruthie tells the truth.

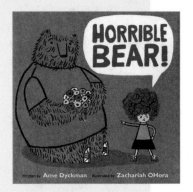

HORRIBLE BEAR!

Written by Ame Dyckman Illustrated by Zachariah OHora

online resources

View the book trailer at resources.corwin.com/rampedup-readaloud

Learning Targets:

- I can use illustrations, text clues, and my schema to infer how a character is feeling.

- I can talk, write, or draw about how the characters in the story responded to events.

- I can talk, write, or draw about how I can use what I've learned from this story in my own life.

Apply New Understandings

Book Title: *Horrible Bear!* (Dyckman, 2016)

About the Book: A red-headed girl gets VERY upset and yells at bear when he accidentally breaks her kite. Bear is *indignant* and plots to get her back. Use this book when discussing how to work out misunderstandings with peers.

To find a book like this one, look for the following:

- Illustrations that clearly reflect the characters' feelings
- Characters who get angry and figure out how to calm themselves down
- Characters who have a misunderstanding and work it out

Comprehension Conversation:

Before Reading

Notice the Cover Illustration:

- What do you notice about the title on the cover? [The title is in a speech bubble.] Why do you think the illustrator chose to do that?

- How do Zachariah OHora's bold illustrations help you to infer how the girl is feeling?

Set a Purpose: As we read this story together, notice the characters' faces and think about their emotions. We'll also ponder what we can learn from this story and how we can use this new learning in our own lives.

During Reading

- *Bear was indignant.* page: Look at the illustration. What is Bear's reaction? It says he's *indignant*. That means he's mad because he believes he is being blamed for something he didn't do. Do you agree?

- *"SHE woke ME up!"* page: Now let's look closely at Bear's face on this page; how is it different than the page before? Do you have any predictions about Bear's horrible idea?

- *"Oh."* page: Why do you think the girl is saying, "Oh"? How is she feeling now? What do you suppose made her change her thinking about Bear's actions?

- *And together, they patched everything up.* page: When you "patch things up" with your friends what does that mean? Can you infer from their faces how they are feeling now?

After Reading

- Let's go back, look at, and talk about the front and back end papers, the front and back of the book jacket, and the front and back of the book case. [The front end papers show the girl's bright red hair and the back end papers picture the top of bear's head.]

Extend the Experience:

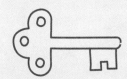

- *But she was too upset to nap.* page: Let's turn back to this page. When the girl went back to her house, she tried to do a few things to cool off, such as drawing, reading, talking to her "stuffie." What are some different ways you can calm down when you are angry? [Co-create an anchor chart with your students or invite them to write about ways they cool off (see below for examples).]

Key Vocabulary:

- barged
- horrible
- ruckus

- Draw a picture of the girl's face at the beginning of the story after Bear broke her kite and at the end of the story when they worked together to fix it. Use your pictures to help you explain to a friend how her feelings changed and what events in the story caused them to change.

Other similar titles:

 Pug & Doug (Breen, 2013)

About the Book: Even pals who both love listening to polka music and have a secret "pawshake" can have their own individual interests. When a misunderstanding threatens their friendship, Pug and Doug agree to "talk things over. Because that's what best friends do." Your students will enjoy the funny ending of this book!

 Shawn Loves Sharks (Manley, 2017)

About the Book: Shawn is obsessed with sharks; he loves to pretend he is one and chase Stacy around the playground. When their teacher announces that each student will each be learning about a different predator, Shawn gets the leopard seal, while Stacy picks the shark. Then, Stacy begins to chase Shawn around the playground. One day, he yells at her and hurts her feelings. In the end, he realizes his mistake, and they learn about predators together.

 What James Said (Rosenberg, 2015)

About the Book: The main character spends a lot of time and energy being mad at James because someone told her that he said, "I think I am perfect." In the end, she discovers that what she heard through the grapevine wasn't exactly true. Rosenberg tells this tale in first-person narrative from the little girl's point of view.

Cool Off chart

Cool Off work sample

story by ADAM REX pictures by CHRISTIAN ROBINSON

Learning Targets:

- I can use illustrations, text clues, and my schema to infer how a character is feeling.

- I can notice who is telling the story.

- I can ponder why the author chose to tell the story from a certain point of view.

Consider Different Points of View

Book Title: *School's First Day of School* (Rex, 2016)

About the Book: Newly constructed Frederick Douglass Elementary is ready to open. But it (yes, the school) is a little nervous about the students' arrival. Reassured by his friend Janitor, School opens its doors and experiences many of the emotions your students feel on the first day of school. Adam Rex and Caldecott-winner Christian Robinson have created a distinctive beginning-of-the-year book told from the point of view of the school.

To find a book like this one, look for the following:

- Illustrations that clearly reflect the characters' feelings
- Characters experiencing a wide range of emotions
- Stories told from a unique point of view

Comprehension Conversation:

Before Reading

Notice the Cover Illustration:

- Look at the wrap-around cover that Christian Robinson created using paint and collage techniques. Collage is when the illustrator cuts and glues different papers or other materials together to create a picture. What is happening on this cover?

- The title of this story is *School's First Day of School.* Think about that for a minute. Who do you think this story will be about? Is that different than other first-day-of-school books we've read?

- Title page: What do you notice on this page? [The school is under construction.]

Set a Purpose: Listeners, as I'm reading, we're going to think about who is telling you the story, that's called *point of view*. Also, notice the different feelings or emotions the characters experience on their first day of school. I can't wait to learn from your questions and thinking about this story!

During Reading

- *A sign above the door read, FREDERICK DOUGLASS ELEMENTARY.* page: Who is thinking aloud on this page? That's right, it's the school!

- *The school creaked.* page: How is the school feeling about children coming? [nervous, worried] Did any of you feel that way on your first day?

- *Some of the older kids gathered. . .* page: Can you infer how school is feeling on this page? What do you think the author means by, "The school sagged a little?"

- *He was so embarrassed.* page: Think of a time when you were embarrassed. What happened to make you feel embarrassed? What sometimes happens to a person's face when he or she is embarrassed? [cheeks turn red]

After Reading

- Why do you think the author chose to write this story from the school's point of view?

- Did you notice that school and the children had many different feelings on the first day of school? Let's look back and see if we can find some different ways characters were feeling in this story. [nervous, worried, amazed, sad, angry, sorry, scared, embarrassed, happy, proud, lucky]

Extend the Experience:

- Using the *My First Day of School Reproducible Response Page* located on the companion website, think about how the school felt on the first day of school. Write about how you felt on your first day.

- Justin Roberts made it seem as if the school was a living thing. Are there other inanimate (or non-living) things you could write about on the first day of school? Let's make a quick list in our writer's notebooks [or on a piece of chart paper].

- [Some possibilities include Pencil's First Day of School, Backpack's First Day of School, Lunchbox's First Day of School]

Other similar titles:

 Dog Days of School (DiPucchio, 2014)

About the Book: When Charlie's wish comes true and he becomes a dog, Norman, his dog, goes off to school. Charlie soon discovers that being a dog isn't as relaxing as he thought!

 First Day Jitters (Danneburg, 2000)

About the Book: Sarah Jane Hartwell does not want to go to school because she doesn't know anybody, and she predicts it's going to be hard. After much cajoling, Mr. Hartwell gets her into the car and drops her off at school. Once in the classroom, readers discover, she is not a student—instead she's the teacher.

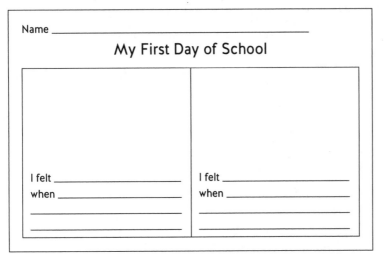

My First Day of School Reproducible Response Page

Download this form at resources.corwin.com/rampedup-readaloud

Key Vocabulary:

- bored
- embarrassed
- worry

Nerdy Birdy

STORY BY Aaron Reynolds PICTURES BY Matt Davies

Learning Targets:

- I can imagine how book characters might feel.
- I can talk, write, or draw about the characters' feelings in a book.

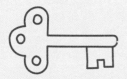

Key Vocabulary:

- confused
- exhausting
- lonely

Imagine Characters' Feelings

Book Title: *Nerdy Birdy* (Reynolds, 2015)

About the Book: Nerdy Birdy is not like the other cool birdies. One day, a group of nerdy birdies invite him to join their flock. But when Nerdy Birdy tries to welcome another unusual bird (Vulture) to join the group, the flock refuses. So, Nerdy Birdy decides to befriend Vulture on his own.

To find a book like this one, look for the following:

- Characters who display empathy, kindness, and understanding
- Characters who are excluded by others
- Characters who face moral dilemmas

Comprehension Conversation:

Before Reading

Notice the Cover Illustration:

- Look at the bird on the back of the book. What do you infer is going on? [They are teasing Nerdy Birdy.] How do you think the bird on the cover is feeling? Turn and tell your friend if you've ever felt that way. Then, ask your friend the same question.

Set a Purpose: People who show empathy think about how others are feeling. As we read *Nerdy Birdy*, we will zoom in on the characters' emotions and ponder how it might feel to be in the same situation.

During Reading

- *Three things Nerdy Birdy is good at. . .* page: I see that Matt Davies has made a funny joke in his illustrations on the page. See the computer, instead of an apple logo, like some computers, it has a banana on it!

- *One day, Eagle flew off to hunt.* page: Can you imagine how Nerdy Birdy is feeling? Have you ever felt the same way?

- *One thing was clear.* page: Wait! Where or who do you think that question is coming from?

- *And then he realized something.* page: Do you think Nerdy Birdy is feeling differently now? Why do you think that?

- *"Right, guys?"* page: Hmmm! Look at Vulture's face. Do you think the Nerdy Birdies are going to agree?

- *Nerdy Birdy looked at his flock of friends.* page: What do you suppose Nerdy Birdy is going to do? Why?

- *This is Nerdy Birdy.* page: Why do you think Nerdy Birdy chose to befriend Vulture? [You might choose to discuss empathy here. Nerdy Birdy remembered how it felt to be lonely.]

After Reading

- Do you have any lingering questions?
- What do you think Nerdy Birdy and Vulture are going to do next?

Extend the Experience:

- As we look through the book again, let's make a list of some of the feelings and emotions we noticed and imagined. [Some possibilities might include proud, stuck-up, mean, unkind, cruel, lonely, nice, friendly, kind, confused, and disappointed.]

- On this sticky note, write the words you think Nerdy Birdy or Vulture might say on the last page. Share your idea with a friend.

Other similar titles:

 ***Ally-Saurus and the First Day of School* (Torrey, 2015)**

About the Book: During lunch, Ally, who loves dinosaurs, is turned away by a group of princesses but finds another group of friends—each with their own unique interest. At the end, the teacher takes the class to the library where they all select books to match their interest.

 ***One* (Otoshi, 2008)**

About the Book: This is an amazing book about bullying! When you first begin reading, you may think it is a book about colors until you realize that the quiet color blue and his buddies are being bullied by the hot-headed color red. Fortunately, "one" shows up and teaches the colors to stand up for themselves.

Read These!
Books Where Characters Display Empathy and Kindness

 ***How to Heal a Broken Wing* (Graham, 2008)**

About the Book: This book begins before the title page, when a bird flies into a building, breaks its wing, and plummets to the ground. No one notices, except a young boy named Will who, with help from his parents, nurses the bird back to health.

 ***Little Fox in the Forest* (Graegin, 2017)**

About the Book: In this wordless picture book, a little girl brings her favorite stuffed animal, a fox, to school for show and tell. After school, she leaves it near the swings. Little Fox grabs it and runs into the forest. After searching through the forest, the girl and her friend find Little Fox's house in a magical forest town. Upon seeing how upset the Little Fox is when she takes the stuffed toy away, she lets him keep it. He returns the favor by giving her a stuffed unicorn.

 ***Samson in the Snow* (Stead, 2016)**

About the Book: As Samson lovingly cares for his dandelion patch, he longs for a companion. One day, a little red bird appears and asks Samson if she can have some flowers to give to her friend who is having a bad day. Samson gives her the flowers and she flies away. That evening a snowstorm blows in. Samson, worried about red bird, sets off to find her. On his quest he saves red bird and her pal mouse, and the trio become friends.

 ***Stick and Stone* (Ferry, 2015)**

About the Book: Stick and Stone become buddies when Stick stands up to Pinecone who is bullying Stone. Tom Lichtenheld's expressive illustrations offer plenty of opportunities to ask students, "Can you infer how the character is feeling?"

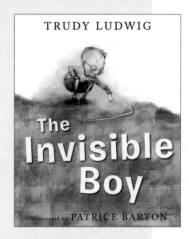

TRUDY LUDWIG

The Invisible Boy

Illustrated by PATRICE BARTON

Learning Targets:

- I can empathize (understand or share another's feelings or situation) with book characters.

- I think about how I would show empathy in situations at school and at home.

Empathize With Characters' Feelings

Book Title: *The Invisible Boy* (Ludwig, 2013)

About the Book: Quiet, shy, Brian has difficulty making friends. He's not included at lunch or on the playground. When a new boy, Justin, joins the class, Brian treats him nicely. Justin returns the kindness and invites him to join the group.

To find a book like this one, look for the following:

- Characters who display empathy, kindness, and understanding
- Characters who are different than their peers

 ## Comprehension Conversation:

Before Reading

Notice the Cover Illustration:

- Think about the title *The Invisible Boy* while you're looking carefully at the cover illustration. Do you see an invisible boy? [No, he looks like a regular boy.]

- I wonder why Trudy Ludwig called this book *The Invisible Boy*.

- Are you wondering anything else?

Set a Purpose: How would you feel if you were invisible? [Some children might think it would be cool to be invisible. Try to steer their conversation toward how it would feel if no one paid attention to them.] I wonder how he feels? Understanding how another person is feeling is called empathy. Let's see if we can better understand how it might feel to be *The Invisible Boy*.

During Reading

- *Can you see Brian, the invisible boy?* page: What did the illustrator, Patrice Barton, do to make Brian look different from the rest of the kids? [He's drawn in black, white, and gray, and everyone else is drawn in full color.] Look at his face. Can you imagine how it feels to have your teacher not notice you? Can you empathize with Brian?

- *Nathan and Sophie take up a lot of space.* page: What does the author mean when she says they "take up a lot of space." Are they bigger than Brian? [No, they just take up more of her time because she is always having to remind them to do what is expected.]

- *J.T. glances in Brian's direction and. . .* page: Look at Brian's face. How do you think he is feeling? Have you ever felt that way? When you can understand how Brian is feeling in this situation, you are showing empathy. What are the other kids doing to make him feel like that? [J.T. and the other kids don't include him in their play.]

- *And the kids laugh.* page: What words might you use to describe J.T.? [mean, bully, unkind]

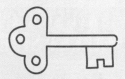

- *The next day, when Justin goes to his cubby. . .* page: How do you suppose Brian's note made Justin feel? Could you do something like that when you see a friend feeling sad?

After Reading

- Now that you've heard the story, talk to your neighbor about the title *The Invisible Boy*. Remember to take turns sharing your thinking and learning from your neighbor. Did empathizing or thinking about Brian's feelings help you better understand the story?

- Look back at the cover illustration. What do you notice? [Brian is drawn in color on the cover.] Why do you suppose he's drawn in color here?

- In the story, what things did Justin do to make Brian feel less invisible? [tells Brian his drawing is cool, invites Brian into the group project with Emilio, has Brian do the drawing because he knows he's good at it, waves Brian over at lunch time]

Key Vocabulary:

- invisible
- glances

Extend the Experience:

- The kids in Brian's class *excluded* him. That means they didn't invite him to join in on their conversations or play. Think about how you would feel if you were excluded. What can you do if you see someone being excluded? Write or draw a picture to share with the class.

- One of Brian's special talents was drawing. What are your special talents? [Students can either draw a picture of themselves and draw or write their talents around the picture, or you can take a picture of them, print it, and have them do the same. Another option is to have learners make a "word cloud" about themselves using Wordle ™ http://www.wordle.net/.]

Other similar titles:

 ***The Bad Seed* (John, 2017)**

About the Book: A sunflower seed acknowledges that he makes bad choices, and therefore, others view him as *a bad seed*. Then, readers learn about why he has chosen to be a bad seed (he was packaged and almost eaten by a baseball fan). Eventually, he decides to try hard to change his ways. Notice that the other characters that surround the bad seed are also seeds like peanuts, pistachios, coconuts, and corn kernels!

 ***We're All Wonders* (Palacio, 2017)**

About the Book: Conceptually based on the themes in the novel *Wonder* (Palacio, 2012), this picture book features Auggie who looks different than his peers. Written in first-person voice, Auggie shares how it feels to be unique and his hopes that others will change the way they see and accept him as a "wonder."

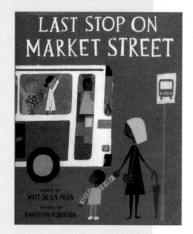

LAST STOP ON MARKET STREET

WORDS BY
MATT DE LA PEÑA
PICTURES BY
CHRISTIAN ROBINSON

Learning Targets:

- I can empathize (understand or share another's feelings or situation) with book characters.

- I think about how I would show empathy in situations at school and at home.

- I can talk, write, or draw about how I can use what I've learned from this story in my own life.

Learn From Characters' Experiences

Book Title: *Last Stop on Market Street* (de la Peña, 2015)

About the Book: Although the reader doesn't know it, CJ and his grandmother are taking the city bus to a soup kitchen on the other side of town. Along the way, nana teaches CJ some important life lessons.

To find a book like this one, look for the following:

- Intergenerational family stories
- Characters who display empathy, kindness, and understanding

Comprehension Conversation:

Before Reading

Notice the Cover Illustration:

[Christian Robinson created the illustrations using acrylic paint, collage, and a bit of digital manipulation.]

- Look at the illustration on the wrap-around cover and think about the title *Last Stop on Market Street*. What do you predict this book might be about?

- Have you ever ridden on a city bus? Tell us one detail about your ride. [After a few children share their schema about city bus rides say, "Thanks for sharing. That helps us all understand a bit more about the story."]

Set a Purpose: I'm wondering where CJ and his grandma are going and what might happen along the way. As we travel with them, I'm going to think about how I would feel if I were in their situation. Do you remember what that's called? [Empathy!]

During Reading

- *The bus lurched forward and stopped, lurched forward and stopped.* page: Where do you think CJ and his nana might be going? Any ideas?

- *"I feel sorry for those boys," she told him.* page: Why do you think CJ is feeling sorry for himself? [Because his friends Miguel and Colby don't have to go "here" after church.] Have you wished you could do something your friends were doing? If you understand that feeling, you are empathizing with CJ.

- *And in the darkness, the rhythm lifted CJ. . .* page: Turn and talk with your friend about the clues that help you infer how the music changes CJ's mood. [He closed his eyes and imagined flying; the sound gave him "the feeling of magic."] Have you ever heard music that changed your mood?

- *CJ saw the perfect rainbow arching over the soup kitchen.* page: Do you have schema for a soup kitchen? What do people do at a soup kitchen? What do you notice about CJ's nana? [She always finds the beautiful or looks on the bright side.]

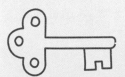
After Reading

- How did CJ's attitude change from the beginning to the end of the story? Could you empathize or understand why he was feeling the way he did?

- What lessons can we learn from CJ's grandmother? [look at the bright side; show empathy; be kind; find the beautiful]

- How might you use those lessons in our classroom?

- How might you use them in your life?

Extend the Experience:

- Let's create a chart that shows all the acts of kindness found in this book.

- Write and illustrate a lesson you learned from either CJ or his nana.

Key Vocabulary:

- aboard

- lurched

- rhythm

View the book trailer at resources.corwin.com/rampedup-readaloud

Other similar titles:

 ***Come With Me* (McGhee, 2017)**

About the Book: A little girl who is frightened by what she hears and sees on the news asks both her dad and mom what she can do to change the world. Each parent says, "Come with me" and takes her out to experience their diverse neighborhood. Then, her parents let her go out to walk the dog, so she invites a neighbor and others to join her.

 ***Something Beautiful* (Wyeth, 1998)**

About the Book: A young girl looks around her neighborhood searching for something beautiful. Each of the people she encounters share the beauty they've found in everyday occurrences. This book is written in first-person narrative from an African-American girl's point of view.

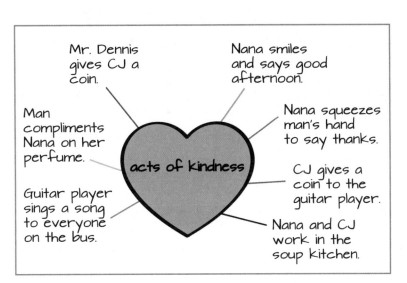

Kindness Chart

Understand Characters' Life Lessons

Book Title: *Marisol McDonald Doesn't Match/Marisol McDonald no combina* (Brown, 2011)

About the Book: Marisol is a multiracial girl who likes to do things her own unique way. Tired of everyone telling her that she doesn't match, Marisol decides to try to match. After noticing a change in Marisol's attitude and artwork, Ms. Apple, the art teacher, writes a note encouraging Marisol to be her own creative self.

To find a book like this one, look for the following:

• Characters who come to appreciate themselves

• Theme of embracing differences

Comprehension Conversation:

Before Reading

Notice the Cover Illustration:

Look carefully at the illustration on the cover. The title is *Marisol McDonald Doesn't Match.* Can you see anything on Marisol that doesn't match? Did you notice that the title is in English and Spanish? This book is written in both languages so whether you read in English, Spanish, or both, you can read this book!

Set a Purpose: Let's read so you can help me figure out why Monica Brown chose the title *Marisol McDonald Doesn't Match* and what Marisol learns about herself in this book.

During Reading

• *My name is Marisol McDonald, and I don't match.* page: How do you think it makes Marisol feel that everyone tells her she doesn't match? Let's read some more to find out.

• *I also love peanut butter and jelly. . .* page: [If you and the kids don't already know who speaks more than one language, you could ask the following question.] How many of you speak more than one language like Marisol and her family?

• *The next day, I wake up. . .* page: Look at Marisol's face. How do you suppose trying to match is making her feel?

• *At the end of the day, Mrs. Apple hands me a note.* page: What does Ms. Apple do to make Marisol skip home? [Reassures her that is okay to be unique. Also, notice that Ms. Apple also writes her name in cursive and printing!]

After Reading

• Let's go back to page 16 where Ollie scrunches his nose at Marisol's sandwich. If you saw Ollie doing that, what might you say to him?

Learning Targets:

• I can figure out the lessons the characters' learned.

• I can talk, write, or draw about the lessons the characters' learned.

Extend the Experience:

- What do you think Marisol learned about herself in this book? Write and/or draw to explain your thinking.

- Marisol didn't like to match. What is something you don't like to do?

Other similar titles:

 Antoinette (DiPucchio, 2017)

About the Book: Antoinette isn't quite sure what makes her special until her doggie friend Ooh-La-La goes missing. With persistence and courage, Antoinette follows Ooh-La-La into the Louvre and saves her from a *perilous fall*.

 I Don't Want to Be a Frog (Petty, 2015)

About the Book: This amusing story, told all in speech bubbles, is about self-acceptance. A small frog is convinced he no longer wants to be a frog, but his wise father and a hungry wolf set him straight.

 We Are Growing (Keller, 2016)

About the Book: One of the books in the Mo Willems's Elephant and Piggie Like Reading series featuring a blade of grass named Walt. Walt's friends are all growing and becoming the "something-est" but he isn't. When the blades are all mowed down and Walt helps clean up, he discovers that he is the neatest!

Read These!
Books About Embracing Differences

 Be Who You Are (Parr, 2016)

About the Book: In his brightly-colored signature style, Todd Parr reminds readers to "be the best you can be!"

 Exclamation Mark (Rosenthal, 2013)

About the Book: Feeling alone in a world of periods, the exclamation mark tries everything to fit in and is about to give up when he meets the question mark. Question mark helps him discover his unique talent—exclaiming! Notice that the book does not have a title on the cover and the pages are made out of children's handwriting paper.

 Why Am I Me? (Britt, 2017)

About the Book: A celebration of diversity and of who we are, not only as individuals but also as a collective *we* in the world.

View the book trailer at resources.corwin.com/rampedup-readaloud

Learning Targets:

- I can figure out the lesson, moral, or big idea.
- I can find clues in the text to support my thinking.
- I can talk, write, or draw about the lesson, moral, or big idea.

Key Vocabulary:

- brave (verb)
- coax
- strictly

Find Clues to Infer Life Lessons

Book Title: *Strictly No Elephants* (Mantchev, 2015)

About the Book: A boy and his tiny elephant don't fit in with the other members of the The Pet Club, so he and a skunk-owning girl start their own club where all are welcome.

To find a book like this one, look for the following:

- Theme of embracing differences
- Characters who appreciate and include others even when they are different from themselves

Comprehension Conversation:

Before Reading

Notice the Cover Illustration:

- In Taeeun Yoo's cover illustration, we can't see the boy's face, but we can read the title and infer how he is feeling.

- Notice that she put the title on a sign, and it reads, *Strictly No Elephants*. The word *strictly* means you absolutely need to follow that direction. At our school, we have a rule in the winter—strictly no snowball throwing. Do you have any rules like that at home? Share one with your neighbor. Say, "Strictly No _____."

Set a Purpose: Did you know that sometimes authors write books, and they hide lessons or messages inside of them? As readers, we can talk together and figure out what messages are hidden in the book. Get ready to try it today!

During Reading

- *I always go back and help him over.* page: What does the boy mean when he says friends "lift each other over the cracks?" What is the author trying to tell us about friendship? What clues help you to know that?

- *When I look up, there's a sign on the door.* page: Now we get to see a similar illustration as the one of the cover, but we can see the boy's face. Do you remember what the sign said? Let's look back at the cover. Wow! How would that make you feel if you had an elephant for a pet?

- *"The sign didn't mention skunks . . ."* page: What do you think the boy means by "they don't know any better?"

- *So we paint our own sign.* page: What does their sign read? Does this sign help you to figure out the author's message or lesson? [First they wrote, "Strictly No Strangers, No Spoilsports." Then they changed the sign to read, "All Are Welcome." They went from excluding to including.]

After Reading

- What do you think the hidden lessons or messages are in *Strictly No Elephants?* Can you find places in the book that helped you to figure them out? [Be a good friend (all the tips about friendship), include others (they start their own club), and other lessons your children find and share.]

Extend the Experience:

- Write and/or draw a picture of the lesson you learned from this book.

- Let's go back and look at the different things that *friends do* in this book [lift each other over cracks, brave the scary things, never leave anyone behind]. Can you think of other things that friends do for each other? Let's make a list together! [To extend this conversation about friendship, read aloud other books about friendship.]

Other similar titles:

 Janine (Cocca-Leffler, 2015)

About the Book: Janine is excluded from a party because she is different, but instead of being upset, she has her own party and invites EVERYONE! The author wrote this book about her daughter, Janine, who has bravely navigated her life with disabilities.

 Odd Velvet (Whitcomb, 1998)

About the Book: Velvet, who begins the school year without a new dress and without friends, is slowly appreciated for her uniqueness.

BE A
FRIEND

SALINA YOON

View the book trailer at resources.corwin.com/rampedup-readaloud

Learning Targets:

- I can figure out the lesson, moral, or big idea.
- I can talk, write, or draw about how I can apply the lesson, moral, or big idea in my own life.

Key Vocabulary:

- invisible
- lonely
- ordinary

Apply Life Lessons

Book Title: *Be a Friend* (Yoon, 2016)

About the Book: Dennis chooses to express himself using mime. Unable to communicate with his peers, he feels lonely and invisible. The other children don't try to get to know him until he meets Joy. Together, he and Joy find a nonverbal way to communicate and play together.

To find a book like this one, look for the following:

- Theme of embracing differences
- Characters who appreciate and include others even when they are different from themselves

Comprehension Conversation:

Before Reading

- [To engage readers, you might choose to introduce the concept of miming by miming, rather than talking, for a few minutes.]

Notice the Cover Illustration:

- Notice the way the boy is dressed. Have you even seen someone dressed like this before? [If needed, introduce the word *mime* and talk a little bit about what mimes do.]
- Why do you think Salina Yoon drew the flower with red dotted lines?
- Think about the title *Be a Friend*. Talk with a neighbor about what you think is happening on the cover. [Perhaps the boy is giving the flower to the girl because he wants to be her friend.]
- [If you have a hardcover book and can remove the book jacket, notice that the book case is the same design as the boy's shirt and has the red heart *pinned* to it.]

Set a Purpose: Friendship is an important part of our lives. Think about what it means to "Be a Friend" as we read and talk about this book.

During Reading

- *. . . who expressed himself in EXTRAORDINARY ways.* page: What do you notice about the clothes in his closet? Why do you think he wears white gloves?
- *Everyone called him MIME BOY.* page: Why do you think Dennis chooses to mime?
- Two-page spread of Dennis miming page: Let's stand up and do some of Dennis's actions together. Stay in your own space and remember when you are miming you are not making any sounds. Are you up for the challenge?

Maria's Thinking: When reading to wiggly children, it is essential to provide time for brain breaks and movement. In this book, for a movement break, you might choose to invite students to stand up and mime the activities that Dennis is miming.

- *It was as if he were standing on the other side of a WALL.* page: What do you notice about the other children? What might happen next? [The girl is looking at Dennis. If you turn back to the previous pages where she appears, she is also doing her own thing.]

- *There was no wall between Dennis and Joy.* page: Why do you think Salina Yoon chose to name the girl "Joy"?

- *But they laughed out loud with JAZZ HANDS . . .* page: Hmmm! Look carefully at their shirts. What do you notice? [The red heart that was on Dennis's shirt is now on Joy's shirt.]

After Reading

- What happened in the end? [All of the children joined Dennis and Joy in their play.]

- Think back to title. What are the big ideas in this book? What lesson can we learn from reading this book?

 ## Extend the Experience:

- What does it mean to *be a friend*? [Encourage your students to dig deeper than simply, "be nice" or "play together." See the chart and work sample for some of the ideas my first graders came up with.

- What is the big idea of this book? Using the *Big Idea Reproducible Response Page* located on the companion website, write about how you felt on the first day of school.

Other similar titles:

 ***Tommy Can't Stop* (Federle, 2015)**

About the Book: "Tommy's gotta bop." He also likes to bounce, kick, clomp, and hurdle. He is so full of energy that his family looks for ways to tire him out. Finally, a reluctant Tommy tries tap dancing and discovers that he's got talent.

Be a Friend Chart

Be a Friend Work Sample

The Sandwich Swap (Al Abdullah & DiPucchio, 2010)

About the Book: In this story of tolerance and acceptance, Salma and Lily eat different kinds of sandwiches, and each girl voices her distaste for the other's food. This attitude snowballs resulting in a school-wide food fight. In the end, the best friends work together to organize a multicultural feast for all.

Big Idea Reproducible Response Page

Download this form at resources.corwin.com/rampedup-readaloud

My Favorite Read Alouds for Developing Empathy and Embracing Differences

Identify the Problem

Book Title: *Rulers of the Playground* (Kuefler, 2017)

About the Book: Jonah and Lennox both want to be rulers of the playground. So, they divide the playground in half and try to conquer their side by telling the other kids what to do. Soon the other children get tired of being bossed around, so they leave. Realizing their mistake, the rulers work together to solve the problem. Read this book if you have children who LOVE being in charge.

Learning Targets:

- I can identify the problem in a story.

- I can think about the actions the character took to solve a problem.

- I can use what I've learned from books to help me solve problems.

To find a book like this one, look for the following:

- Plots with a clear problem and solution

- Characters who look for different ways to solve a problem

- Setting that includes a playground

Comprehension Conversation:

Before Reading

Notice the Cover Illustration:

- Look closely at Joseph Kuefler's illustration on the cover. Which children do you think are the "Rulers of the Playground?" Now look at the expressions of the other kids on the swings. Are they all feeling the same way? Turn and chat about this with your friend.

Set a Purpose: Can you predict what the problem might be in this story? Let's read to find out if your prediction matches Joseph Kuefler's thinking.

During Reading

- *Jonah's kingdom had slides, so everyone pinkie promised.* page: Does it look like the other kids are okay with Jonah being the ruler of the playground? Do you think it is fair? Share your thinking with a partner. Don't forget to ask them what they think and why.

- *Everyone except for Lennox. . .* page: You can tell Lennox's mood by looking at the picture. What do you imagine she will do next?

- *"This side of the playground is not mine," announced Lennox.* page: What do you suppose her friends were thinking when Lennox *announced* this to them. Do you like when your friends tell you what to do? How might you handle this situation?

- *King Jonah and Queen Lennox claimed the entire playground.* page: Talk with your friend about what happened on this page. [Nobody wants to play with Jonah and Lennox anymore.]

- *"We're done conquering," said Jonah.* page: How did Lennox and Jonah solve the problem?

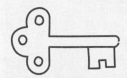
After Reading

- I heard you all say, "Oh no!" and "Not again!" when I read the ending. Why did you say that? [Because now Augustine wants to rule the playground!]

- What did you learn from this book that you can use when you play on the playground?

- Look at the end papers. The front end papers show Jonah's version of the playground and the back end papers show Lennox's. Let's see if they are the same or different.

Extend the Experience:

- Draw the characters on the playground. Label the playground problems you noticed in the story.

- After reading this book, what playground advice do you have for your friends? Write it on this speech bubble and we'll put it up in the hallway near the playground to remind us.

Key Vocabulary:

- conquer
- hollered
- rule (verb)

Other similar titles:

 ***King of the Playground* (Naylor, 1991)**

About the Book: Kevin wants to go to the playground, but he knows if his Sammy "king of the playground" is there, he won't let Kevin play on the equipment. Each time this happens, Kevin's father gives him strategies or encouragement for dealing with Sammy. Finally, Kevin faces Sammy, and they end up playing together.

 ***The Recess Queen* (O'Neill, 2002)**

About the Book: Mean Jean was Recess Queen, and no one said any different until a new student came and decided to change things.

Advice Work Sample

Learning Targets:

- I can think about the actions the character took to solve a problem.

- I can use what I've learned from books to help me solve problems.

Consider Possible Solutions

Book Title: *Charlotte the Scientist Is Squished* (Andros, 2017)

About the Book: Charlotte, the bunny scientist, doesn't have enough room to do her experiments. To solve her problem, she employs the scientific method and engineers a carrot-shaped rocket to blast her into space. When she finds space too lonely, she concludes she just needs her own space and finds it inside her rocket next to the crowded house.

To find a book like this one, look for the following:

- Plots with a clear problem and solution

- Characters who look for different ways to solve a problem

Comprehension Conversation:

Before Reading

Notice the Cover Illustration:

- What clues in Brianne Farley's cover illustration help you to know that Charlotte is a scientist?

- Think about the title, *Charlotte the Scientist Is Squished*. What might the book be about? Ask a friend what he or she thinks.

Set a Purpose: Being squished sounds like a problem. Let's read, ponder, and talk to find out how Charlotte solves the problem.

During Reading

- *Charlotte was a serious scientist.* page: How did Charlotte solve problems?

- *STEP 1: Ask a question.* page: Can you imagine how Charlotte is feeling about her problem? Do you ever feel that way? What can you do to calm yourself down when you're feeling angry or frustrated?

- Two-page spread where Charlotte is in space page: Have her feelings changed? How is she feeling now that she's alone? Do you like being alone? Why or why not?

- *Observations* page: Can you name other words (synonyms) that mean the same thing as the word splendid [excellent, great, outstanding, super, superb]?

- *And what was Charlotte supposed to do when she ran out of toilet paper?* page: Hmmm! It looks like Charlotte's mood is changing again. What's going on? What do you predict she'll do next?

After Reading

- What was Charlotte's big conclusion at the end of the story? [She needed her own space.]

- Do you ever feel like you need your own space? When do you feel that way? Where do you go?

Extend the Experience:

- Identify a problem that you have at home or at school. Think about how you might solve that problem. Explain your procedure step-by-step.

- In the back of the book, Charlotte has invited us to do our own experiment and e-mail her to tell her about it. Next time we do an experiment in science, we'll do that!

Other similar titles:

  Leave Me Alone! **(Brosgol, 2016)**

About the Book: Graphic novelist, Vera Brosgol, won the 2017 Caldecott Honor for this, her first picture book. *Leave Me Alone!* is a combination of folktale and futuristic story. In it, an old woman, searching for somewhere to do her knitting, lands on the moon and travels through a worm hole. Her repeated plea, "Leave me alone!" is sure to be ringing in your students' ears after you read this book.

Lion and Tiger and Bear: Tag! You're It! **(Long, 2016)**

About the Book: Lion is painting a masterpiece in his "Alone Spot" when both Bear and Tiger disturb him by trying to get him to play tag. Even when Lion builds a fence around his easel, his friends still tag him. Finally, he convinces his friends to let him finish his painting and then they all play tag.

Key Vocabulary:

- essential
- splendid

View the book trailer at resources.corwin.com/rampedup-readaloud

Learning Targets:

- I can think about the actions the character took to solve the problem or resolve the conflict.

- I can notice the impact that solution had on other characters.

- I can use my schema and clues from the text to infer the theme or big idea of a story.

Connect Problem, Solution, Impact, and Big Ideas

Book Title: *The Smallest Girl in the Smallest Grade* (Roberts, 2014)

About the Book: Sally McCabe notices everything, even the unkind behavior of the other children at her school. One day she's had enough and stands up for those who were bullied. Read this book at the beginning of the school year or later if/ when you observe children being bullied.

To find a book like this one, look for the following:

- Plots with a clear conflict and resolution
- Characters who stand up to bullies

Comprehension Conversation:

Before Reading

Notice the Cover Illustration:

- Before we read, let's compare the way the kids' faces look on the cover to the way they look on the title page. [Robinson's colored-pencil illustrations clearly show the emotions of each of the children in "the smallest girl's" class—on the cover, they are all happy, on the title page some children are not being kind, so they look mean. Also, notice that "the smallest girl" is watching the unkind kids.] It looks like there are some unkind acts happening in her class.

- [If/when a child notices Sally with her finger up on the cover, ask, "Why do you think she is pointing her finger? Turn and talk to your neighbor about that."]

Set a Purpose: Let's read to find out more about the "Smallest Girl," what is happening at her school, and if that is the reason that she is pointing her finger up. I'm wondering if we can learn any lessons that might help us in our classroom.

During Reading

- *Hardly anyone noticed young Sally McCabe.* page: What is happening on the playground? [Notice the unkind acts.] What do you think is the problem?

- *She said, "I'm tired of seeing this terrible stuff."* page: What does Sally do to try to solve the problem? Do you think it will work? [She tells her friends to stop hurting each other.]

- *The swings soon resumed their rhythm . . .* page: What do you notice about the playground now? How is different from the playground at the beginning of the story? [Look back and forth between the two pages to compare.] Why do you suppose it is different? [Because Sally had the courage to stand up when she saw something bad happening.]

After Reading

- How did Sally's actions impact her friends at school?

- What lesson can we learn from reading this book?

- How can we use this understanding at our school?
- Does this book remind you of any other books we've read? How is it the same or different?

Extend the Experience:

- On this chart we'll record the problem (or conflict), solution (or resolution), the impact, and the big idea. Then, we can compare it to other books we read about bullying. (See example below.)
- Divide your paper in half. On one side draw and/or write about an unkind act you've seen happening at school. On the other side draw and/or write what you might say or do to stop an act like that from happening.

Other similar titles:

● **Peanut Butter and Jellyfish** (Krosoczka, 2014)

About the Book: Best friends, Peanut Butter and Jellyfish, are endlessly taunted by Crabby. One day, Crabby gets caught in a lobster trap. When the duo sets Crabby free, he apologizes for his behavior, and they all become friends.

● **Two of a Kind** (Robbins, 2009)

About the Book: If you are looking for a book to spark a conversation about kindness and healthy friendships, this is the one! Kayla and Melanie are exclusive friends and known as "two of a kind." Julisa and Anna are also friends. When Melanie *befriends* Anna, Anna discovers that being friends with Kayla and Melanie means making choices that exclude her friend Julisa.

Key Vocabulary:

- attention
- notice
- transform

What is the CONFLICT (problem)?			
Mean Jean is being rude, bossy and a bully.	Crabby is yelling mean words all the time. He's a bully.	Kayla and Melanie don't let kids play, make fun of Julisa and Anna and are bossy to Anna	Sally is noticing a lot of bullying
↓ How did they solve the problem? RESOLUTION ↓			
Katie Sue asked Mean Jean to play with her.	Peanut Butter and Jellyfish saved Crabby from the trap.	Anna chose to join her friend Julisa.	Sally said, "Stop!"
↓ How did the solution IMPACT others? ↓			
Everybody is playing together and Mean Jean is being nice.	They all became friends.	Julisa and Anna were kind friends and helpful students	Kids are being nice, kind, and respectful.
↓ What is the BIG IDEA? (theme, moral, lesson) ↓			
Ask friends to play!	Help friends when they're in trouble. Find new friends and play with them.	Ignore bullies and troublemakers, they will only get you into trouble!	Stand up to bullies. Say "STOP!"

Conflict Chart

Notice Characters' Mindsets

Book Title: *Chicken in Space* (Lehrhaupt, 2016)

About the Book: An adventurous, positive-thinking chicken is determined to travel to space. Although her mission doesn't go quite as expected, she's already planning the next one. This is the first book in a series.

To find a book like this one, look for the following:

- Characters with an adventurous spirit
- Characters that overcomes obstacles to reach a goal

Learning Targets:

- I can notice how characters think and act.
- I can talk, write, or draw about how I can use what I've learned from this story in my own life.

Comprehension Conversation:

Before Reading

Notice the Cover Illustration:

- At first when you look at this cover you might think that this chicken is really in space, but look closely as I open the book to view the wrap-around illustration.
- What other details do you notice in Shahar Kober's illustration? Do you still think the chicken is in space? Where do you think she is?
- What is the setting for this story? If you look on the verso page [where you find the copyright information], it often says how the illustrations were created. This artist created the illustrations for the cover and the rest of the book digitally (that means on a device like a laptop or tablet).

Set a Purpose: Today, as we're enjoying this fun book, let's think about Zoey's attitude or mind set—how she approaches problems and challenges.

During Reading

- *"Pip," said Zoey, "come to space with us."* page: What does Zoey mean when she says that it is not dangerous to go to space; rather, it's an adventure? What other adventures can you think of that might be a little dangerous?
- *"Not a problem!"* page: What does Zoey mean when she says that it is not a problem that she doesn't have a ship; rather, she looks at it as an opportunity? Have you ever had a problem that turned into a learning opportunity?
- *"Watch out for the birds!"* page: Wow! Zoey is really good at using her imagination. What did she imagine? [She imagined that the birds were alien attack ships.]

After Reading

- Is this book real or make-believe? Can you go back into the book to find proof to support your answer?

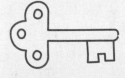

- How did Zoey approach the problems or challenges she faced in the book? What lessons can we learn from her that we might use in our own lives [have a plan, use your imagination, go on adventures, view problems as opportunities, find your own way]?

Extend the Experience:

- Zoey stretched her brain by trying new things. What can you do or try to make your brain grow?

- What do you predict will be Zoey's next big adventure? Create your own version of the cover of the next book.

Key Vocabulary:

- adventure
- gathered
- impressed

....

Other similar titles:

 Chicken in School (Lehrhaupt, 2017)

About the Book: Zoey the chicken is back in her second adventure. When Sam, the pig, says he wants to go to school, Zoey makes a plan, creates a classroom, and invites all her barnyard friends.

 What Do You Do With an Idea? (Yamada, 2013)

About the Book: A child has an idea. At first, worried about what others might think, he hides the idea. Then, after giving the idea attention, he decides to show it to others. Even after hearing it is a waste of time, the child nurtures the idea and discovers that ideas change the world.

Helping Your Brain Grow Work Sample

Learning Targets:

- I can notice how characters think and act.

- I can learn how to think flexibly.

- I can talk, write, or draw about how I can use what I've learned from this story in my own life.

Learn to Think Flexibly

Book Title: *A Perfectly Messed-Up Story* (McDonnell, 2014)

About the Book: Louie is trying to tell his story when someone messes it up. In the end, he realizes that everything is just fine. This book is ideal for kids who need to be a bit more flexible in their thinking.

To find a book like this one, look for the following:

- Characters who are flexible thinkers

- Plots that encourage readers to learn from or celebrate problems and mistakes

Comprehension Conversation:

Before Reading

Notice the Cover Illustration:

- Hmmm! It looks like there are some things on the cover that don't belong. What do you see?

- I noticed that Patrick McDonnell used a lot of different art tools to create his illustrations. Look carefully at the title. What do you notice?

Set a Purpose: Let's read to find out why this book is called *The Perfectly Messed-Up Story* instead of *The Perfect Story*. After reading, we'll think about the title and how it connects to what we can learn from the story.

Maria's Thinking: Young children, particularly students with special needs, find it a challenge to think flexibly or smoothly adjust when unexpected events occur or things don't go their way. Reading books like the three listed in this experience are ideal for introducing a flexible mindset. Then, as teachers, it is essential to model your reactions to unplanned occurrences throughout the year. For example, when a learning experience takes longer than the time you allotted, verbalize your flexible mindset by saying something like, "Oh! It looks like we ran out of time for [a particular activity]. Even though I really wanted you to finish, I'm going to have to be a flexible thinker and figure out what to do. My new plan is to stop and put everything away until first thing tomorrow morning. Does that make sense? Thanks for being flexible."

During Reading

- *Plop!* page: Uh-oh! What's happening to Louie's story? [Jelly and peanut butter have landed on the page.] How would that make you feel? How could Louie solve the problem?

- *Orange juice!* page: Can you imagine how Louie is feeling now?

- *AAAIIEEEE . . .* page: Look at Louie's face and body language. Can you figure out how he is feeling now? Let's go back and compare the orange juice page to this page. On which page are Louie's feelings more intense? Would you use different words to describe his feelings? Why?

- *This is Louie's story. Who cares.* page: What are some words you might use to describe Louie's mood now [defeated, crushed, miserable, depressed, gloomy, and so on]?

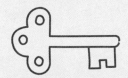
After Reading

- How did Louie's attitude change at the end of the story? What happened to make it change? [He realized that even though things were messed up, his story was fine. He changed his thinking (his mindset).]

- Talk about the title *The Perfectly Messed-Up Story*. What do you think Patrick McDonnell is trying to tell us? [It's okay to mess up, messy stories can still be *perfect*.] [This book can also open a conversation about the concept of *perfect*. Is anything ever perfect?]

Extend the Experience:

- Let's write down some of the flexible thoughts Louie has in this book. [Co-create a flexible thinking anchor chart with your students using some of Louie's quotes like "Everything IS fine." "Nothing is going to stop ME!" Add to these as you read other books about flexible thinking throughout the year.]

- Pick a flexible thought that you want to work on this quarter. Write it on this index card. We'll put the index card in a special place to remind you to use that thinking when you have a problem or make a mistake.

Other similar titles:

 The Book of Mistakes (Luyken, 2017)

About the Book: In this celebration of mistakes, readers watch as page by page the artist draws a girl and makes mistakes. Then, by adding a detail such as eyeglasses or a fancy collar, she fixes them up. It continues as the illustrator adds items that are both mistakes and revisions until readers see a fantastical scene that leads to the beginning of another drawing.

 What Do You Do With a Problem? (Yamada, 2016)

About the Book: The creators of *What Do You Do with an Idea?* (Yamada, 2013), share the story of a child with a problem that won't go away. After worrying and avoiding it, the child finally tackles the problem. In doing this, he learns that his problem held an opportunity for something good.

Flexible Thoughts Chart

Key Vocabulary:

- awful
- inspire
- merrily

View the book trailer at resources.corwin.com/rampedup-readaloud

Learning Targets:

- I can notice how characters think and act.

- I can look for new and different ways to solve problems.

- I can keep working even when something doesn't go well.

Learn to Problem Solve and Persevere

Book Title: *Rosie Revere, Engineer* (Beaty, 2013)

About the Book: Rosie Revere "dreamed of becoming a great engineer" until her uncle laughed at her latest invention. Fortunately, her great-great aunt Rose came to her rescue and helped her to see that "the only true failure can come if you quit."

To find a book like this one, look for the following:

- Characters who persevere

- Characters who think *outside of the box*

Comprehension Conversation:

Before Reading

Notice the Cover Illustration:

- I'll open the book so we can look carefully at the wrap-around cover. David Roberts used pen, ink, and watercolor paints to draw a lot of things on this cover. What do you see? [If you are able to take off the book jacket your students can see more objects on the book case.]

- Think about the title, *Rosie Revere, Engineer*. Does anyone know what an engineer does? This kind of engineer does not drive a train; this engineer is a person who makes plans to build things like bridges, buildings, or machines. Engineers try to figure out how and why things work, they solve problems, and they create new things or improve old ones. Now that you know what an engineer does, what do you think Rosie is going to do with all of that stuff?

Set a Purpose: Today, while you're listening to this story, I want you to notice how Rosie thinks and acts. I'm wondering if we can learn anything from her to use in our work at school and at home.

During Reading

- *And when it was finished, young Rosie* . . . page: How did Uncle Fred make Rosie feel [embarrassed, perplexed, and dismayed]? [If needed, take a moment to define those words for your students.] What do you think she's going to do next?

- *Then Rosie heard laughter* . . . page: Oh no! Rosie's aunt is laughing at her too. Turn and talk with your neighbor about that.

- *"Your brilliant first flop was a raging success!"* page: What does Rosie's aunt mean when she says, "The only true failure can come if you quit?" [You can learn a lot from mistakes and you will make or do things better the next time you try. But, if you just give up, then you don't get a chance to use what you've learned.]

- *With each perfect failure, they all stand and cheer.* page: I'm going to turn to the copyright page to see why Rosie is so proud. [Her aunt is flying in the new "heli-o-cheese-copter" she made.] Why do you think Rosie feels proud? [She didn't give up, she finally made a flying vehicle for her aunt.]

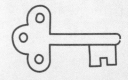
After Reading

- How many of you use your eraser when you're writing or drawing? What would happen if you just gave up every time you had to erase? Have any of you learned to ride your bike without training wheels, tie your shoes, or do something else that has taken a lot of tries? When you don't give up, that is called perseverance. Do you think Rosie had perseverance? Share your thinking with your neighbor.

- To strengthen students' concept of opinion, you might choose to occasionally have students rate the book either using fingers or stars on paper. (See example below.)

Key Vocabulary:

- embarrassed
- failure
- invention

Extend the Experience:

- What did Rosie learn about being an engineer? What are some of the *engineering* actions you noticed Rosie do that you might use to solve problems? [She built things, made inventions, worked hard, tried out her inventions, drew plans, kept trying, and looked for new ways to make things.]

- Draw a picture of an invention you want to create and write to tell us what it will do.

Other similar titles:

 Going Places **(Reynolds & Reynolds, 2014) [out-of-the-box thinking]**

About the Book: The "Going Places" contest is underway and Rafael wants to win. So, he builds his go-cart to the exact specifications. Then, he notices that Maya has taken a different approach. Together, they create their own unique vehicle.

 The Most Magnificent Thing **(Spires, 2014) [characters who persevere]**

About the Book: A little girl has a "wonderful idea," she and her canine assistant are going to make "the most magnificent thing." Although she knows exactly what it is going to look like and how it is going to work, she is unable to get it just right. After many attempts, she gets frustrated and gives up. Then they take a walk to calm down, and she is able to regroup and create a near-perfect magnificent thing.

Rate the Book Work Sample

"And then . . . if it was a really good story . . . go right back to the beginning and start all over again."

—*How to Read a Story*
by Kate Messner and Mark Siegel

Converse About Literary Elements—Fiction

Reading *Really Good* Stories

I'm sure, by now, you know which students in your classroom have a strong sense of story and which learners will benefit from more interactions with books to build their story schema. Cunningham & Zibulsky (2014) stress why a working knowledge of literary elements is key for readers, "Like the border pieces of a jigsaw puzzle, the story schema acts as a framework that makes it easier to understand, organize, and store information in a meaningful context" (p. 229). Helping children understand the separate puzzle pieces and showing them how they fit together is the focus of this chapter. The stories, conversations, and extensions in Chapter 2 will focus on the following literary concepts:

- Describe and Understand Characters
- Build Schema for Story Structure (Compare and Contrast)
- Engage in Illustration Study
- Ponder Point of View
- Infer Themes and Big Ideas

On the next page, you will find the concepts you will introduce or review while enjoying the stories in this chapter. To support you in using these terms, I've included kid-friendly definitions. Be confident in the fact that every story you read and discuss is going to have a positive impact on the children you teach.

Use and Explain Key Comprehension Strategies

Infer: When you infer, you use your schema along with the clues from the text and pictures to figure out what is happening in the story. Some people call inferring "reading between the lines" that means figuring out what the author didn't tell you with his or her words.

Predict: Use clues from the pictures and words to think ahead of your reading or to think about what might happen next.

Schema: Your schema is everything you've experienced so far in your life. The places you've visited, the experiences you've had, and the stories you've heard. Thinking about what you already know, or using your schema, helps you better understand stories and situations.

Foster a Growth Mindset

Discuss: Talk with others to help grow your thinking.

Notice: Pay attention to what is happening in the world around you or in the words and pictures in a book.

Study: To look closely at, think deeply about, or investigate something.

Converse About Literary Elements—Fiction

Develop Students' Social and Emotional Learning

Characters and People Grow and Change: You are always growing and changing. You are smarter today than you were yesterday.

Kindness: Being nice to, helping, or thinking about others.

Relationship: The way in which you get along with others. You have relationships with your family, friends, teachers, and others. Like people, relationships grow and change.

Understanding Different Perspectives: Thinking about how others feel. Some people call this *putting yourself in someone else's shoes*. That means imagining how that person might think or feel about a situation, event, or idea.

Teach Literary Language

Beginning: The part of the story where readers usually learn a little about the characters, setting, and problem.

Compare: Notice how things are alike or different.

End: The part of the story where the problem is solved.

Events: The actions the character takes to try to solve the problem.

Image: A picture of a person, place, thing, animal, or idea.

Main Characters: The person, animal, or other object that the story is mostly about.

Make-Believe Stories: Stories that can't happen in real life. They might have talking animals, animals wearing clothes, objects acting like people, or other imaginary characters.

Middle: The part of the story where the character is attempting to solve the problem.

Problem/Conflict: The struggle between the character and himself or herself, a character and another character, a character and nature, or a character and their community/world.

Real Stories: Stories with people acting, talking, and doing things that people normally do.

Setting: The time and place in which the story happens.

Solution: When the character figures out how to solve the problem or reach his or her goal.

Story Elements: The parts of a story such as character, setting, problem, solution.

Traditional Tales: Stories that have been passed down over time.

Turning Point: An event or situation in a story that causes the character to change.

Chapter 2 Concepts, Terms, and Kid-Friendly Definitions

My Favorite Read Alouds for Literary Elements—Fiction

Notice How Characters Change

Book Title: *Tek: The Modern Cave Boy* (McDonnell, 2016)

About the Book: Much to his parents' and friends' chagrin, Tek refuses to leave his cave and all of his electronic gadgets until a volcano explodes and he is disconnected. Outside of his cave, Tek discovers friendship and "THE BIG BEAUTIFUL WORLD!"

To find a book like this one, look for the following:

- Characters who change over the course of the story
- Characters who discover that face-to-face interaction is more satisfying than face-to-screen interaction
- Illustrations that include digital elements

Comprehension Conversation:

Before Reading

Notice the Cover Illustration:

- Notice that Patrick McDonnell chose to design the front cover, spine, and part of the inside of the book to look exactly like a tablet. Why do you think he chose to do that?
- Why do you suppose Patrick McDonnell chose to name the cave boy Tek?

Set a Purpose: As we read, think, and talk about this story, pay attention to Tek's actions and feelings. See if you notice any changes in his attitude.

During Reading

- *Tek stayed alone in his cave . . .* page: Does Tek remind you of any kids you know? Why?
- *Big Poppa, the village volcano, had an idea.* page: What do you predict Big Poppa is going to do? What clues led to your prediction?
- *He was totally . . . disconnected.* page: What do you notice about these two pages? What do you think the author is showing you here? [The left page is still black like a tablet, and the right page white because he's outside.]

After Reading

- What did Tek discover after he left his cave? [He discovered creatures and the "big beautiful world. He laughed and played with his friends.] What lesson do you think he learned?
- Was Tek the same at the end of the book as he was at the beginning? What happened along the way to change the way he was feeling and acting?

Learning Targets:

- I can notice how characters change from the beginning to the end of a story.
- I can think about the differences in the way characters' think and act during a story.
- I can talk, write, or draw about how characters' change.

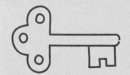

Extend the Experience:

- Divide your paper in half. Draw two pictures of Tek, one showing how he spent his time at the beginning of the story and the other showing what he was doing at the end of the story. Explain to someone how he changed over the course of the story.

- Would you tell your friend to read this book? Use ideas from the book to tell why or why not.

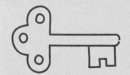

Key Vocabulary:

- budge
- eerie
- invent

Other similar titles:

 Doug Unplugged (Yaccarino, 2013)

About the Book: Before Doug's parents leave for work, they plug him in so he can download a lot of facts. As he's learning about the city, a pigeon outside the window catches his eye. So, Doug unplugs himself and experiences the sights and sounds of the city firsthand.

 Hello! Hello! (Cordell, 2012)

About the Book: Tired of her electronic devices and of being ignored by her family, Lydia ventures outside to discover a world of wonder and adventure. In the end, she entices her family to join her.

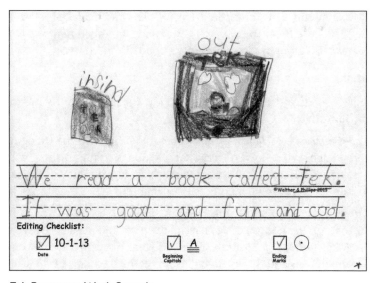

Tek Response Work Sample

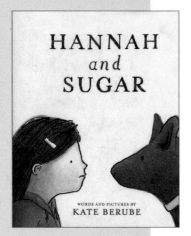

HANNAH
and
SUGAR

WORDS AND PICTURES BY
KATE BERUBE

online
resources

View the book trailer at
resources.corwin.com/
rampedup-readaloud

Learning Targets:

- I can notice how characters change from the beginning to the end of a story.
- I can think about the events that caused the change.
- I can talk, write, or draw about how characters' change.

Key Vocabulary:

- gasped
- searched
- strange

Ponder When Characters Change

Book Title: *Hannah and Sugar* (Berube, 2016)

About the Book: Every day, Hannah's papa picks her up from the bus, and her friend's dog Sugar is always waiting too. Hannah is afraid to pet Sugar. One day, Sugar is missing, and Hannah finds her in the bushes. Hannah overcomes her fear to bring Sugar safely home.

To find a book like this one, look for the following:

- Characters who change over the course of a story
- Characters who overcome fears

Comprehension Conversation:

Before Reading

Notice the Cover Illustration:

- The title of this story is *Hannah and Sugar*. So who do you think Kate Berube drew and painted on the cover?

- Look at the back cover, what do you notice? [Hannah isn't in the illustration where all the children are petting Sugar.] Hmmm! I wonder why Hannah isn't there? Talk with a friend about that.

Set a Purpose: Sometimes in stories, an event happens and characters learn new ways of thinking that cause them to change. These events are called *turning points*. As you listen to *Hannah and Sugar*, notice any turning points in the story.

During Reading

- Title page: Look at Hannah's face and body. Can you infer how Hannah feels about Sugar here?

- *Every day after school, Hannah's papa picked her up. . .* [with the changing seasons pictures] page: What do you think Kate Berube is trying to show you in these four pictures? Is Hannah's attitude toward Sugar any different? [No, her face still looks sad; she's crossing her arms across her chest.]

- *Sugar!* page: Why do you think Hannah stopped? What do you suppose was going through her mind? Let's go back in the book and reread the page that starts with "After dinner . . ." I can't wait to see what happens next. I wonder if the way Hannah feels and thinks about Sugar is going to change. Let's keep reading!

After Reading

- Did you notice if any of the characters changed? What was the *turning point* or the event in the story that helped Hannah overcome her fear of Sugar.

Extend the Experience:

- Using the *Pondering When Characters Change Reproducible Response Page* located on the companion website, draw and/or write about Hannah at the beginning of the story, the turning point, and the end of the story.

- Write about something you used to be afraid of and what happened to make you braver.

Other similar titles:

 A Small Thing . . . but Big **(Johnston, 2016)**

About the Book: On the way to the park (look carefully at wrap-around front cover) Lizzie and her mom meet an "old man" and his dog, Cecile. Unfortunately, Lizzie is afraid of dogs. The kind man helps Lizzie overcome her fear through small steps that eventually turn into something big.

 The Thing Lou Couldn't Do **(Spires, 2017)**

About the Book: Lou's friends want to play pirate ship up in a tree, but she has never climbed a tree. After making many excuses, she gives it a try. Even though she falls, she's planning to try again. [I enjoyed the fact that once her friends realized she couldn't climb the tree they decide to play a different game that she could join.]

Name _____

Pondering When Characters Change

Beginning	Turning Point	End

Pondering When Characters Change Reproducible Response Page

Download this form at resources.corwin.com/ rampedup-readaloud

Read These!
Books Where Characters Overcome Fears

 After the Fall: How Humpty Dumpty Got Back Up Again **(Santat, 2017)**

About the Book: Bird-watching Humpty Dumpty's accident "changed his life." Even though the king's men put him back together, he was afraid of heights and could no longer watch the birds from his wall. So, Humpty replaces his beloved birds with paper airplanes. When an airplane gets stuck on the wall, Humpty has to overcome his fear to rescue it.

 The Darkest Dark **(Hadfield & Fillion, 2016)**

About the Book: Young Chris is afraid of the dark and having difficulty staying in his own bed. Then his parents remind him that he'll be too tired to enjoy the *special day* tomorrow unless he falls asleep. After he sleeps and dreams of going to the moon, he and his fellow island dwellers gather to watch the first lunar landing, and he realizes the beauty of the darkness. Don't forget to check out the author's note at the back of the book that includes photographs of Chris throughout his life.

 I Used to Be Afraid **(Seeger, 2015)**

About the Book: Using the see-saw structure, "I used to be afraid of _____ /but not anymore." Laura Vaccaro Seeger explores typical childhood fears like the dark, shadows, mistakes, and change. Read this book aloud, and then invite students to write their own "I Used to Be Afraid" book.

 Nope! A Tale of First Flight **(Sheneman, 2017)**

About the Book: In this nearly wordless book, a young bird lives with his mama in a tall, tall tree. Afraid to fly, the bird imagines all kinds of dangers below until his mother lovingly gives him the nudge he needs to fly.

Ponder How Relationships Change

Book Title: *Mango, Abuela, and Me* (Medina, 2015)

About the Book: Mia's Abuela moves in with the family. Because Mia and Abuela speak different languages, they are having trouble communicating with each other. Mia's wise mother reminds Mia of how her bilingual friend learned English at school. Using the strategies her teacher employed, Mia and Abuela teach each other their native language.

To find a book like this one, look for the following:

- Relationships that change over the course of the story
- Intergenerational family stories

Learning Targets:

- I can notice how the characters' relationships change from the beginning to the end of the story.
- I can think about the events cause the change.
- I can talk, write, or draw about how the characters' relationship changed.

Comprehension Conversation:

Before Reading

Notice the Cover Illustration:

- If needed, explain (or ask a child who speaks Spanish to explain) that Abuela means grandmother in Spanish.

Set a Purpose: Sometimes in stories, characters change, and this can affect their relationships with other characters. As you listen to *Mango, Abuela, and Me*, think about if any of the characters change from the beginning to the end of the story and how this change affects their relationships.

During Reading

- *!Pín pán pún!* page: Can you imagine how Mia's Abuela is feeling? Why do you think she feels this way?
- *And her English is too poquito . . .* page: What does Mia mean when she says, "With our mouths as empty as our bread baskets?" [They don't have the words to talk with each other.]
- *When we bring him home . . .* page: Look at Abuela's face. What is Abuela's reaction to getting the parrot?

After Reading

- How did Mia and her Abuela's relationship change from the beginning to the end of the story? What important events led to that change?

Extend the Experience:

- Using the *Noticing How Relationships Change Reproducible* located on the companion website, draw and/or write about how Mia felt about Abuela at the beginning of the story [shy/unsure/can't communicate], the important events that happened to change their relationship [learning each others' language/getting the parrot], and how they both feel at the end of the story [like friends, talking, sharing stories.]

online resources

View the book trailer at resources.corwin.com/rampedup-readaloud

- If someone joins our class who speaks a language different from what you speak, what can you do to teach and learn from each other?

Key Vocabulary:

- bundle (verb) & Spanish words, as needed

Other similar titles:

 Bella's Fall Coat **(Plourde, 2016) [Intergenerational family stories]**

About the Book: Bella is getting too small for the coat that Grams made her, but she is also too busy playing outside in the beautiful fall day to care. Then, while *flying* with geese, her coat finally rips. As she sleeps, Grams sews her a new coat—just in time for the first snow. This book is brimming with verb pairs like "twirled and whirled" and energetic onomatopoeias as Bella runs outside to play.

 Drawn Together **(Lê, 2018)**

About the Book: When a young boy goes to visit his grandfather, they have difficulty communicating because they speak different languages. Just when they give up trying, they discover a new way to connect—through their shared love of drawing.

 In Plain Sight **(Jackson, 2016) [Intergenerational family stories]**

About the Book: Grandpa lives with Sophie and her family in a room filled with the things he loves. Each day, after school, Sophie visits her grandpa in his room. He cleverly hides an object, in plain sight, for her to find. On Sunday morning, Sophie sneaks into her grandpa's room while he's sleeping and hides herself. Your students will enjoy taking a close look at Jerry Pinkney's illustrations to find the hidden objects before Sophie does.

Name _____

Noticing How Relationships Change

Beginning	Important Event	Important Event	End

Noticing How Relationships Change Reproducible Response Page

Download this form at resources.corwin.com/rampedup-readaloud

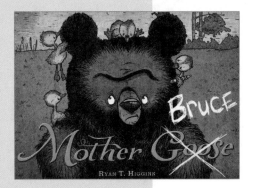

online resources

View the book trailer at resources.corwin.com/rampedup-readaloud

Learning Targets:

- I can identify the character, setting, problem, events, and solution in a story.

- I can talk, write, or draw about the elements of a story.

Identify Story Elements

Book Title: *Mother Bruce* (Higgins, 2015)

About the Book: Bruce, the grumpy bear, likes his eggs cooked in fancy recipes. One day, Bruce finds a recipe for boiled goose eggs, but instead of a delicious meal, he finds himself the mother to four goslings. After trying to scare them away, Bruce decides to make the best of the situation.

To find a book like this one, look for the following:

- Straightforward plots with clearly identifiable story elements

- Humorous stories

Comprehension Conversation:

Before Reading

Notice the Cover Illustration:

- Does anyone notice anything about the title of this book? Turn and tell your friend what you notice.

- Why do you think this story is called *Mother Bruce*? So, you're inferring this bear's name is Bruce. Look at Bruce's face. Turn and tell someone how you would describe Bruce's mood.

- [If you can take the dust jacket off of the book, you can show the book case with a close up illustration of Bruce.]

Set a Purpose: As we read this story we are going to think about the characters, location, action, problem, and solution. (C.L.A.P.S.; See Maria's Thinking for explanation.) This will help us to better understand and remember the elements of the story.

During Reading

- *He did NOT like cute little animals.* page: Who is the main character? What do you we know about Bruce so far?

- *Bruce only liked one thing—eggs!* page: Where does Bruce live? Where does this story take place?

- *But the fire in his stove fizzled.* page: Yikes! What do you predict is "the unwelcome surprise?"

- *MAMA!* page: What is the problem? [the goslings think Bruce is their mother]

- *Bruce left the goslings there anyway and went back home.* page: It sounds like Bruce solved the problem. Do you think he did?

- *. . . and migrated to Miami.* [If you have a map handy you can show students where Miami is located.] Wow! Bruce sure tried a lot of different solutions. How did he finally solve his problem? Let's turn the page and see what happens next.

After Reading

- Did that ending surprise you? It made me laugh. I like when authors do that, don't you?

- Does that story remind you of any other stories we've read?

Extend the Experience:

- Let's write down the characters, locations, action, problem, and solution.

- What are some other ways Bruce could have tried to solve his problem? Work with a partner to draw or write down some of your ideas.

Key Vocabulary:

- appetite
- pesky
- unwelcome

Maria's Thinking: To introduce readers to the elements of a story, I use a *secret formula* I learned from talented children's author Candace Fleming. When she helps young writers create stories, she uses a strategy she's dubbed C.L.A.P.S. The clever acronym serves as a graphic organizer for students by reminding them that a story must include Characters, Location/Setting, Action, Problem, and Solution (Fuhler & Walther, 2007). When using this acronym, I'm always careful to explain that the setting of a story is more than just the location of the story, but as Candace says, "C.S.A.P.S. doesn't make a word!"

Other similar titles:

Bruce's Big Move (Higgins, 2017)

About the Book: Bruce, the grumpy bear, is tired of his "crowded, chaotic, and loud" house so he decides that he and the geese are going to move away from the three pesky mice. In their new, quiet home by the lake, Bruce realizes how much the geese miss the mice. Luckily, for the geese (but not for Bruce), the mice decide to join the family again.

Hotel Bruce (Higgins, 2016)

About the Book: When Bruce and his goslings return from wintering in Miami, they discover their house has been transformed into a woodland hotel.

The Perfect Nest (Friend, 2007)

About the Book: Jack, the farm cat, builds the perfect nest to attract a perfect chicken who will lay the perfect egg for his omelet. Much to his surprise, he lures a chicken, duck, and goose into the nest. When they all lay eggs, Jack is ecstatic and shoos them to the next farm. Soon, he finds that instead of three eggs, he has three babies who need a lot of attention.

ALAN'S BIG, SCARY TEETH
by JARVIS

online resources

View the book trailer at resources.corwin.com/rampedup-readaloud

Learning Targets:

- I can identify and describe the character, setting, problem, events, and solution in a story.
- I can compare two stories with similar elements.

Comparing Story Elements

Book Title: *Alan's Big, Scary Teeth* (Jarvis, 2016)

About the Book: Alan the alligator is best known for scaring creatures with his *razor-sharp* teeth. Find out what happens when the animals discover Alan's secret—his teeth are fake.

To find a book like this one, look for the following:

- Straightforward plots with clearly identifiable story elements
- Humorous books about (false) teeth

Comprehension Conversation:

Before Reading

Notice the Cover Illustration:

- Let's read the title and the back cover blurb. Notice how author/illustrator, Jarvis, put those marks around frog and snail's head. What do you think those marks mean?

Set a Purpose: As we read, think about the different elements of the story. After reading we'll use these words: *somebody, wanted, but, so, finally,* and *in the end* to compare this story to another familiar story.

During Reading

- *Alan came from a long line of very scary alligators.* page: What do we already know about the main character?
- *TAKE OUT HIS FALSE TEETH!* page: Oh my goodness, I didn't expect that! Turn and talk to your partner about the surprise.
- *When Alan awoke his teeth were GONE.* page: What's the problem? How do you predict he will solve it?
- *Next morning . . .* page: How was the problem solved? Did your prediction match the author's thinking?

After Reading

- Let's talk about the elements of this story.
  - **Somebody (character):** *Alan*
  - **Wanted** *to scare the animals*
  - **But (problem)** *he lost his scary teeth*
  - **So** *he cried*
  - **Finally (solution),** *the animals gave them back (with rules)*
  - **In the end,** *he let Barry borrow his teeth.*

Extend the Experience:

- To prepare for this extension, read and record the elements of another similar story. (See other similar stories section.) After retelling two stories, compare the story elements in each story and tell how they are the same and different.

- Which story did you prefer and why?

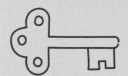

Key Vocabulary:

- familiar

- polishing

- terrified (terror, terrifying)

Comparing Story Elements Chart

Other similar titles:

 Bear's Loose Tooth **(Wilson, 2011)**

About the Book: Bear has his first loose tooth. His animal friends try to help him pull it out without success. Finally, Bear gives it a *nudge* with his tongue and out it pops! That night, the tooth fairy comes and leaves him blueberries. The next day, Bear discovers he has another loose tooth!

 Grandpa's Teeth **(Clement, 1997)**

About the Book: It's a "dis*thasth*ter!" [Note: This is the correct spelling because you have to read it like you have false teeth!] Someone has stolen Grandpa's false teeth. The police are called, everyone in town is a suspect, but they still can't find the teeth. Finally, the townspeople pitch in to buy Grandpa a new set so he can smile again. Guess who else is smiling? Grandpa's old dog Gump who has had the teeth in his mouth the whole time.

Read These! A Sampling of Paired Texts	
A Chip Off the Old Block (Shaffer, 2018)	*Cloudette* (Lichtenheld, 2011)
Creepy Carrots (Reynolds, 2012)	*Muncha! Muncha! Muncha!* (Fleming, 2002)
A Perfect Day (Smith, 2017)	*My Lucky Day* (Kasza, 2003)
Woolbur (Helakoski, 2008)	*Naked Mole Rat Gets Dressed* (Willems, 2009)

Notice How Authors Change Elements

Book Title: *The Turnip* (Brett, 2015)

About the Book: Badger Girl finds a giant turnip in her vegetable patch. Her family and friends, including a *cocky little rooster* attempt to help her pull it out of the ground. Finally, a family of bears living underground push the turnip up at the same time Rooster is pulling it out, so the critters all think rooster was the hero.

Maria's Thinking: To prepare for this read-aloud experience, gather and read a few different retellings of the Russian folktale about an enormous turnip. The version I like to read first is *The Gigantic Turnip* (1998). Then, I read the retellings listed in the "Other Similar Titles" section. This experience will also work with any collection of different versions of the same traditional tale like The Three Pigs, Little Red Riding Hood, or Goldilocks and the Three Bears.

To find a book like this one, look for the following:

- Straightforward plots with easily identifiable story elements
- Traditional tales with a unique twist

Comprehension Conversation:

Before Reading

Notice the Cover Illustration:

- If you've read a book by Jan Brett before, you know that she has distinctive illustrations. That means you can tell just by looking at the book that she created the pictures. What are some of the clues?
- What does it look like the animals are doing?
- Back Cover Illustration: What do you see inside the turnip shape?

Set a Purpose: To create a story, authors carefully put together parts or elements like characters, setting, problem, events, and solution. When rewriting a traditional tale, authors such as Jan Brett might change an element or elements of the story to create a new version.

Traditional tales are stories that have been told for many years like "Little Red Riding Hood" or "Goldilocks and the Three Bears." Have you heard either of those traditional tales before? Let's see if Jan Brett changed any of the elements in her version of the story of *The Turnip*.

During Reading

- *Badger Girl . . .* page: What do you see in the turn on the left-hand side of the page? Do you think it is the same bear family we noticed on the back cover? [As the story progresses, continue noticing the bear mother's actions as she prepares her cubs for bed.]
- *One autumn morning, the air turned chilly.* page: What animal do you see in the turnip shape on the right-hand side of the page? I wonder why Badger Boy is shown there.
- [As the story progresses, continue noticing that the characters who appear in the turnip on the right-hand side of the page are those who will appear next in the story.]

Learning Targets:

- I can identify and describe the character, setting, problem, events, and solution in a story.
- I can compare two stories with similar elements.
- I can notice how the author changed elements of a traditional tale.

- *Down in their winter den, the bears found . . .* page: Look at what the bear family is doing! [They are pushing the turnip up as the rooster is pulling on it.]

After Reading

- Was the rooster really as useful as they thought?

- What did you think of Jan Brett's surprise ending of this "Turnip Tale?" How did changing the ending change the story?

- Work with a partner to write and illustrate another turnip version using a different problem and different characters.

Extend the Experience:

- If your students have read or are reading other versions of the turnip tales, they can compare and contrast the tales to notice that when authors choose to change certain elements of a story, they create a new version of the story.

Comparing Different Turnip Versions Chart

Other similar titles:

  Grandma Lena's Big Ol' Turnip (Hester, 2005)

About the Book: Grandma Lena has planted turnips to make turnip stew. When the Big 'Ol turnip won't budge, she enlists the help of her family. As with the other versions, eventually the turnip comes out, and Grandma Lena makes a feast to feed the neighborhood. My students' favorite character is Baby Pearl!

  Kumak's Fish (Bania, 2004)

About the Book: Another variation of the turnip tale, set in the Arctic. In this story, Kumak and his family go ice fishing using "Uncle Aglu's amazing hooking stick." Kumak is sure he'll catch a gigantic fish. Soon, his poll begins to bend. Eventually, everyone in the village join in to pull the fish out only to discover that, instead of one big fish, there is a *village* of fish under water pulling right back.

Key Vocabulary:

- budge
- fond
- useful

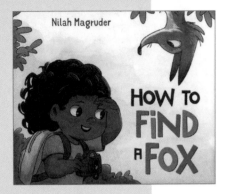

Nilah Magruder

HOW TO FIND A FOX

Study Images to Understand Characters

Book Title: *How to Find a Fox* (Magruder, 2016)

About the Book: Do you know how to find a fox? In this book, a girl shows readers exactly how to find a sly fox, but she doesn't notice that he is hiding in plain sight on almost every page.

To find a book like this one, look for the following:

- Illustrations that enhance or extend readers' understanding of characters, settings, and events
- Illustrations that help readers imagine how the characters are feeling

Learning Targets:

- I can study the illustrations to learn more about characters' feelings and actions.
- I can study and discuss the illustrations to better understand the story.

Key Vocabulary:

- bait
- search
- sneakier

Comprehension Conversation:

Before Reading

Notice the Cover Illustration:

- Nilah Magruder created the illustrations for this book using a computer. That is amazing. I would have guessed that she drew and painted them by hand.
- Wait! Isn't the title *How to Find a Fox*? The fox is right there. I wonder why the girl doesn't see it.

Set a Purpose: I'm predicting that the illustrations are going to be very important to this story. As we learn how to find a fox, zoom in on the illustrations to figure out more about what is happening in the story and to notice how the girl is feeling.

During Reading

- *Find a fox hole.* page: Oh boy! Do you see a fox on this page? Why doesn't the girl see the fox? [As the story continues, your students will enjoy noticing the fox hiding in plain sight!]
- *Wait a little longer.* page: Can you infer how she is feeling here? How did the illustrations help you figure that out?
- *Maybe you need a change of perspective.* page: What is the girl doing to get a "change of perspective"? Changing perspective means looking at things in a new way. Let's see what she does on the next page.
- *Maybe you should just give up.* page: Instead of giving up, what does she do?

After Reading

- Was that the ending you expected? What other ways could this story have ended? Turn and talk with your friend about the possibilities.
- How did studying the illustrations and learning from your friends help you to better understand the main character and what happened in this story?

Extend the Experience:

- In this story, the girl taught you the steps in finding a fox. Pick another creature you might want to find. Draw a "How to Find a _____" to share with your friend.

- Draw a picture and write another possible ending to this story.

How to Find a _____ Work Sample

Other similar titles:

How to Find an Elephant **(Banks, 2017)**

About the Book: From the team who brought you *Max's Words* (Banks, 2006), comes an innovative and eye-appealing adventure. A young boy takes readers along as he searches for an elephant. Your children will delight in finding the hidden elephant pictured on every page and on the wrap-around cover.

How to Wash a Woolly Mammoth **(Robinson, 2013)**

About the Book: A young girl shares her step-by-step guide to bathing a pet woolly mammoth. This book would be an ideal mentor text for informational how-to pieces.

Read These!
More Books for Illustration Study

Are We There Yet?
(Santat, 2016)

About the Book: A boy and his family are headed on the long car ride to grandma's birthday party. As their car travels through time and space, you will read upside down and backward (don't forget to scan the QR Codes). In the end, the boy discovers that "there's no greater gift than the present."

Breaking News: Bear Alert
(Biedrzycki, 2014)

About the Book: Told in the style of a news report, readers follow two bears enjoying a day in the city. Causing panic all around them, the bears calmly take in the sights and unwittingly become heroes. Once you've introduced this book to learners, it works well for individual illustration study. Students will pour over the bold and busy illustrations to find clues and bear-related humor.

Sam and Dave Dig a Hole
(Barnett, 2014)

About the Book: Sam and Dave are in search of *something spectacular*, so they set off to dig a hole. What readers see, but Sam and Dave don't, are the jewels hidden beneath the earth that they keep missing as they change directions. Kids gasp in disbelief each time the diggers miss the buried gems.

The Fan Brothers

Learning Targets:

- I can study and discuss the illustrations to better understand the story.

- I can talk, write, or draw about how the illustrations change over the course of the story.

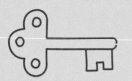

Key Vocabulary:

- admire

- commotion

- masterpiece

Notice How Images Change

Book Title: *The Night Gardener* (Fan & Fan, 2016)

About the Book: William lives in an orphanage on downtrodden Grimloch Lane. One morning, he wakes to a surprise topiary created by the night gardener. Each day, a new topiary appears bringing hope and happiness to the townsfolk. After William learns from the night gardener, the gardener leaves town and gifts his clippers to William so he can continue the work.

To find a book like this one, look for the following:

- Illustrations that enhance or extend readers' understanding of characters, settings, and events

- Illustrations that change over the course of the book

Comprehension Conversation:

Before Reading

- [To build background, you might want to have an image of a *topiary* handy to help define the text-specific word for your students.]

Notice the Cover Illustration:

- Look closely at the owl on the cover. What do you see? I notice that the illustration is so detailed you can see almost every leaf on the tree. I wonder if all the illustrations in the book will be this way. I can't wait to find out.

- Verso/copyright page: When you look at this illustration, how does it make you feel? Why? Tell a friend some details you notice in this two-page spread. [man with ladder, "watch for children" sign (why would that be there?), someone sitting on a log/bench in distance, girl with pigtails, Grimloch Lane sign]

- Dedication page: Wait! The illustrations are changing. [There is a little more color.] I wonder why the Fan brothers chose to do that.

- Title page: Turn and tell your friend what is happening on this page. Wow! We've already learned so much about this story and we're not even on the first page. I notice the sign says, "Grimloch Orphanage." Do you have any schema for orphanages? [If not, share that an orphanage is a place where children live whose family can't take care of them.]

Set a Purpose: As readers, it is so important to take time to look carefully at both the illustrations and words on all of the pages to better understand the story. Let's study the illustrations to see if they continue to change as we read this magical book.

During Reading

- *and he continued to stare. . .* page: When you picture a *night gardener* in your mind who do you see? Do you think this man is "The Night Gardener?" What makes you think so? What do you suppose he might create next? Why?

- *The following morning, William was not disappointed.* page: Discuss with a friend what you see on this page. [Notice the girl with pigtails from verso page is peeking over the fence.]

- *The next day, William dashed out of his home.* page: What good things are happening on this page? [The workers are fixing up the house. If you go back to the rabbit topiary page you can compare how the house looked before.]

- *William awoke . . .* page: Look! The Night Gardener left William his clippers. Why would he do that? Try and figure that out with a friend.

After Reading

- How had the town changed? How did the illustrations in this book help you to understand the changes?

 ### Extend the Experience:

- Fold your paper into three sections. In the first section, draw a picture of Grimloch Lane at the beginning of the story. In the third section, draw a picture of Grimloch Lane at the end of the story. Label your illustration to show the differences. In the middle, draw or write what happened to cause the changes (See the examples here).

- Think of things you could do to fix up our classroom, school, playground, or neighborhood. Work with a friend to make a list of ideas. Then, as a class we'll pick one and make a plan to do it.

Other similar titles:

 ***The Curious Garden* (Brown, 2009) (See read-aloud experience on page 94)**

About the Book: A curious boy named Liam discovers a struggling garden growing atop an abandoned railway line. After a few mishaps, he teaches himself how to garden so that can nurture the plants. Soon gardens are popping up all over the city. Be sure to read Peter Brown's Author's Note where he talks about the questions that led him to write this book.

Start/Change/End Work Sample

 ***Maybe Something Beautiful:
How Art Transformed a Neighborhood
(Campoy & Howell, 2016)***

About the Book: The city is drab and gray until Mira begins to share her paintings with people and catches the eye of a muralist. Together, along with the community, they transform the neighborhood into something beautiful. This joyful celebration of art and community is based on the true story of how Rafael López and his wife Candice revived the East Village near downtown San Diego, California, by turning the neighborhood into a work of art.

 ***The Napping House* (Wood, 1984)**

About the Book: In this classic cumulative tale, the snoring granny, the dozing child, and their animal friends are taking a nap on a rainy day. As the story progresses, the rain slows to a stop and the sun comes shining through the window. Notice how the perspective changes in the illustrations from an eye-level vantage point to a bird's eye view and back down again. It is helpful to look at the water pitcher and chair to watch this happen.

My Favorite Read Alouds for Illustration Study

BLUE SKY
WHITE STARS

online
resources

Read background
information about the book
at resources.corwin.com/
rampedup-readaloud

Learning Targets:

- I can study
and discuss the
illustrations to
better understand
the story.

- I can think
beyond the text
and illustrations
to figure out the
theme or big idea.

Think Beyond Images to Big Ideas

Book Title: *Blue Sky White Stars* (Naberhaus, 2017)

About the Book: Naberhaus wrote this story to illuminate the parallels between America and its flag. She poetically uses the same or similar words to describe our country and its most prominent symbol. Kadir Nelson's stunning paintings help to make her words glow. To fully understand this book, your students will benefit from background knowledge about key points in American history. It will also be helpful for you to read the book background information in the back matter and on the author's website.

To find a book like this one, look for the following:

- Illustrations that enhance and extend the meaning of the text

- Lyrical text

- Illustrations that support the understanding of the theme or big idea of the story

Comprehension Conversation:

Before Reading

Notice the Cover Illustration:

- [Open the book so your students can see the front and back cover at the same time.]

- What do you notice about Kadir Nelson's oil paintings on the front and back cover?

- What holiday do you think these people are celebrating?

- Can you think of anything else in our world that is blue with white stars? Turn and tell your neighbor.

Set a Purpose: We're going to begin by reading this book straight through with no stopping or talking so we can enjoy Sarvinder Naberhaus's words and Kadir Nelson's paintings. Then, we'll go back and look and think carefully how they work together to help us better understand the big ideas.

Maria's Thinking: Because this book has sparse text, you will have enough time to it read aloud once without stopping, and then go back to look, think, and talk about the illustrations. When doing this in my classroom, I spend no more than ten minutes exploring the illustrations. This means it takes me a few read-aloud experiences to enjoy the beauty of the book either over the course of one day or over a few days in a row.

During Reading

- *WHITE ROWS* page: What is making the white rows on the left-hand side of the page? [the covered wagons] How about on the right-hand side? [the stripes on the flag] How many stripes are on the flag? What do they stand for?

- *OLD GLORY* page: Did you know that our nation's flag is sometimes called "Old Glory?" Why do you think the Grand Canyon is called "OLD GLORY"?

- *SEA WAVES* page: Let's talk about how the author played with words on this page. What is the difference between "SEA WAVES" and "SEE WAVES"?

- *SO TOGETHER* page: Look how she did a similar thing with the words on these pages. Let's talk about the meaning behind the words and pictures.

- [Continue in the same fashion as the book continues highlighting historical events, discussing the meaning behind the words and paintings, and thinking about the big ideas.]

After Reading

- This book gave us a lot to think and talk about. What are some of the big ideas you learned about America?

Extend the Experience:

- On this index card, write two words that you would use to describe America. This is called the *Two-Word Strategy*. You can use it to help you remember and retell the key ideas of a text (Hoyt, 1999, p. 4).

- Pick an image in the book that you want to learn more about. Do some research and find one fun fact to share with your classmates. [Some possible images include the Statue of Liberty, covered wagons, the Grand Canyon, the first flag, Abe Lincoln, the March on Washington, Wrigley Field, a bald eagle, and Neil Armstrong's first step on the moon.]

Other similar titles:

 ***Before She Was Harriet* (Cline-Ransome, 2017)**

About the Book: A poetic tribute to Harriet Tubman that traces her life accomplishments backward in history from suffragist to childhood. It will be helpful if children have some background knowledge about Harriet Tubman before reading this book.

 ***Climbing Lincoln's Steps: The African American Journey* (Slade, 2010)**

About the Book: Using the marble steps of the Lincoln Memorial as a backdrop, Slade retells key moments in African-American history. She repeats the powerful lines, "Change. It happens slowly. One small step at a time." This gives the text a lyrical feel.

YOU WILL BE MY FRIEND!

Peter Brown

online resources

View an interview with Peter Brown at resources .corwin.com/rampedup-readaloud

Learning Targets:

- I can identify who is telling the story at different points.

- I can think about how knowing who is talking helps me better understand the story.

Key Vocabulary:

- critter

- decided

- ridiculous

Identify Who Is Talking

Book Title: *You Will Be My Friend!* (Brown, 2011)

About the Book: Lucy, the bear, is determined to find a new friend. She's a little overzealous and scares away many of the animals. Finally, she finds a friend who has the same interests as she does.

To find a book like this one, look for the following:

- To highlight point of view—books where different speakers' dialogue is marked in different ways

- If friendship is your focus—characters who comes to an understanding that you shouldn't have to be someone else to find a true friend

Comprehension Conversation:

Before Reading

Notice the Cover Illustration:

- Let's read this title carefully, *You Will Be My Friend!* At first I thought it read, *Will You Be My Friend?*

- Let me write those sentences so you can look at them. What do you notice? Look at all other animals? How are they reacting to the bear? Why? What do you see behind Peter Brown's drawings? [wood] Wow! I wonder if there is wood behind all the pages.

Set a Purpose: Sometimes stories are told from different characters' points of view. That means that sometimes one character or the narrator will tell the story as he or she sees or experiences it. Sometimes more than one character tells the story. That is true for *You Will Be My Friend.* As we read, I need you to help me figure out who is telling the story.

During Reading

- *So Lucy went outside to begin her search.* page: Let's go back to the beginning and notice who is telling the story at different points. How has Peter Brown helped us to know this as readers? [The narrator's words are blue, Lucy's are orange, and Mom's are pink.]

- *Lucy did her best to win over the forest animals.* page: What is Lucy doing to *win over* the forest animals? *Win over* is another way of saying she is trying to convince or talk them into being her friend. Let's keep reading to see what else is she does to win over the forest animals.

- *Come back here and have fun with me!* page: Think about all the things Lucy is doing. Do you think she should have to win over or fit in to find a friend? Maybe there is a different way to find friends. Any ideas?

- *DOESN'T ANYBODY WANT TO BE MY FRIEND?!* page: Look carefully at this illustration. What do you notice? [One of the flamingos looks different/worried/sad.]

After Reading

- That book had a happy ending! I enjoy books with happy endings; how about you?

- How did Peter Brown help you as the reader identify who was talking at different points of the story? How did that help you better understand the story?

Extend the Experience:

- Writers, think about what you learned from Peter Brown about point of view. Maybe when your characters are talking you could write their words in different colors.

- What do you do when you want to find a friend? Let's help Lucy by writing a three-step guide to friend finding.

  o How to Find a Friend

    - Step 1:
    - Step 2:
    - Step 3:

Other similar titles:

 Goodbye Summer, Hello Autumn (Pak, 2016) [point of view]

About the Book: A girl with a bright red scarf greets all the signs of the coming season and each responds. The dialogue is not marked in any way, so readers have to infer from the structure of the story and the text whether it's the girl or the natural world doing the talking. Later in the year, you can read *Goodbye Autumn, Hello Winter* (Pak, 2017).

 I Love You Already (John, 2016) [point of view and friendship]

About the Book: Bear wants to spend a relaxing morning by himself, but his energetic friend Duck has other ideas. The back and forth banter is humorous and begs to be read with two voices. Bear's words appear in a chunky bold font, while Duck's dialogue is a different font clearly indicating who is talking throughout the story.

 My Best Friend (Rodman, 2005) [friendship]

About the Book: When Lilly is at the pool, she tries hard to act like Tamika (who is one year older) so that Tamika will be her friend. Tamika isn't nice to Lilly until her friend Shanice is away for the day. The next day, when Shanice returns, Lilly realizes that she should find a different friend. Luckily, same-age Keesha, who has been around all along, is ready to play. Mary Ann Rodman highlights the same theme as Peter Brown did in *You Will Be My Friend!* (Brown, 2011).

puddle

HYEWON YUM

Learning Targets:

- I can identify who is telling the story at different points.

- I can think about how knowing who is talking helps me better understand the story.

- I can tell which parts of the book are real and which parts are imaginary or part of a dream.

Distinguish Between Real and Make Believe

Book Title: *Puddle* (Yum, 2016)

About the Book: One drizzly day, a grumpy boy is bored until his mom coaxes him to draw with her. Later, after drawing about walking in the rain, the boy and the mom go for a rainy-day walk. Notice that the dialogue of the boy and the mom are differentiated by the colors of the text.

To find a book like this one, look for the following:

- Plots where two different characters' points of view that are clearly portrayed

- Illustrations that differentiate between dream scenes and reality

Comprehension Conversation:

Before Reading

Notice the Cover Illustration:

- What do you enjoy doing on rainy days? See the boy and the dog on the cover of this book called *Puddle*? The puddle almost looks like real water. I wonder how Hyewon Yum made it look that way. Do you think this story is real or make believe?

- Do you think the boy and the dog are the only characters in this book? Who else might be in this story?

Set a Purpose: When readers pay attention to who is talking in the story, it helps them to better understand the plot (or what is happening). Let's find out if the boy is the only character who talks in this story and whether this story is a real or a make-believe.

During Reading

- *Don't be so grumpy.* page: Do you notice something different about the text (that means words) on this page? [It's red.] Why do you think it is a different color? [Because the mom is talking on this page.]

- *There!* page: I notice two different colored text on this page. Can you help me figure out what the author is trying to show me? [That when the mom is talking her words are in a red font, and when the boy is talking his words are in a black font so that even though we can't see who is talking we can figure it out.]

- *Thanks, Mom!* page: How can you tell who is drawing on this page? [You can see the boy's hand holding the blue crayon.]

- *No, no, no, NO, NO!* page: Let's read this together the way the author wants it to sound.

- *I said not to go in there.* Ponder for a minute. Is this part happening in real life? What are your clues? [The boy says, "Mom, it's just a picture."]

- Two-page spread where they are really outside walking: Is this really happening? What are the clues? What do you predict might happen next? What happened so far in the story to make you think that? [Yes, it's really happening because

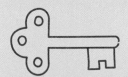
you can see apartments in the background (you didn't see those in their picture). I think he's going to jump in the puddle because he has a sneaky expression on his face, and he did that in their drawing.]

After Reading

- How did the mom change the boy's mind about the rain? [She got him interested in going outside by drawing about it.]

- Which parts of the story were real, and which parts were make believe?

- How did thinking about who is talking help you to better understand what was happening in the story?

Extend the Experience:

- Writers, when you are creating a story with two characters, you might choose to put their words in two different colors to help your readers better understand who is talking.

- The boy and his mom liked rainy days. Pick your three favorite kinds of weather. Survey the kids in class to see which they prefer. See *Take a Survey! Reproducible Response Page* located on the companion website.

Key Vocabulary:

- grumpy
- pouring [rain]
- tricky

∙∙

Other similar titles:

 Goodnight, Hockey Fans (Larsen, 2017) [Font that differentiates between dream scenes and reality]

About the Book: A young hockey fan is having difficulty falling asleep. So he turns on his dad's old radio to listen to the game. He drifts off to sleep and dreams that he scores a big goal. The dream sequence is written in a different font than the story, helping readers differentiate between the two.

 I Will Take a Nap (Willems, 2015) [Illustrations that differentiate between dream scenes and reality]

About the Book: Elephant is desperate to take a nap. Is Piggie disturbing his sleep or is it all a dream? Notice that the dream sequence, beginning on page 9, is illustrated with a muted green background.

 Rain! (Ashman, 2013) [point of view]

About the Book: An enthusiastic young boy and a grumpy old man both experience rain in their own way. In the end, the boy shows the man kindness and his attitude toward the rain changes a bit. The fonts differ depending on who is doing the talking and the illustrations clearly show the characters' moods.

Take a Survey!

Take a Survey! Reproducible Response Page

Download this form at resources.corwin.com/rampedup-readaloud

THEY ALL SAW A CAT

BRENDAN WENZEL

View the book trailer at
resources.corwin.com/
rampedup-readaloud

Learning Targets:

- I can notice that there are different ways to look at or think about things (different perspectives).

- I can ponder why people have different perspectives.

Understanding Different Perspectives

Book Title: *They All Saw a Cat* (Wenzel, 2016)

About the Book: A cat walks through the world and each animal it encounters views the cat from a different perspective. Wenzel uses a range of art media and techniques to depict each animal's unique viewpoint. This book was a 2017 Caldecott Honor Book.

To find a book like this one, look for the following:

- Illustrations that invite multiple viewpoints
- Text that sparks a dialogue about perspective

Comprehension Conversation:

Before Reading

Notice the Cover Illustration:

- [Before showing students the cover of the book, have the following conversation.] Close your eyes and picture a cat. Turn and tell your friend about the cat you pictured. [Invite a few students to share with the group.] Why do you think we all have a different picture of a cat in our brains? We have different pictures because we all have our own perspectives. That means because of our experiences with cats, we all picture a different kind of cat.

- Brendan Wenzel's illustrations in this book won the Caldecott Honor in 2017. That means a group of experts decided that his illustrations helped to better tell the story and were written especially for kids.

- Consider the title of this book—*They All Saw a Cat*. Who might *they* be?

Set a Purpose: As we enjoy the words and art in this book, I want you to help me figure out why Brendan Wenzel chose the title *They All Saw a Cat* and whether *they* are all going to see that cat from the same perspective.

During Reading

- *and the fish saw . . .* page: Talk about this illustration with a friend. Why do you think it looks this way? [Perhaps the fish is looking out of his fishbowl at the cat.]

- *and the mouse saw . . .* page: Do you think this picture shows you how mice feel about cats? [Yes, because the background is red and the cat looks really scary. The cat's teeth and claws are extra sharp and long.]

- *and the bird saw . . .* page: Talk about the bird's view. Why do you think it looks like this? Do you spot any other animals on this page? [The bird is flying above the cat looking down so you can only see the top of the cat. You can also see the clouds around the bird, the fish in the pond, and the mouse hiding by a bush.]

- *YES, THEY ALL SAW A CAT!* page: I bet if you went back to each page you could match a part of this cat to a page.

After Reading

- So, now that we've read and talked about this book, what are you thinking or wondering about the title?

- Why do you think each creature saw the cat in a different way? [They had different experiences; they felt different ways about a cat; they had different perspectives.]

- Turn to a friend and finish this sentence. They all saw a cat, but. . .

Extend the Experience:

- When I saw the word "WATER" [or other noun that has multiple interpretations like BALL, BIRD, CAKE, PET, TOY] what do you see? Draw a picture on your whiteboard (or piece of paper) to show us what you visualize. [Compare and discuss drawings to continue the conversation about how your experiences, beliefs, and attitudes shape your perspective.]

- If you had to give this book a different title what would it be? Draw a new cover for the book using your title and illustration.

Key Vocabulary:

- imagine, perspective* [*This word does not appear in the book, but it will be helpful when discussing the book.]

Other similar titles:

Duck! Rabbit! **(Rosenthal, 2009)**

About the Book: Two unseen narrators debate whether the creature they see is a duck or a rabbit. You can use this book to spark conversations about mental images and multiple perspectives. Because kids love reading it so much, it is a perfect book for rereading with a partner to strengthen fluency.

Picture a Tree **(Reid, 2011)**

About the Book: Barbara Reid's unique Plasticine illustrations celebrate trees in all seasons and settings. She wrote this book in second person to invite readers to slow down and notice that "there is more than one way to picture a tree."

Seven Blind Mice **(Young, 1992)**

About the Book: In Ed Young's 1992 Caldecott Honor book, he tells a variation of the fable where the blind men try to identify an elephant. In his version, six of the blind mice focus on one separate part of the elephant and disagree on what it is. In the end, the seventh blind mouse takes the time to experience the whole elephant and helps the others to do the same. The book ends with a *mouse moral* that provides a jumping-off point for rich discussions.

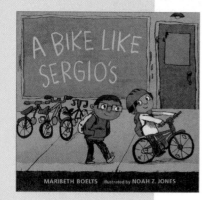

Learning Targets:

- I can think about how the main character responds to the challenges he faces in the book.

- I can understand the big ideas, lessons, or morals of this story.

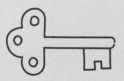

Key Vocabulary:

- appear
- mumble
- proud

Understand Big Ideas

Book Title: *A Bike Like Sergio's* (Boelts, 2016)

About the Book: Ruben is longing for a bike just like his friend Sergio's, but his family can't afford one. While he and his friend are shopping, a woman drops some money. Ruben, thinking it's a dollar bill, puts it in his pocket. When he gets home, he realizes it is a $100 bill. In the end, Ruben does the right thing and returns to the money to the woman.

To find a book like this one, look for the following:

- Books with diverse characters
- Characters who have to decide whether or not to do the right thing

Comprehension Conversation:

Before Reading

Notice the Cover Illustration:

- Think about the title *A Bike Like Sergio's* and look carefully at the cover illustration that Noah Jones created using watercolor, pencil, ink, and a computer. What do you think this book might be about?

- As we read, we'll see if your before-reading predictions match the author's thinking or if they are different than the author's thinking.

Set a Purpose: In this book, Ruben has some choices to make. Let's pay attention to what he chooses to do and what events in the story lead him to that decision.

During Reading

- *"I wish," I say, but I know that wishes. . .* page: On these two pages, we learned a little more about Rubin's family. What did you learn?

- *Later, when I'm alone . . .* page: Instead of writing Ruben feels _____, Maribeth Boelts wrote, "My hands are shaking." As a reader, you have to use the clues from the pictures and the words to infer how Ruben is feeling. Turn and talk about what you're thinking. What do you think Ruben should do with the money he found?

- *I walk hunched and draggy to school. . .* page: What words on this page help you to know how Ruben is feeling now?

- *And like a hot blast, I remember. . .* page: What events happened that made Ruben change his mind?

After Reading

- Why are Ruben's parents *so proud*? Think of a time when you were proud of yourself and share that with your neighbor.

- What are the big ideas, lessons, or morals that we can learn from this story?

Maria's Thinking: As you can see from work sample A, some children find it challenging to figure out the big idea. You may also have children who are having difficulty with the abstract concept of the big idea or moral. If so, you might choose to pull together a small group to scaffold their understanding. With book in hand, so you can refer to key pages, have a conversation such as the following:

T: What did Ruben **do** near the end of the story?

S: Give the money back.

T: Why do you think he did that?

S: I don't know.

T: Let's look at this picture. Look at her face. How is she feeling when Ruben gave her the money?

S: Happy

T: So, you're saying what he did made her feel happy?

S: Yes.

T: Then, maybe we should all do things that make people happy. What do you think?

S: I think we should do stuff to make people happy.

T: That's so smart. You just taught me a lesson, just like the author was trying to teach you a lesson. Work with your friends to see if you can figure out any other lessons in this story.

A Bike Like Sergio's Work Sample A

 ### Extend the Experience:

- Make a poster to share with your classmates about the lesson or big idea you learned from reading this book.

- Draw a picture or write some words to finish this sentence: I felt proud when . . .

Other similar titles:

 ***The Can Man* (Williams, 2010)**

About the Book: Tim's parents can't afford to buy him a new skateboard for his birthday, so he is looking for ways to earn money. Along comes Mr. Peters, a homeless man known as "The Can Man," who gives Tim an idea. But Tim soon discovers that he has taken away Mr. Peters' only source of income. Pair and compare this book with *Fly Away Home* (Bunting, 1991).

 ***Those Shoes* (Boelts, 2007)**

About the Book: Jeremy really wants *those shoes*—the pair of high-tops that everyone else has, but Grandma can't afford them. Later, Jeremy finds a pair in a thrift store that are much too small but gets them anyway. After much debate, Jeremy ends up giving his too-small shoes to another boy in need.

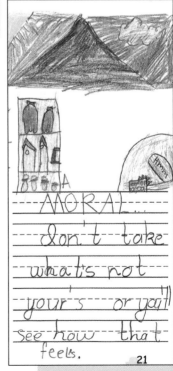

A Bike Like Sergio's Work Sample B

The Curious Garden

PETER BROWN

View the book trailer at resources.corwin.com/rampedup-readaloud

Learning Targets:

- I can infer the big ideas, lessons, or morals of this story.

- I can talk, write, or draw about how the big ideas in the story.

Infer Big Ideas

Book Title: *The Curious Garden* (Brown, 2009)

About the Book: A curious boy named Liam discovers a struggling garden growing atop an abandoned railway line. After a few mishaps, he teaches himself how to garden so that can nurture the plants. Soon gardens are popping up all over the city. Be sure to read Peter Brown's Author's Note where he talks about the questions that led him to write this book.

To find a book like this one, look for the following:

- Themes related to protecting the environment

- Characters who choose to act in environmentally friendly ways

Comprehension Conversation:

Before Reading

Notice the Cover Illustration:

- When I look at the cover illustration, I'm curious. Where is this garden? Who is this boy? Are there any clues in Peter Brown's illustration that might help me to answer these questions? [There is a wall around the garden and clouds behind the boy. Maybe the garden is up high. There is a watering can next to the boy. Perhaps he is taking care of the plants in the garden. He's reading a book with the same flower on the cover as the flowers in the garden. It might be a book about how to grow or take care of flowers.] Do you have any other questions?

Set a Purpose: Let's read to find the answers to our questions, and as we answer these questions, we can think together about the theme or big idea of this story.

During Reading

- *There once was a city without gardens* . . . page: It says the city is a *dreary* place. Look at the illustration, what do you think *dreary* means. [It means dull or gloomy. There isn't a lot of color in the illustration.]

- *Liam ran up the stairs, pushed open the door, and stepped out* . . . page: I'm curious, what do you think Liam might do? Why do you think that?

- *Winter had taken a toll on the garden.* page: What does Peter Brown mean by *taken a toll* on the garden? Use the clues in the illustration to help you figure it out. [The plants look like they did when Liam first found the garden. They're brown instead of green. There aren't any flowers.] So, *taken a toll* means that winter hurt or damaged the garden.

- *Many years later, the entire city had blossomed.* page: Can you infer who is in this picture "many years later"? [Liam is now the dad, and his wife and children are taking care of the garden.]

After Reading

- Let's compare the first page to the last page. How did the city change in the story? [It went from *dreary* to *blossoming*. There were no people outside on the first page, and there are a lot of people outside on the last page. There is a lot of green space, and the sky is blue on the last page, and so forth.]

- What caused the change? What message do you think Peter Brown is sharing in this book?

- [After reading, put the book in a place where students can do a close study of the illustrations and notice the following:

  o Compare the dreary city on the first two-page spread to the blossoming city on the last two-page spread.

  o Find all the different gardens pictured on the "But the most surprising things that popped up. . ." page and the page that follows in the two-page blossoming city spread at the end of the book.

  o On the six-paneled page with the different gardens, notice that a grown-up Liam is having a picnic with his future wife in an old parking lot (see the parking meters and parking space lines!).

  o Notice the garden on top of the bar code on the back of the book!]

Key Vocabulary:

- curious
- delicate
- dreary

Extend the Experience:

- I'm curious to hear what you infer the big ideas or lessons are in this book. Write and draw to share your thinking.

- What can you do to make the world a *greener* place? Draw a diagram showing your idea.

Other similar titles:

 ***Grandpa Green* (Smith, 2011)**

About the Book: Grandpa Green's great grandson tells you about his great grandfather's life as he follows him through the garden. As they meander, the boy helps him with the little things he's forgotten to do and picks up the items he's left along the way.

 ***The Tree* (Layton, 2016)**

About the Book: A couple have a *wonderful plan* to build a house, but a tree stands in their way. As they begin to cut down the tree, they realize that it is home to many animals. Thinking flexibly, they revise their original house plan and create homes for the creatures who share their tree. This book is a powerful Earth Day read aloud! You can also pair and compare it to *The Great Kapok Tree: A Tale of the Amazon Rain Forest* (Cherry, 1990).

Curious Garden Work Sample

words and paintings by KADIR NELSON

Learning Targets:

- I can infer the big ideas, lessons, or morals of this story.
- I can talk, write, or draw about the actions I would take to apply these lessons in my own life.

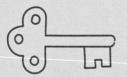

Key Vocabulary:

- kindness
- selfishness

Apply Big Ideas

Book Title: *If You Plant a Seed* (Nelson, 2015)

About the Book: Rabbit and Mouse plant seeds, but their selfishness leads to trouble. They discover that planting a seed of kindness is much sweeter.

To find a book like this one, look for the following:

- Characters faced with a moral dilemma
- Theme of kindness

Comprehension Conversation:

Before Reading

Notice the Cover Illustration:

- The title of this book is *If You Plant a Seed*. What happens when you plant a seed?
- Notice that the cover reads, "Words and Paintings by Kadir Nelson." Notice how his oil paintings are so realistic looking that its seems like the rabbit and mouse are standing right in front of you. I can't wait to see the illustrations inside the book!

Set a Purpose: Listeners, while we're reading together, ponder what happens "if you plant a seed." Let's think and talk together about why Kadir Nelson might have written this book and how what we learn from it might help us in our own lives.

During Reading

- *in time, with love . . .* page: What is Kadir Nelson showing you in these four panels? [the passage of time, what the animals are doing to care for the plant]
- Two-page spread where the birds appear: If the birds had speech or thought bubbles above their heads what would you write in them?
- *If you plant a seed of selfishness, in a very short time . . .* page: Turn and talk with someone to see if, together, you can figure out what is going on here.
- *it will grow, and grow, and grow . . .* page: This page is similar to the "in time" page at the beginning of the book. Let's go back and compare the two pages. What has changed? [the rabbit, mouse, and birds are working together]

After Reading

- So, what happened when rabbit and mouse planted a seed? [Encourage your children to *dig deeper* than simply saying, "Plants grew."] Yes, plants grew. That is one thing that grew, what else grew? [kindness]

Extend the Experience:

- How can we grow kindness in our classroom? I'm going to give you this heart-shaped piece of paper. When you notice someone doing something kind, write it down and give it to that person. Let's see what we can learn from each other's acts. See *Acts of Kindness Reproducible Response Page* located on companion website.

- Write or draw about the big ideas in this book.

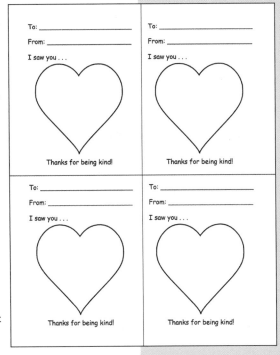

Acts of Kindness Reproducible Response Page

Download this form at resources.corwin.com/rampedup-readaloud

Other similar titles:

 Each Kindness (Woodson, 2012)

About the Book: When the new girl Maya joins the class, Chloe ignores her because she is less fortunate and different. Chloe's wise teacher does an activity that demonstrates the far-reaching power of kindness. After this compelling lesson, Chloe wishes she had shown Maya kindness. Sadly, Chloe never gets the chance because Maya moves away.

 Most People (Leannah, 2017)

About the Book: Most people in this world are helpful, kind, happy, and loving. Readers see examples of people engaging in kind acts and learn that, although some people choose to do bad things, most people want to do good things. After reading, ask children to talk about the acts of kindness they saw in the book.

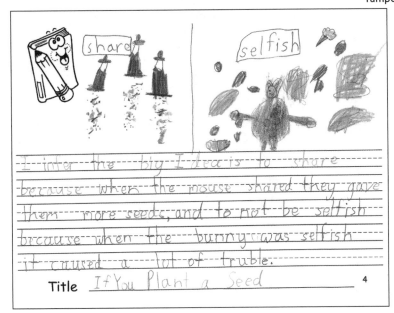

If You Plant a Seed Work Sample

"As he listened, Bunny imagined himself

climbing mountains . . .

captaining a ship . . .

ruling a kingdom . . ."

—*Bunny's Book Club*
by Annie Silvestro and Tatjana Mai-Wyss

Converse About Comprehension–Fiction

Imagining Ourselves Into Books

The read-aloud experience is a welcoming learning event for all of your readers. Whether a child is still striving to make sense of the printed word or is a *word caller* who can read the words but is not deeply comprehending yet, you can offer support. As you read and encourage children to converse with you or with each other, your insights, questions, and prompts call their attention to the goal of reading—comprehension. Stephanie Harvey and Harvey Daniels (2009) stress the importance of comprehension instruction, "Today, we build lessons around what skillful readers do. We teach thinking strategies that help learners understand whenever they read, listen, or view" (p. 25). In Chapter 3, the read-aloud experiences will support you as you model and teach the thinking strategies that follow to help your learners comprehend:

- Make Meaningful Connections
- Predict and Prove
- Question Your Way Through a Text
- Visualize Using Senses and Feelings
- Retell to Demonstrate Understanding

On the next page, you will find the concepts you will introduce or review while zooming in on comprehension strategies. To help you better explain these concepts to your young learners, I've included kid-friendly definitions. View the books in this chapter as your teaching partners. Dig in, debate, nudge your children to think deeply and reflect on how they've figured things out. Note their difficulties and celebrate their successes. Use what you've learned from your informal observations during the next read-aloud experience and when you work with them individually or in small groups. Guide them so that eventually they can imagine themselves into any story.

Use and Explain Key Comprehension Strategies

Connect: Use your schema or what you already know about the topic or an element of the story to help you better understand what you are reading.

Predict: Think ahead of your reading by using clues from the pictures and text to think about what might happen next in the story.

Question: Asking questions before, during, and after reading makes you want to keep reading to find the answers. Questions also help you to think more deeply about the text and better understand the author's message

Visualize/Make Mental Images: To picture in your mind what is happening in the text.

Foster a Growth Mindset

Revise Your Thinking: As flexible thinkers, we are able to revise our thinking. That means first we might think one thing, and then when we listen to our friends, read some more or learn something new, we can change or revise what we first thought. When we talk about revising our thinking we might say, "First I thought _____. Now that I've learned more I think _____."
Revising our thinking helps stretch our brain.

Converse About Comprehension—Fiction

Develop Students' Social and Emotional Learning

Ask Questions: Asking questions means starting with words like *who, what, when, where, why,* and *how* when you are wondering or want to know more about something. Asking questions helps us to learn.

Discuss: When we discuss something with our friends we take turns talking and listening. As we listen, we think about what our friends are saying. When they are done talking, we ask questions or build on their thinking.

Listen: Listening is important for learning. When you are listening to something your brain is thinking about what the person is saying. Also, by looking at the person and nodding your head or making comments when he or she is done, you are showing the person you care about what he or she has to say.

Teach Literary Language

Author's Purpose: Authors write books for different reasons or purposes. Some books entertain us, others share information, and still others are trying to persuade or convince us to do something. Some books teach us lessons that we can use in your own lives.

Figurative Language: When authors use words to help us to better see the world in a new way. Figurative language is frequently used in poetry, and as readers, we often have to infer what the author means rather than use the words' literal or actual meanings.

Retell: Tell the main events in the story in the order that they happened.

Sensory Language: Words the author uses to help us better see, hear, taste, smell, or feel what is happening in the text. Sensory language helps you use your senses to make mental images or visualize what is happening in the text.

Chapter 3 Concepts, Terms, and Kid-Friendly Definitions

My Favorite Read Alouds for Comprehension—Fiction

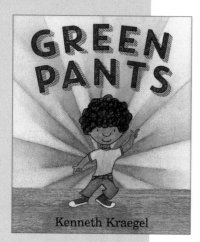

GREEN PANTS

Kenneth Kraegel

View the book trailer at resources.corwin.com/rampedup-readaloud

Learning Targets:

- I can understand how the character is feeling to better understand the story.

- I can think about how I would feel in the same situation.

Connect With Characters' Feelings

Book Title: *Green Pants* (Kraegel, 2017)

About the Book: Green is the only color of pants Jameson will wear. In fact, he believes that his green pants give him the power to do just about anything. When his cousin's fiancée, Jo, who he adores, invites him to be in their wedding, Jamison enthusiastically agrees. Then, his mother informs him he will have to wear a tuxedo with black pants. Jameson is in a quandary, but he eventually agrees to wear the black pants (over his green ones) after seeing how excited Jo is on her wedding day.

To find a book like this one, look for the following:

- Characters or situations that are relatable to children

- Characters whose feelings and emotions change over the course of the story

 ## Comprehension Conversation:

Before Reading

Notice the Cover Illustration:

- When you look at Kenneth Kraegel's cover illustration, what do you see? Perhaps the boy is the main character. What do you think?

- Back Cover Blurb: What do you suppose "Behold the power of green pants!" means? To get you started, I'll tell you that the word *behold* means to look at or observe.

Set a Purpose: When we put ourselves "in the shoes of the character" and consider what he or she is thinking and feeling, it helps us to better comprehend (or understand) the story. Let's think and talk together about how we would feel if we were in same situation as the main character.

During Reading

- *Jameson only ever wore green pants.* page: I notice the word *anything* is in italics. That means the author wants us to emphasize that word. Let's read it the way the author wants us to. Do you have a favorite piece of clothing or item at home that makes you believe you can do anything?

- *But one way . . .* page: Where do you see the pants in this picture? [flying on the flag pole and on the dog!]

- *"Would you like to be in our wedding?"* page: How does Jameson respond to Jo's request? [*Absolutely*] What other words or phrases do you know that mean the same as *absolutely* in this sentence? [Yes! Okay! Sure Thing! Of Course!] Have any of you ever been in a wedding? To help build our schema, share one thing you remember about it.

- *WHAT? Jameson gasped.* page: How does Jameson react when his mom tells him he has to wear black pants? What do you suppose he is going to do? Turn and discuss it with your friend.

After Reading

- Why do you believe Jameson decided to wear the black pants to the wedding? What was the turning point in the story? Let's go back and reread that part.

- What would you have done if you were Jameson? Why? Would anyone have done something different?

Extend the Experience:

- Have you ever had to do something you didn't really want to do? If so, write about it. You can begin like this: I understand how Jameson was feeling because once I had to . . .

- What piece of clothing or object gives you power? Draw a picture of it and add the title: Behold the Power of the _____

Key Vocabulary:

- absolutely
- dashing (adjective)
- lingered

Other similar titles:

 ***Hello Goodbye Dog* (Gianferrari, 2017)**

About the Book: Zara, who uses a wheelchair, has a dog named Moose. Story-loving Moose says "Hello" to school but is repeatedly "Good-byed" by teachers, librarians, and even the principal. Once Zara takes Moose to be trained as a therapy dog, he is welcomed at school to listen to children read. The Author's Note explains a bit more about therapy dogs. Kids who have dogs and those who love to read will relate to this book.

 ***The Ring Bearer* (Cooper, 2017)**

About the Book: It's the day of Mama's wedding and Jackson is worried about how his life will change. As the ring bearer, he is terrified that he might trip when walking down the aisle. His grandpop advises that he and his new stepsister walk slowly down the aisle, but Sophie doesn't listen. When she begins to trip on a stair, Jackson risks losing the rings and catches her. This spur-of-the-moment decision makes everyone, including Jackson, proud. As the wedding concludes, Jackson is no longer as nervous about his new family.

View the book trailer at resources.corwin.com/rampedup-readaloud

Learning Targets:

- I can understand how the character is feeling to better understand the story.

- I can think about how I would feel in the same situation.

- I can consider how the characters' mindsets helped them to be creative.

Connect With Characters' Mindsets

Book Title: *Happy Dreamer* (Reynolds, 2017)

About the Book: A child is a happy dreamer, but the adults in his world don't always approve. Luckily, he is resilient and finds his way back to dreaming "amazing, delightful, happy dreams." Peter Reynolds has filled the end papers with inspirational sayings that would make a powerful anchor chart or bulletin board.

To find a book like this one, look for the following:

- Characters or situations that are relatable to children

- Characters who adjust their mindsets in order to be creative

 Comprehension Conversation:

Before Reading

Notice the Cover Illustration:

- This cover is so bright and colorful. Did you know that Peter Reynolds did the lettering himself? That means he didn't use a computer to make the letters on the cover or in the book. He wrote each word by hand. Wow! That must take a long time.

- What do you dream of doing some day? Ask your neighbor what they dream of doing.

Set a Purpose: When we put ourselves *in the shoes of the character* and ponder how he or she handles or approaches different situations, it helps us to better comprehend (or understand) the story. Let's think and talk together about what we notice about the main character's mindset and how that way of thinking might help us if we were in same situation.

During Reading

- *I AM A HAPPY DREAMER.* page: When you're a creative dreamer you make or create something new or something using your imagination. Give me a thumbs up if you are a creative dreamer. How do you suppose creative dreamers think and act?

- *Sometimes the world tells me sit still.* page: Does this ever happen to you? How does it make you feel? Talk about that with a friend.

- *Sometimes I'm a quiet dreamer . . .* page: Do you ever look at the clouds and see shapes? What shapes do you see on this page?

- *Cleaning up hides my treasures.* page: Can you infer how cleaning up makes him feel? Why do you suppose he reacts that way?

After Reading

- Let's look back at the *magical* gatefold page. What kind of dreamer are you? What kind of happy are you? What's your mindset?

- What strategies can you use when you have to focus or pay attention and you would rather be dreaming?

Extend the Experience:

- Using the examples on the gatefold page, draw a picture to show all of us what kind of dreamer you are or what makes you happy.

- Write, draw, or talk about your dreams. You might want to use these words to get you started: *Someday, I want to* _____.

Key Vocabulary:

- colorful

- creative

Other similar titles:

 ***The Dot* (Reynolds, 2003)**

About the Book: In art class, Vashti stares at her blank paper believing she can't draw. Her caring art teacher asks her to simply make a dot and sign it. The next day, when Vashti returns to art class, her dot is framed. The teacher's small act encourages Vashti to change her mindset and ***make her mark*** as an artist.

 ***Ish* (Reynolds, 2004)**

About the Book: Ramon loves to draw until his older brother Leon laughs at his work. With his brother's laughter echoing in his brain, Ramon can't make anything look *right*. Luckily, his sister Marisol has quietly collected all of Ramon's discarded drawings and displayed them on her wall. When Ramon finally gives up, she shows him how to think "ISH-ly." I read this book at the beginning of the year to introduce the concept of "ISH" writing and spelling. It leads to a helpful conversation for budding writers and students who are perfectionists.

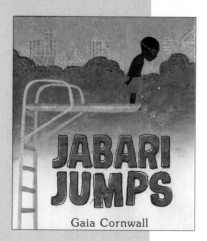

Learn From Characters Who Overcome Fears

Book Title: *Jabari Jumps* (Cornwall, 2017)

About the Book: Jabari has finished swimming lessons, passed his swimming test, and is ready to jump off the high dive, or is he? In Gaia Cornwall's debut picture book, she masterfully addresses the uncertainty children experience when doing something for the first time. My favorite illustration is the one where Jabari has his toes curled around the diving board and is looking down at the water.

To find a book like this one, look for the following:

- Characters or situations that are relatable to children
- Characters who overcome fears

View the book trailer at resources.corwin.com/rampedup-readaloud

Learning Targets:

- I can understand how the character is feeling to better understand the story.
- I can think about how I would feel in the same situation.
- I can use what I've learned from reading this book in my own life.

Comprehension Conversation:

Before Reading

Notice the Cover Illustration:

- What do you notice in the artwork that Gaia Cornwall created for the cover of her book? It says on the copyright page that she used pencil, watercolor paint, and collage and then colored the pictures digitally (that means using computer or tablet.) What did she use to make the buildings? [It looks like newspaper or parts of a book.]

- Look at Jabari on the cover. Can you tell by the way he is standing on the diving board how he might be feeling? Have you ever felt that way? Turn and talk about Jabari's emotions with someone near you.

Set a Purpose: When we put ourselves *in the shoes of the character* and ponder what he or she is thinking and feeling, it helps us to better comprehend (or understand) the story. Let's think about how we would feel if we were in same situation as Jabari and how we might use what we learned from this book in our own life.

During Reading

- *"I'm jumping off . . ."* page: Why do you think his dad said, "Really?" [Maybe he's surprised Jabari is ready to jump or excited to see him do it.]

- *Jabari watched the other kids climb the long ladder.* page: Jabari and his dad squeeze each other's hands. What do you think they are *saying* to each other?

- *Jabari started to climb.* page: How do you think Jabari is feeling right now? Do you think he is really tired or is something else going on?

- *"It's okay to feel a little scared,"* said his dad. page: Let's reread Jabari's dad's advice. Do you think that would help you when you were scared? Has someone in your family given you similar advice?

After Reading

- How did Jabari feel after his jump?

- What did he plan to do next? Why?

- Today we put ourselves in Jabari's shoes. How did connecting with Jabari's character help you to better understand the story?

Extend the Experience:

- What lesson can you learn from Jabari after reading and talking about this book? Divide your paper in half. On one side, draw a picture from the book and write what you learned from Jabari. Start with these words: "From Jabari I learned _____." On the other side, draw something that makes you a little scared and write what you might do next time you're in that situation. Start with these words: "Next time I'm scared I will _____."

- Jabari's dad gave him some advice on what to do when he was scared. Let's do the same for our friends. Make a list of "Things to Do When You're Feeling Scared." [You can choose to do this as a class anchor chart or invite students to do it individually or in pairs.]

Other similar titles:

 Everyone Can Learn to Ride a Bicycle **(Raschka, 2013)**

About the Book: A young girl is learning how to ride a bicycle while her patient father takes her through the process step by step. Raschka's abstract illustrations add visual interest to this story of disappointment and determination. Children who have tried to ride a two-wheel bike will be able to empathize with the girl in the story.

 Hannah and Sugar **(Berube, 2016)**
(See read-aloud experience on page 68)

About the Book: Every day, Hannah's papa picks her up from the bus and her friend's dog Sugar is always waiting too. Hannah is afraid to pet Sugar. One day, Sugar is missing and Hannah finds her in the bushes. Hannah overcomes her fear to bring Sugar safely home.

by Annie Silvestro • Illustrated by Tatjana Mai-Wyss

Learning Targets:

- I can use clues from the text and pictures to help me predict.

- I can talk about my predictions with my friends.

Use Clues to Predict

Book Title: *Bunny's Book Club* (Silvestro, 2017)

About the Book: As a librarian reads aloud to kids outside the library, Bunny listens in. From that day on, Bunny "couldn't live without books." So, he sneaks into the library at night. Soon, his animal friends join him on his late-night library visits. When they're discovered by the librarian, she gives all of the animals a library card, and the animals form "Bunny's Book Club."

To find a book like this one, look for the following:

- Plots with suspense and perfect points for predicting
- Text and illustrations clues that support predictions
- Book-loving characters

 Comprehension Conversation:

Before Reading

Notice the Cover Illustration:

- What are all of the animals doing on the cover? It looks like Bunny just finished painting a sign [the title]. What does it say? What do you predict this book might be about?

- Look! What is this on the end papers? [A library card pocket—some children might not know what this is so you might have to explain!]

Set a Purpose: While reading, let's ponder and predict (or think ahead of our reading). To do this, it's helpful to use clues from the pictures and words.

During Reading

- *Night after night, he could hardly sleep for wishing.* page: What do you predict Bunny might do next? Why do you think that? Share with a partner. Do you have the same thinking or different thinking? I can't wait to keep reading to find out!

- *Until finally he noticed . . .* page: What do you think Bunny noticed? Turn and tell your neighbor. Do you spot any clues in the illustration? Did you and your friend notice the same clues? Did your friend help you find new clues? Let's see if your prediction matched the author's thinking.

- *No one heard the key in the front door.* page: Who do you predict just came into the library? What are the clues that made you think that?

After Reading

- How did talking with your classmates help you better predict and understand the story?

- Do you know anyone in a book club? Why do you think people join book clubs? Our classroom is just like a book club because we love to read and talk about books!

Extend the Experience:

- As we were reading this story, we stopped along the way to predict what might happen next. Which clues helped you more—picture clues or word clues? Jot your thinking on a sticky note to share with your friends.

- Design your own book club sign. Draw a picture of the first few books you would read in your book club.

Key Vocabulary:

- cozied
- curious
- sternly

. . . .

Other similar titles:

 Bear's House of Books **(Bishop, 2017)**

About the Book: Tired of reading their old, worn-out book, four animal friends go on a book hunt for a new story. In the woods, they find a book belonging to Bear and try to return it through Bear's window. Oops! Mouse falls in, and they discover a room full of books. At first, when Bear returns, he is upset. Eventually, Bear realizes books are meant to be shared, and with the help of his new friends, he opens a library.

 Give Me Back My Book! **(Foster & Long, 2017)**

About the Book: While Redd and Bloo are arguing over who owns a green book, a bookworm steals it away. To tempt the bookworm out of her hole, Redd and Bloo create a book that will "blow her mind!" Bookworm takes the bait, the creatures get *their* book back and read it together. Notice that the character Redd is illustrated by Travis Foster and Bloo is illustrated by Ethan Long. Also, their dialogue is marked with different colored speech bubbles.

Learning Targets:

- I can use clues from the text and pictures to help me predict.

- I can talk about my predictions with my friends.

- I can revise my predictions as I learn more from reading.

Predict and Revise

Book Title: *Julia's House of Lost Creatures* (Hatke, 2014)

About the Book: Julia's house is lonely, so she goes into her workshop and makes a sign inviting lost creatures to join her. Eventually, the lost creatures become a bit unruly, so Julia goes into her workshop again and creates a chore chart. Finally, when the house needs to be repaired, she posts her last sign.

To find a book like this one, look for the following:

- Plots with suspense and perfect points for predicting

- Text and illustration clues that support predictions

- Plots with unexpected turns

Comprehension Conversation:

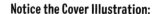

Before Reading

Notice the Cover Illustration:

- [To work on predicting and revising, you may choose to do an activity called Predict the Title (Nations & Alonso, 2001; Walther & Phillips, 2012). To set this activity up, mask the title on the cover and spine with construction paper See example below and provide each child with a sticky note large enough for students to write three different title predictions.]

- Look at Ben Hatke's cover illustration. Do you notice anything unusual about the house? What do you predict the title of this story might be? Write your prediction on your sticky note. Read your prediction to a friend. Does your prediction make sense with the cover illustration?

- Title Page: Wait a second! I need to turn back to the cover. I didn't notice the house was on the shell of a turtle! So, you might choose to revise (or change) your title prediction based on this new information. If you want to revise your prediction, draw a line under you first prediction and write your revised title under the line. Now we're going to put our sticky notes and pencils away until the end of the story.

Set a Purpose: Readers who predict stay focused on the story and better understand what is happening along the way. Thoughtful readers also revise their predictions based on new clues found in the book. I'm not going to tell you the title yet. First, I'm going to read the whole story and see if you want to revise your title prediction again when I'm done.

Predict the Title Photo

During Reading

- *Julia's house came to town.* page: I'm glad we noticed the illustration on the title page; otherwise, this sentence wouldn't really make sense, would it?

- *She made a sign.* page: What do you predict her sign will say? Why do you think she wrote it? [Perhaps she's inviting lost creatures to her house since she said her house was too quiet.]

- *And then she waited.* page: Yikes! What do you suppose is scratching at her door? Turn and predict with your thinking partner. Let's read to find out if your prediction matched Ben Hatke's thinking or if it was different.

- *Before long there was another knock at the door.* page: Wow! What might be going "BOOM, BOOM, BOOM!" at her door? Make a prediction in your head. [It's probably something bigger because the words, "BOOM, BOOM, BOOM!" are much bigger than the "Scritch Scratch" that Patched Up Kitty made.]

- *The creatures stopped what they were doing . . .* page: Hmmm! What could Julia be doing in her workshop now?

- *So Julia got out of bed and made one more sign.* page: What do you predict *this* sign will say?

- *She didn't have to wait for long.* page: Tell your neighbor whether your prediction matched the author's thinking or was different and why.

Key Vocabulary:

- creatures
- guilty

After Reading

- Did anything happen in this book that surprised you?

- How did predicting help you as a reader?

- What would you name the lost creature who came to help repair Julia's house?

Extend the Experience:

- After hearing the whole book, do you want to revise your title again? If so, draw a line under the title and write your revision under the line. What clues in the pictures or words made you change your thinking? Share your revised title with a friend and listen to their title and thinking. [After children have had a chance to share their titles, reveal Ben Hatke's title and compare to the students' titles, discussing similarities, differences, clues, and so on.]

- What do you predict will happen at Julia's house tomorrow? Work with a partner. Talk about what you predict might happen at Julia's house the next day. Once you've agreed, work as a team to draw a picture and write some words to show us your prediction. When you are done, we will share our predictions.

Other similar titles:

 Skyfishing (Sterer, 2017)

About the Book: When grandpa comes to live in the city, he desperately misses fishing. His granddaughter, the narrator, tries to introduce him to different hobbies to no avail. When spring arrives, they decide to use their imagination and fish off of their balcony. The first fish they catch is a "Flying Litterfish." After that, their surprising catches will delight your readers and have them predicting what they might catch next. Notice that the front end papers have real fish and the back end papers have imaginary child-drawn fish. Gideon Sterer's debut picture book is original and creative!

 There's a Lion in My Cornflakes (Robinson, 2014)

About the Book: If you save 100 coupons from cereal boxes, you will get a free lion. At least that is what the narrator and his brother think. After waiting and waiting, their free lion doesn't show up but everyone else's does. By the time the delivery truck arrives at their house, the cereal company is out of lions. Instead the brothers get a bear, a crocodile, and a gorilla. What will they collect coupons for next? Pause and predict on the pages that have ellipses.

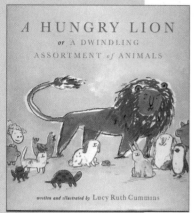

Embrace Unexpected Endings

Book Title: *A Hungry Lion or a Dwindling Assortment of Animals* **(Cummins, 2016)**

About the Book: A hungry lion is surrounded by his assortment of animal friends. After each page turn, a few animals disappear. Is Lion eating the animals or is something else occurring? Readers will be surprised more than once!

To find a book like this one, look for the following:

- Plots with suspense and perfect points for predicting
- Text and illustration clues that support predictions
- Plots with unexpected endings

Learning Targets:

- I can use clues from the text and pictures to help me predict.

- I can talk about my predictions with my friends.

- I can revise my predictions as I learn more from reading.

- I can think and talk about the ending of the story.

Comprehension Conversation:

Before Reading

Notice the Cover Illustration:

- Wow! I see a lot of different animals. Let's read the title *A Hungry Lion or a Dwindling Assortment of Animals*. On the cover, Lucy Ruth Cummins has drawn an *assortment* of animals. The word *assortment* means a collection of different kinds of items. Turn and take turns with your partner naming the animals you see in this assortment.

Set a Purpose: Readers often predict (or think ahead of their reading). This helps them to stay focused on the story and better understand what is happening along the way. Let's do that today as we read this book about a hungry lion.

Maria's Thinking: Although I usually try to include the language from the learning targets in my purpose statement, I chose not to do that here because it would draw attention to the unexpected ending and take away the joy of seeing the kids' faces when they find out what happens to the animals.

During Reading

- *Hold on.* page: Wait a minute. What do you notice? [There are fewer animals.] I agree. The animals are dwindling. There are fewer of them on this page than there were on the page before. What do you predict will happen when we turn the page?

- *It seems there was just . . .* page: Oh no! They dwindled even more! What do you suppose is happening to the animals? Turn and ponder with your friends. See what you can learn from them.

- *Hello, there . . .* page: Have you revised your prediction or are you still thinking the same thing?

- *Surprise!* page: Hmmmmm! Turn and talk with your neighbor about this surprising page! Did your prediction match the author's thinking or was it different?

- *and . . .* page: What do you predict will happen next?

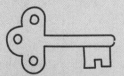
After Reading

- Yikes! That was an unexpected ending! Show me with your thumbs [thumbs up = liked the ending, thumbs in the middle = OK ending, thumbs down = not my favorite ending] how you felt about the ending. What made you feel that way? [Invite a few children to share the reasons behind their opinion.]

Extend the Experience:

- Using the *Share Your Opinion Reproducible Response Page* provided on the companion website. Rate this book based on how you felt about the ending. Draw a picture and write some words to support your opinion. Once we're done, we'll share so we can hear the different opinions of the students in our class.

- Write a different ending for this story.

Key Vocabulary:

- assortment
- dwindling
- ravenous

Share Your Opinion Reproducible Response Page

Download this form at resources.corwin.com/rampedup-readaloud

Other similar titles:

That Is Not a Good Idea! (Willems, 2013)

About the Book: From the opening two-page spread where fox and goose are staring at each other, readers assume that fox is going to eat the goose. Each time the fox lures the goose closer to the soup the goslings interject, "That is not a good idea!" Readers are always surprised at the end when the goose pushes the fox into the soup!

The Woods (Hoppe, 2011)

About the Book: Before he goes to sleep, a boy always hugs his bunny. Tonight, his bunny is missing so he goes searching in the woods. Each time he runs into a frightened creature, the boy shares one of the items from his bedroom. When all the creatures come back to bed with him, they appear as stuffed animals, and you realize that he was just making up the story. Notice the items in the bedroom like the red blanket (his cape), trash can (his hat), sword and so on that were part of his imaginary trek.

View the book trailer at resources.corwin.com/rampedup-readaloud

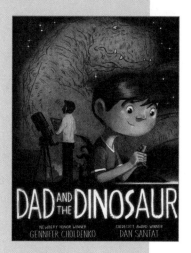

View the book trailer at
resources.corwin.com/
rampedup-readaloud

Learning Targets:

- I can notice how my teacher asks questions.
- I can ask questions to help me better understand the text.

Ask Questions to Understand

Book Title: *Dad and the Dinosaur* **(Choldenko, 2017)**

About the Book: Nicholas is afraid of the dark, bugs, and manhole covers, but his dad isn't afraid of anything. To boost his confidence, Nicholas carries a small plastic dinosaur everywhere he goes. One night, he loses his dinosaur and his dad comes to the rescue.

To find a book like this one, look for the following:

- A plot that causes readers to stop and wonder
- Characters who overcome fears or obstacles

 Comprehension Conversation:

Before Reading

Notice the Cover Illustration:

- Look at Dan Santat's illustrations and think about the title. Do you have any questions? [If none of your children have questions you might query, "I'm looking at the picture and wondering why the title is *Dad and the Dinosaur* if the boy is holding the toy dinosaur in his hands."]
- Do you notice any other dinosaurs in the illustration? Talk about what else you see on the cover with your friend. Do you have any questions?
- The back cover blurb says, "Dads get it. They just do." What do you think that means?

Set a Purpose: As a reader, I'm always thinking and wondering to help me better understand the story. Sometimes my questions are answered as I continue reading and other times I have to infer (or figure out using clues) what is happening. Today while I'm reading, I'm going to think aloud so you can peek into my brain. When I'm thinking aloud, I will point to my brain. If I have a question for you, I will point to you.

During Reading

- *Nicholas tried to be brave . . .* page: [Point to your brain.] I'm wondering how the dinosaur helps him be brave. [Point to kids.] Do any of you have something at home that helps you be brave? Thanks for sharing, that helped me to better understand this part of the story! I'm glad I asked you to help me with that question.
- *Then one day at soccer, Nicholas played . . .* page: [Point to your brain.] I'm wondering what the word *fearless* means. Let's see if I can figure it out using context clues, word part clues, and picture clues. I already know that *fear* means *afraid* and the suffix -less means *without*. So I'm inferring *fearless* means *without fear*. Let's see if that makes sense in the sentence and matches the picture. [Point to kids.] What do you think?

- *Nicholas's face lit up like a glow stick.* page: Hmmm! [Point to your brain.] I'm wondering what the author means when she says, "Nicholas's face lit up like a glow stick." [Point to kids.] Look carefully at the illustration and share your ideas with a partner.

Key Vocabulary:

- fearless
- incredible

Maria's Thinking: Your *literal* thinkers might say it is because the boy is talking on a cell phone, but your *inferential* thinkers will dig deeper and talk about his feelings—he feels proud, happy and so on. If not, demonstrate your inferential thinking for the benefit of all.

- *What are you doing, Nick?* page: [Point to your brain.] I wonder why Nicholas doesn't tell his mother about the missing dinosaur. Perhaps he wants her to think he is big and brave like his dad.

- *Sure enough, there was Nicholas's dinosaur, as big as ever.* page: [Point to your brain.] Hmmmm! Nicholas's dinosaur isn't big. Why does he say "as big as ever?" Maybe because it makes him feel big and brave.

After Reading

- [Point to your brain.] Now I'm wondering why Gennifer Choldenko wrote this book. What is she trying to tell us as readers? What are her messages/big ideas? [Point to kids.] Think and talk about that with your friend.

- Do you have any after-reading questions that you want to ask the class?

Extend the Experience:

- What did you notice about the different types of questions I asked while I read? We can write these ideas on a chart to help us remember.

- Write or draw something you have or do to help make you feel braver.

Readers Ask Questions About . . .

- pictures
- meaning of words or phrases
- what is going to happen next
- big ideas
- parts of the book they don't understand

Other similar titles:

 Dogosaurus Rex (Staniszewski, 2017)

About the Book: Determined to find the best pet at the shelter, Ben selects large, green, roaring Sadie. When Ben takes her out for a walk, she creates chaos. Once home, she causes more trouble. After mom threatens to return Sadie to the shelter, she and Ben go to town and Sadie catches a thief. Then, she becomes "the most popular dog in town." The thief scene in *Dogosaurus Rex* reminds me of the ending in *Pinkerton, Behave* by Steven Kellogg (1979).

 Hattie and Hudson (Van Dusen, 2017)

About the Book: Hattie McFadden loves to explore the lake in her canoe. In fact, it makes her so happy that she sings a bouncy song that catches Hudson's (the creature's) ear. When he emerges to hear her song, the other boaters are in a tizzy. After a town hall meeting where they decide to get rid of the beast, Hattie and Hudson devise a plan. The rich vocabulary found in *Hattie and Hudson* draws attention to one of the many benefits of reading aloud–vocabulary development. Some of the words kids will hear as you read aloud include *mysterious, elusive, ventured, astounded, commotion, massive, emerged, peril,* and *frolicked.*

View the book trailer at resources.corwin.com/rampedup-readaloud

Learning Targets:

- I can ask questions to help me better understand the text.
- I can listen to my friends' answers and ideas to help me better understand the text.

Think, Talk, and Wonder

Book Title: Double Take! A New Look at Opposites (Hood, 2017)

About the Book: At first glance this book appears to be a simple text about opposites, but the complexity increases as the book unfolds. Transitioning from opposites to relative words, to perspective and point of view, this book offers plentiful opportunities for thinking, conversing, and asking questions. For additional titles highlighting point of view and perspective see pages 86–91.

To find a book like this one, look for the following:

- A text that causes readers to stop and wonder
- Texts that teach concepts
- Texts with surprising twists

Comprehension Conversation:

Before Reading

Notice the Cover Illustration:

- Look carefully at the cover Jay Fleck creating using digital tools. What do you see?
- Do you know what the phrase *double take* means? It means to take a second look at something or to rethink something you saw, said, or understood in a new way. For example, when I first looked at this cover I thought I saw two elephants, two boys, and two cats. But when I did a double take or looked at it again closely, I saw that they were looking at their reflections in the water.

Set a Purpose: The subtitle says, *A New Look at Opposites*. I wonder what that means? Sometimes readers ask questions to help them focus on their reading and clear up misunderstandings. When we listen to each other's answers and thinking, it helps us get even smarter. We can try that together today as we read this book.

During Reading

- Copyright page: Look! Do you notice that the pier on which the boy is sitting on the title page is also right here on the copyright page? I wonder if the other places and animals on this page will appear in the story. Sometimes readers ask questions about the pictures.

- *and NIGHT, not every duo is so BLACK and WHITE.* page: I wonder what the author means by "not every duo is so BLACK and WHITE." Sometimes readers ask questions about the meaning of the words.

- *A racer's called FAST when rivals are SLOW.* page: I'm wondering what *relative words* means. Are those words puzzling to anyone else? Let's look back at some of the words and the pictures on the two pages before this page: *big-small, short-tall, high-low, fast-slow*. Hmmm! I'm noticing that you have to compare one object to another to decide which is which. So, it seems like *relative words* are words that have to be compared to something else to understand what they mean. Let's keep reading and see if that makes sense.

- *Point of view* . . . page: I wonder what we'll see when we back up. What do you think? Turn and tell a friend. Wondering about that really makes me want to turn the page. Ready?

- [Continue the questions and conversation about relative words and point of view as you enjoy the rest of the story.]

After Reading

- Now I'm wondering why Susan Hood wrote this book. What is she trying to tell us as readers? What are her messages/big ideas?

- I'll turn back to the copyright page. Did we see all of these places and animals in the book?

Extend the Experience:

- Share something your partner said, asked, or noticed that made you ponder or think about the book in a different way.

- Work with a partner. Pick a pair of words that are opposites. Divide your paper in half. Each of you write and illustrate one of the words. When we're done we'll hang our words on the bulletin board for all of our friends to see. [Some opposite words that work well for this response include: *adult/child, asleep/awake, beginning/end, cry/laugh, dry/wet, empty/full, happy/sad, hot/cold, little/big, night/day, noisy/quiet, old/young, sweet/sour.*]

Other similar titles:

 Found Dogs **(Sirotich, 2017) [texts that teach concepts–counting forward and backward]**

About the Book: Set in the city shelter, groups of dogs are waiting to be adopted. The rhyming text begins, "1 dog, long and low. 2 dogs, silver and slow." The counting up continues until ten people arrive to adopt the ten dogs. Then, the pages count back down as all of the dogs are adopted. Notice that the new owners often *match* the dogs. For example, the greyhounds are adopted by runners. Also, the final two-page spread shows all the dogs in numbered dwellings.

 Where Do You Look? **(Jocelyn & Jocelyn, 2013) [texts that teach concepts–homonyms]**

About the Book: A playful and colorful look at homonyms written with young learners in mind. The book asks question after question beginning with "Where do you look for a cap?" "On a tube of toothpaste?" "Or on your head?" The exploration of homonyms leads to rich vocabulary-related discussions and activities. After reading, children can search for other homonyms not found in the book and draw pictures to represent their different meanings.

Key Vocabulary:

- opposite
- reflection (verb)
- relative (words)

Jenny Sue Kostecki-Shaw
Luna & Me
The True Story of a Girl Who Lived in a Tree to Save a Forest

online resources

View a film about Luna at resources.corwin.com/rampedup-readaloud

Learning Targets:

- I can ask questions to help me better understand the text.
- I can listen to my friends' answers and ideas to help me better understand the text.
- I can ponder the author's purpose.

Question to Determine Author's Purpose

Book Title: *Luna and Me: The True Story of a Girl Who Lived in a Tree to Save a Forest* (Kostecki-Shaw, 2015)

About the Book: This is the true story of a brave young woman who lived in a Redwood tree named Luna for two years in order to protect it and its surrounding grove. Although Julia Butterfly Hill was in her twenties when she sat in Luna, the author/illustrator depicts her as a young girl which helps to make this book easily relatable for children.

To find a book like this one, look for the following:

- A text that causes readers to stop and wonder
- True stories about people who have made a difference

 ## Comprehension Conversation:

Before Reading

Notice the Cover Illustration:

- You are never going to believe one of the things that Jenny Sue used to make her illustrations—salt! Along with paints, pencil, and collage, she used something you find right in your kitchen. When artists use a variety of tools to make their pictures it is called a *mixed-media* illustration. What might you use to create mixed-media illustrations for your books?

- If we read the title, subtitle, and back cover blurb we can learn a bit more about this book.

Do you have any questions before we begin reading?

> **Maria's Thinking:** If your students need scaffolding and support to ask before reading questions, model questions such as, "Hmmm! I'm wondering who Luna is in this story." "How can you live in a tree?" "What do you eat?" "Where do you sleep?"

Set a Purpose: Readers ask questions to help them focus on their reading and clear up misunderstandings. When you talk with your friends about questions, they can help you to grow your thinking. As you're asking questions and talking, dig a bit deeper and ponder why we think the author wrote this book.

During Reading

- *"Hello?" a curious Butterfly called up into Luna.* page: Let's talk about the big blue X. What are you thinking? What are you wondering?

- *The redwood quivered . . .* page: Wow! Why do you think the author chose to design the page this way? Could you do that in your books? [The two-page spread is designed to be viewed vertically rather than horizontally to show readers how tall the redwood tree looked compared to Butterfly.]

- *Butterfly realized what the blue X meant on Luna's trunk.* page: Talk with your partner about how Butterfly figured out what the blue X means. Think back to the title and subtitle. What do you think Butterfly will do next?

- *Suddenly, an idea sprouted deep inside Butterfly.* page: Her friends were *eager* or wanted to help her. What do you see them doing?

- *When she awoke, she discovered the sun.* page: Talk with your neighbor about what you think the author means when she says that Butterfly discovered her wings.

After Reading

- Do you have any after-reading questions? Look, here an author's note gives us extra information. Maybe we can find some of the answers to your questions in here. Would a few of you like to read it together and share what you learn? [As this is a dense piece of text, you will need to choose children who, together, can read it.]

Extend the Experience:

- Why do you think the author wrote this book about Julia Butterfly Hill? What was her purpose for telling Julia's story? Write your thinking on a sticky note and get ready to share with the class.

- What are some words you might use to describe Julia Butterfly Hill? We can look back in the book to see if we can find any descriptive words and make a chart to capture our thinking. (See below.)

Key Vocabulary:

- eager
- marveled
- quivered

....

Other similar titles:

 ***Biblioburro: A True Story From Colombia* (Winter, 2010)**

About the Book: Winter introduces readers to Luis and his trusty "Biblioburros" Alfa and Beta, who faithfully carry books to children in the remote villages of rural Colombia.

 ***One Plastic Bag: Isatou Ceesay and the Recycling Women of the Gambia* (Paul, 2015)**

About the Book: When young Isatou is walking home, her palm leaf basket breaks, and she leaves it to naturally decompose. Then, she finds a plastic bag drifting by and begins using it. When it breaks, she leaves it on the ground but notices it, and many others, are building up. Later, when she is an adult, she discovers her goats are eating the bags and dying. Determined to do something, she and group of women wash the bags and use them as *thread* to crochet purses to sell at the market. Elizabeth Zunon used colorful papers and leftover shopping bags to create her collage illustrations. The back matter includes a Wolof Glossary and Pronunciation Guide and a timeline.

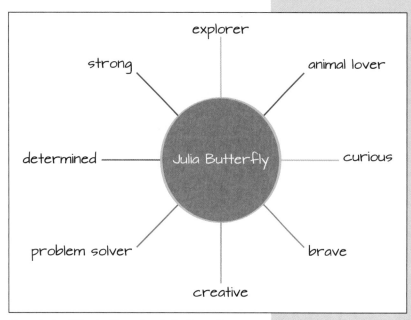

Descriptive Words Chart for Julia Butterfly

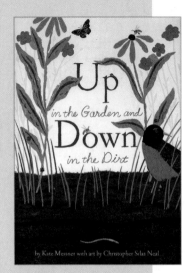

by Kate Messner with art by Christopher Silas Neal

Learning Targets:

- I can find sensory words or phrases in a poem or story.

- I can think about how sensory language helps me visualize.

Notice Sensory Language

Book Title: *Up in the Garden and Down in the Dirt* (Messner, 2015)

About the Book: A girl and her grandmother plant, care for, and harvest their garden while readers learn about what is happening under the ground. Read this book in the spring, during a science unit on plants, or to inspire writers to use sensory language. You can also help listeners notice the repetitive *see-saw* structure, "Up in the garden/Down in the dirt" that they could borrow in their own writing.

To find a book like this one, look for the following:

- Written in first-person point of view

- Events are described using sensory language

- Main character is curious, asks questions, and/or explores nature

 ## Comprehension Conversation:

Before Reading

Notice the Cover Illustration:

- Let's open the book so you can see the front and back cover. What do you see? [A wrap-around cover]

- The illustrator used different types of art tools to make this picture, that's called a mixed-media illustration. What plants and creatures can you find above and below the dirt?

Set a Purpose: Today as we are reading, let's think and talk about how the author, Kate Messner, helps us to experience what the girl is seeing, hearing, and feeling as she works in the garden. Let's record when she uses words that connect to your five senses. When writers use words like this, it is called using sensory language.

During Reading

- After the first few pages: Who do you think is telling you this story? What clues help you figure this out?

- [Pause at different points and provide time for students to either share or record the author's use of sensory language on a piece of paper or device. Some examples appear in the Sensory Language Chart on the facing page.]

After Reading

- Why do you think Kate Messner chose to write this book from the girl's point of view?

- How did her use of sensory language help you to experience what it was like when she was working in the garden?

See

orange pumpkins

bowing sunflowers

colored leaves

autumn moon

Hear

wind whistles

chickens squabble & scratch

Touch/Feel

sun shines

mud sucks at boots

juice dribbles

cool wind

Key Vocabulary:

- feast (verb)
- gobble
- munch

Sensory Language Chart

Extend the Experience:

- Draw and label an *over/under* diagram of a garden, our playground, your backyard, or another place of your choice. What do you think is down in the dirt? Challenge yourself to label the diagram using words or phrases that help us use our senses to picture your place.

- Pick an animal you want to learn more about. Read more about it in the "About the Animals" section. Write the two most interesting facts you learned.

Other similar titles:

Over and Under the Pond (Messner, 2017)

About the Book: In the third book of the Over and Under series, a mother and her son are out paddling around the pond when, like the other books, the secret world hiding under the water is illuminated. In the Author's Note, Kate Messner briefly describes how, in the book, she's shown the interactions among the organisms that thrive in a mountain pond ecosystem and invites readers to return to the text to look for such interactions. This book would pair nicely with Denise Fleming's Caldecott Honor Book *In the Small, Small Pond* (1993).

Over and Under the Snow (Messner, 2011)

About the Book: A girl and her dad are cross-country skiing through the woods on a snowy day. When squirrel disappears down a crack in the snow, the girl asks her dad where the squirrel went. He tells her that there is a "whole secret kingdom" under the snow. With the same repetitive pattern as the other books in this series, readers learn about the creatures who dwell above and below the snow.

Learning Targets:

- I can notice and discuss sensory words or phrases in a poem or story.

- I can think about how sensory language helps me visualize.

- I can use sensory words in my own writing.

Use Sensory Language That Creates Mental Images

Book Title: *A Small Blue Whale* (Ferry, 2017)

About the Book: A small blue whale is waiting to find a friend. Along comes small pink cloud who whale thinks might be his friend. Then whale meets the penguins and discovers what true friendship is all about. Beth Ferry, author of *Stick and Stone* (found in the "Read These!" section on page 37), cleverly has the whale describe friendship using his senses.

To find a book like this one, look for the following:

- Experiences are described using sensory language
- Main character is searching, wishing, or waiting for something

Comprehension Conversation:

Before Reading

Notice the Cover Illustration:

- I'll open the wrap-around cover so that we can look at Lisa Mundorff's illustrations. Did you know that this is the first picture book she has illustrated? I bet she's excited about it.

- Let's read the back cover blurb and see if we can get an idea of what this book is about.

- It sounds like the whale is looking for a friend. I wonder if he'll find one. What do you think? Talk with your neighbor about that.

Set a Purpose: Sometimes authors use sensory language to help us better experience a story.

Sensory language contains words that help us picture things using our senses. What are your five senses? Listen as I'm reading to see if you notice any sensory language.

During Reading

- *As the sun rose, he glimpsed a glint of gold.* page: How did Beth Ferry describe the sun? [As the sun rose, she used colors to describe what whale saw.] Do her words help you to make a picture of the sun in your mind?

- *The sun grew stronger.* page: How does the sun make you feel when you're out on the playground? Is this the same feeling you have when you are with your friends?

- *The cloud drifted . . .* page: What other things taste sweet and cool to you?

- *They leapt and swooped.* page: What does friendship sound like to you?

After Reading

- Look back one page. I'm going to reread this sentence, "Finally, the whale knew *exactly* what friendship . . ." Why do you think Beth Ferry chose to put the word

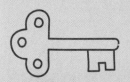
exactly in italics? [Because she wants us to stress that word when we read it. Let's read it the way she wants it to sound.]

- Talk about the whale's friendship with cloud and whale's friendship with the penguins? [Some might say the whale's friendship with the cloud was *one-sided* because they never really did anything together, but perhaps the cloud led him to the penguins. The whale helped the penguins and when he got stuck, the penguins helped him. They played together.]

- What can you learn about friendship from this book?

Extend the Experience:

- In this story, the author used senses to describe friendship. Pick a sense or two and use them to describe what friendship means to you:

  o Friendship looks like _____

  o Friendship tastes like _____

  o Friendship sounds like _____

  o Friendship feels like _____

- To challenge ourselves, let's pick an idea other than friendship to describe using our senses. Some examples might include bullying, kindness, happiness, sadness, love, anger, and so forth.

First, we'll try one together. (See example below.) Then, you can work with a friend to write your own.

Use these words to help you get started:

_____ looks like _____

_____ tastes like _____

_____ sounds like _____

_____ feels like _____

Key Vocabulary:
- heaved
- glimpsed
- radiant

Peace

Peace looks like a blue sky.

Peace tastes like cool water.

Peace sounds like the ocean waves.

Peace feels like a warm breeze.

Example Sensory Descriptions

Other similar titles:

 The Black Book of Colors (Cottin, 2006/2008)

About the Book: How you would describe the color blue to a person who is blind? In this distinctive book, Thomas describes colors using his senses of touch, taste, smell, or hearing. The written text is translated into Braille and the illustrations are raised black line drawings on black pages.

Owl Moon (Yolen, 1987)

About the Book: A child and her Pa go owling on a frigid winter night. Will they see an owl? Notice Jane Yolen's use of descriptive, sensory language and also the way the text on the pages appear and read like poetry.

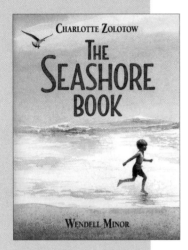

Learning Targets:

- I can notice and discuss figurative language in a poem or story.

- I can think about how figurative language helps me visualize.

- I can use figurative language in my own writing.

Notice Figurative Language That Creates Mental Images

Book Title: *The Seashore Book* (Zolotow, 2017)

About the Book: A boy who lives in the mountains asks his mom to describe the seashore for him. She does so using vivid figurative language.

To find a book like this one, look for the following:

- Settings or events described using sensory language
- Text contains similes, metaphors, or other figurative language

Comprehension Conversation:

Before Reading

Notice the Cover Illustration:

- Look at Wendell Minor's cover painting. Close your eyes and pretend you are at the seashore with this boy. What might you see? What do you hear? How would the water and sand feel on your feet? What would your mood be like? Turn and share your sensory images with a friend.

- How many of you have been to the seashore or the beach? Was it easier to imagine being at the seashore if you had been there before? Tell us more about that.

Set a Purpose: Sometimes authors use figurative language to help us better experience a place or feeling in a story. Figurative language is text made up of phrases that help us picture parts of the story using our senses or feelings. Instead of telling us exactly how something looks or feels an author might compare it to something else so that we have to infer. Let's see if we can notice any phrases like this in *The Seashore Book*.

During Reading

- *"What is the seashore like?" a little boy asked his mother.* page: Let's pretend along with the boy and see if can visualize what his mom is telling him about the seashore.

- *"You bend over and pick up a stone washed smooth by the sea."* page: Yikes! How would you react if a clam snapped the shell shut while it was in your hand?

- *"You lie down in the hot noonday sun . . ."* page: The author says the "swish-swashing sound" of the waves. Did the onomatopoeia she used help you to better imagine what the waves sound like?

- *"An airplane flies low in the sky."* page: Can you picture what the airplane's shadow looks like? What words helped you to do that?

After Reading

- After hearing that book, could you also close your eyes and *be there* just like the boy? Are there pages in the book that helped you to do that? Which ones? Let's go back and reread them again.

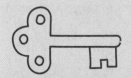

Compared to some of the other books we've read this year, I'd call this book a *quiet* book. Turn and discuss with your neighbor whether you agree or disagree and what other ways you might describe *The Seashore Book*.

Extend the Experience:

- [Depending on the attention span of your listeners, you may want to do this close-reading lesson at a different time.] I want to go back and reread some of the descriptive sentences in this book and see what you notice. [To help children better see the comparison words *like* and *as*, you might consider quickly jotting the phrases on a chart or interactive whiteboard document:]

   o "The cold water makes your skin feel like peppermint"

   o "It [the sun] feels as warm as a big, soft cat covering you"

   o "Claw prints [of a sandpiper] like pencil lines in the sand"

   o "Its [an airplane's] shadow on the sand is like a gigantic bird"

   o "[The fishing pier] is as white as snowfall"

- What did Charlotte Zolotow do in these phrases to help you better imagine what it is like at the seashore? [Scaffold and prompt students to notice the similes or comparisons using *like* or *as*.]

- Describe a familiar place or thing using a simile.

Key Vocabulary:

- lulls
- pretend
- wade

Other similar titles:

 Hello Ocean (Ryan, 2001)

About the Book: Pam Muñoz Ryan celebrate the mysterious beauty of the ocean by taking readers on a sensory outing to the sea. When reading this book, I often invite listeners to sketch what they see, hear, taste, and feel.

 Twilight Comes Twice (Fletcher, 1997)

About the Book: Writing guru, Ralph Fletcher's poetic book about the happenings in a town at dusk and dawn. This book is filled with figurative language to notice and discuss.

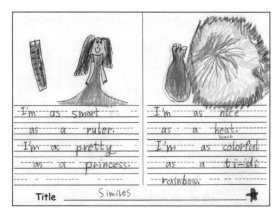

Simile Work Sample

View the book trailer at
resources.corwin.com/
rampedup-readaloud

Learning Targets:

- I can identify the elements of a story.

- I can use story elements to help me retell a story.

Use Story Elements to Retell

Book Title: *Creepy Pair of Underwear* (Reynolds, 2017)

About the Book: Older and braver, Jasper Rabbit from the book *Creepy Carrots* (2012) is back. When shopping for underwear, he convinces his unwilling mom to buy him one pair of Creepy Underwear. When he discovers that they glow in the dark, he makes many attempts to get rid of them, but they keep coming back. After burying the underwear deep underground, he realizes that their "gentle, greenish glow" helped him sleep.

To find a book like this one, look for the following:

- Straightforward plots with clearly identifiable story elements

- Plots with places to predict

- Plots with a humorous ending

 Comprehension Conversation:

Before Reading

Notice the Cover Illustration:

- That is one creepy pair of underwear. What did the illustrator, Peter Brown, do to make the underwear look creepy? What colors did he choose to use?

Set a Purpose: When Aaron Reynolds wrote this story, he used important parts or elements. Those elements are characters, setting, events, problem, and solution. As we read this creepy book, we'll notice the elements, and after reading, we'll use those elements as we tell someone what happened in *Creepy Pair of Underwear*.

During Reading

- *Jasper Rabbit needed new underwear.* page: What do you think Jasper spotted in the underwear store? Tell your friend. What clues helped you make that prediction? [The creepy underwear on the cover!] Let's turn the page to find out what happens next.

- *Mom! Mom! Can we get these?* page: Can you infer how mom is feeling on this page? What did you notice in her facial expressions to help you figure that out?

- *That night Jasper wore his cool new underwear to bed.* page: Who is the main character in this story? What do we know about him so far? [Jasper Rabbit is "not a little bunny anymore!"]

- *Do you want me to leave the hallway light on?* page: What do you suppose Jasper noticed?

- *. . . the underwear glowed.* page: What is the problem in the story? How might Jasper solve the problem? I can't wait to see how Jasper tries to solve the problem.

- *He reached for the handle.* page: Ahhhh! How did Jasper finally solve the problem? [He buried them deep underground.]

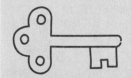
- *There was just one problem. . . . It was really dark in there.* page: Oh no! Now Jasper has another problem. How do you suppose he'll solve this one?

- [Continue pausing and inviting students to predict at points that make sense and/or where you see ellipses.]

After Reading

- Did the ending surprise you? Make you laugh? Don't you love when an author adds a funny ending like that?

- This story was so fun to read that I know you are going to want to tell your friends about it. Let's practice retelling what happened in the story. Who was the story about? What did he want? What was the problem? How did he solve the problem? What was your favorite part? Turn and retell *Creepy Pair of Underwear* to your neighbor.

Extend the Experience:

- Let's retell the story using the parts or elements we noticed. (See example below.)

- I noticed that Aaron Reynolds used vivid verbs to tell what Jasper Rabbit did with the underwear. Let's see if we can find some of them. [stuffed, threw, snatched, seized, dropped] Why do you think he chose to do this?

Key Vocabulary:
- ghoulish
- gleamed
- yelped

Other similar titles:

 ***Creepy Carrots* (Reynolds, 2012)**

About the Book: Jasper Rabbit loves eating the carrots from Crackenhopper field. In fact, he is *always* munching on them until the creepy carrots begin appearing everywhere. After many creepy encounters, Jasper fences in the carrots. In a surprising twist, the carrots celebrate that their plan worked and Jasper can't eat them anymore!

 ***Muncha! Muncha! Muncha!* (Fleming, 2002)**

About the Book: Mr. McGreely dreams of planting a garden, but once he does so, three hungry bunnies get in and "Muncha! Muncha! Muncha!" Mr. McGreely builds fences, digs trenches, and constructs a wall. In the amusing ending, the bunnies sneak into his basket, and he carries them over the wall and into the garden.

In A Creepy Pair of Underwear . . .

Somebody (character): Jasper Rabbit

Wanted: creepy underwear

But: they glowed in the dark

So: he tried to get rid of them many different ways

Finally, he realized he liked the glow!

In the end, he filled his room with Creepy Underwear!

NANETTE'S BAGUETTE
words and pictures by **Mo Willems**

View the book trailer at resources.corwin.com/rampedup-readaloud

Learning Targets:

- I can use clues from the text and pictures to help me predict.

- I can revise my predictions as I learn more from reading.

- I can use story elements to help me retell a story.

Predict, Revise, Retell

Book Title: *Nanette's Baguette* (Willems, 2016)

About the Book: Nanette's mom sends her off to get a baguette from the bakery. The warm, wonderful baguette is too tempting so Nanette eats it all. "Beset with regret," Nanette heads home to face her mom, only to discover that her mom can't resist the baguette either. What other author could write a book filled with words that rhyme with Nanette? *Nanette's Baguette* is hilarious, has perfect points for predicting, and is simply fun to read aloud!

To find a book like this one, look for the following:

- Straightforward plots with clearly identifiable story elements
- Plot with a surprise ending

Comprehension Conversation:

Before Reading

Notice the Cover Illustration:

- The title of this story is *Nanette's Baguette*. Do you know what a baguette is? See this bread on the cover. This is a baguette. It is a long, thin loaf of French bread.

- So, I'm thinking this story might happen in France. Let me show you where France is on the map.

- Title Page: Can you find Nanette in this illustration? Look back and see if we can figure out where she is on the cover. Mo Willems created this three-dimensional village in his studio and then took photographs of it to put it in the book.

Set a Purpose: Stories have important parts or elements. Those parts are characters, setting, events, problem, and solution. As we're reading, we can predict what might happen to the character and revise our predictions as events occur. After we enjoy this funny book, we'll use all of the elements to help us tell someone more about *Nanette's Baguette*.

During Reading

- *YOU BET!* page [the first one where she is holding the coin]: What do you notice about the words in this book? [They rhyme with baguette.] Do you think that was challenging for Mo to do?

- *YOU BET!* page [where she has the baguette]: What do you predict will happen next? Why do you think that? Talk it over with a friend. After you talked with your friend, did you revise your prediction? What did your friend say that makes you rethink your ideas?

- [As you are reading, offer a few more opportunities for students to predict what might happen next and revise their predictions based on picture and text clues.]

- *There is no more baguette!* page: Look at the picture and think about what is happening in the story. What do you think the word *fret* means?

- *"Where is the baguette, Nanette?" asked Mom.* page: See if your students notice Mo Willems's pigeon character in the umbrella stand!

After Reading

- Did the ending surprise you? What do you suppose Nanette and her mom will do next?

- Who do you know that might enjoy the story *Nanette's Baguette*? To get that person excited about the story, you might tell them a little about the story. Let's practice using the elements of character, problem, and solution to retell *Nanette's Baguette* so that you are ready to tell someone else about it.

Extend the Experience:

- Depending on how much experience your students have had with retelling, you can either complete the response together as a class (see example below from *Nanette's Baguette*), with partners, or independently. To record students' retelling, use an interactive whiteboard, chart paper, or *Retell the Story Reproducible Response Page* provided on the companion website.

- Invite your students to bring in empty cereal boxes and other items and construct their own village in a makerspace or other area of your school or classroom.

Key Vocabulary:

- fret

- regret

- responsibility

Other similar titles:

 ***Clever Jack Takes the Cake* (Fleming, 2010)**

About the Book: Jack bakes a special cake to bring to the princess for her 10th birthday party. Along the way, his cake is eaten bit by bit by different characters. In the end, he tells the princess about his adventures, giving her the best gift of all—a story.

 ***Strega Nona* (dePaola, 1975)**

About the Book: In the town of Calabria, lives Strega Nona (Grandma Witch) who helps the townspeople with headaches, warts, and finding husbands. When she hires Big Anthony to help her, the trouble begins. Big Anthony wants to show everyone how Strega Nona's magic pasta pot works, but he doesn't know that he has to blow three kisses to turn it off. Soon, the town is filled with pasta, and Strega Nona makes Big Anthony eat it all up!

In *Nanette's Baguette* . . .

Somebody: Nanette

Wanted: to get a baguette

But: it was warm and wonderful

So: she ate it

Finally, she told her mom

In the end, her mom ate one too!

Retell the Story: _____

Somebody: _____

wanted _____

but _____

_____

so _____

_____

Finally, _____

_____

In the end _____

_____

Name_____

Draw a picture of the main character.

Retell the Story Reproducible Response Page

Download this form at resources.corwin.com/rampedup-readaloud

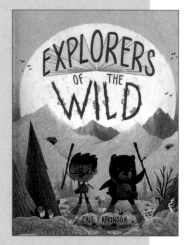

Learning Targets:

- I can use story elements to help me retell a story.
- I can think beyond story elements to ponder big ideas.

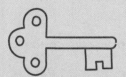

Key Vocabulary:

- adventure
- conquer
- discovery

Think Beyond Retelling to Big Ideas

Book Title: *Explorers of the Wild* (Atkinson, 2016)

About the Book: An adventurous boy and an equally curious bear roam the wild forest. When they bump into each other, they discover that exploring together is much more fun! Can you find the snail hidden on every page?

To find a book like this one, look for the following:

- Straightforward plots with clearly identifiable story elements
- Characters who are adventurous

 Comprehension Conversation:

Before Reading

Notice the Cover Illustration:

- Compare the front cover and the back cover. What do you notice about the two characters? Do you think these characters will be the main characters in the book? Why do you think that?

- Do you see the snail on the cover? After we read *Explorers of the Wild*, I'll put it in the reading area so that you can search and find the snail hidden on the inside pages.

- [If you are able to remove the book jacket, you can show the kids the book case that looks like a travel journal.]

Set a Purpose: Authors create stories using certain parts or elements. Those parts are characters, setting, events, problem, and solution. After we enjoy this adventurous book, we'll notice and talk about how those parts help us to tell someone what happened in the story and what we learned from reading the story (the big idea).

During Reading

- *My parents tell me to be careful.* page: Where does this story take place? [the wild] How would you describe *the wild* to someone who hasn't read this book?

- *I say I'm an explorer, and explorers are prepared for anything.* page: What is Cale Atkinson showing you on these two pages? [The contents of the boy's backpack and the bear's messenger bag.] I'm thinking you can use the same technique to show items that are hidden inside of something in your own books.

- *I run and run until one day I ran right into . . .* page: What do you predict will happen on the next page? Make a prediction in your head.

- Next page where the boy and bear meet: Did what happened in the story match your prediction? Can you infer how the characters are feeling? So, what is the problem in the story?

- *I saw we were both explorers.* page: What do you suppose might happen next? Do you think the boy and the bear will solve their problem?

After Reading

- With your partner, take turns retelling the story. Partner 1 will begin with the character, then Partner 2 will continue to share the problem, and so forth. [Demonstrate doing this with one of your students.] Get ready, begin!

- In the end, what did the boy and the bear discover? [Prompt students to dig deeper than "they were kings of the wild" or "the top of a mountain" to some of the big ideas that appear in the example from *Explorers of the Wild*.]

Extend the Experience:

- Let's retell the story using the parts or elements we noticed and record some of your big ideas.

- Look at the endpapers. See how Cale Atkinson drew different places to explore. Draw your own exploration map to share with your friends.

. . . .

Other similar titles:

 ***Garcia and Colette Go Exploring* (Barnaby, 2017)**

About the Book: The story begins with a disagreement. Garcia, the rabbit, wants to explore space, but Colette, the fox, prefers to venture to the sea. Separately, they build their own vehicles and blast off. After a while, they realize it would be more fun to explore together, so they do. This book would team up nicely with either *Going Places* (Reynolds & Reynolds, 2014) or *Chicken in Space* (Lehrhaupt, 2016) (See read-aloud experience on page 56).

 ***Robinson* (Sis, 2017)**

About the Book: For a school costume party, Peter's mom makes him a Robinson Crusoe costume. His friends laugh and tease him, so he goes home. At home in bed, he dreams of adventures on an island. Later, his friends come to apologize, and he tells them all about Robinson Crusoe. In the Author's Note, readers discover that this story is based on an actual event from Peter Sis's boyhood.

In *Explorers of the Wild* . . .

<u>Somebody (character)</u>: The boy and the bear

<u>Wanted</u>: to explore

<u>But</u>: they ran into each other and were scared

<u>So</u>: they decided to explore together

<u>Finally</u>, they had an amazing adventure.

<u>In the end</u>, they took a picture to help them remember.

THE BIG IDEAS WERE . . . be adventurous, explore the wild, it's fun to explore with friends, you never know where you might find a friend.

Exploration Map Work Sample

"But the sharks were only in her mind, for now.

Eugenie decided to learn everything she could about them.

So she dove . . .

. . . this time into books."

—*Shark Lady*
by Jess Keating and Marta Àlvarez Miguéns

Converse About Comprehension–Informational and Narrative Nonfiction

Diving Into Informational Texts

Sharks. Giant Squids. Wolf Pups. Books that contain information about these animals and many others fly off the shelves. Like Eugenie Clark in the opening quote, children want to learn everything they can about their favorite topics. Reading aloud fascinating texts while helping children learn how to navigate a nonfiction text is a necessity. Longtime advocate of nonfiction reading Nell Duke (2014) emphasizes, "Reading aloud informational text provides students with exposure to content, syntax, and vocabulary they simply can't grapple with entirely on their own" (p. 101). In Chapter 4, you will help your student better comprehend nonfiction texts by focusing on these strategies and skills:

- Identify Main Topics
- Uncover Key Details
- Wonder about the World
- Connect to the Past

On the next page, you will find the concepts you will introduce or review while zooming in on nonfiction comprehension strategies. To support you in using these terms, I've included kid-friendly definitions. As you know, it isn't always easy to find nonfiction texts that make engaging read-aloud fare. To help you in this pursuit, I've scoured the shelves to locate books that both you and your students will enjoy. Dive in and learn together. It is my hope that the books in this chapter will inspire wonder and propel students to ask questions that lead to further research and reading.

Use and Explain Key Comprehension Strategies

Predict: Think ahead of your reading

Question: Asking questions before, during, and after reading makes you want to keep reading to find the answers. Questions also help you to think more deeply about the text and better understand the facts being presented.

Visualize/Make Mental Images: To picture in your mind what is happening in the text such as how an animal is behaving or what the inside of a machine looks like.

Foster a Growth Mindset

Ask Questions: Asking questions means starting with words like *who, what, when, where, why,* and *how* when we are wondering or want to know more about something. Asking questions helps us to learn.

Wonder: When we wonder, we are curious about something. Curiosity makes us smarter.

Converse About Comprehension—Informational and Nonfiction Narrative

Develop Students' Social and Emotional Learning

Explain: When you explain something to someone you try to make an idea, situation, or problem more clear. You tell them details to help them better understand.

Life Lessons: A life lesson is something you learn from a book or an experience that you can use when you have that same experience.

Life Choices: Life choices are decisions you will make when you get older like whether you want to go to college or not, where you want to live, or what kind of job you might want to do.

Teach Literary Language

Character Traits: Adjectives that describe how characters act in certain situations.

Diagram: A drawing that shows what something looks like, its parts, or how it works.

Infographic: An image that tells about a topic using very little text.

Key Details: Sentences or images that show or tell more information about the main topic.

Main Topic: The overall idea of a text or a section of a text.

Text Features: All the parts of a book that do not appear in the text like images, diagrams, graphs, maps, tables, and so forth.

Chapter 4 Concepts, Terms, and Kid-Friendly Definitions

My Favorite Read Alouds for Comprehension–Informational and Narrative Nonfiction

_____

_____

_____

_____

_____

_____

_____

_____

_____

_____

_____

_____

_____

_____

_____

_____

_____

_____

_____

_____

_____

_____

_____

_____

_____

_____

_____

_____

_____

_____

_____

_____

_____

_____

Rick Chrustowski

online
resources

View "The Making of *Bee Dance*" slide show at resources.corwin.com/rampedup-readaloud

Learning Targets:

- I can explain what the book is mainly about.
- I can share details about the topic.

Zoom in on the Topic

Book Title: *Bee Dance* (Chrustowski, 2015)

About the Book: A scout bee finds a prairie in bloom and returns to the hive to perform a bee dance. See the "Why do honeybees dance?" section at the back of the book for more specific information about the dance.

To find a book like this one, look for the following:

- Accessible facts and supportive illustrations
- Informational text about one aspect of a topic

Comprehension Conversation:

Before Reading

Notice the Cover Illustration:

- Rick Chrustowski used cut paper collage and pastel pencils to create his illustrations. Can you find the parts of the picture where he cut things out?
- How does he show you that the bee on the cover is moving?

Set a Purpose: As nonfiction readers, it is helpful to pay attention to what the book is mainly about. Thinking about the details you've learned about the main topic helps you to add new information to your schema. Sometimes authors give you a clue to the main topic in the title. Ponder the title *Bee Dance* as we read this book together.

During Reading

- *When sunlight warms* . . . page: What do you think bees do when they go on flower *patrol*?
- *Follow a sweet scent* . . . page: What would a *gold mine* be for a honeybee?
- *Waggle faster, honeybee!* page: What important detail do we learn on this page? [The length of time bees waggle their bodies tells the other bees how far to go.]
- *Go to work, forager bees!* page: What two things do bees collect from flowers? [nectar to make honey and pollen]

After Reading

- What did the author teach you about in *Bee Dance*?
- Why do you think he chose to focus mainly on the bee's dance?
- What important details did you learn about a bee's dance? [They fly in a figure eight; they waggle their bodies back and forth; how long the bee waggles equals how far the bees have to fly to get to the flowers.]

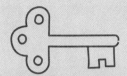

Extend the Experience:

- To help our brains better remember the main event in the book, let's go back to the back of the book where there is a diagram and details to help us act the dance out with our bodies. Ready to do the bee boogie?

- What else do you want to learn about bees? How can we go about getting more information? [Make a list of possible sources of information that students could access to learn more about bees such as bee experts, online data bases, informational books, visits to zoos or parks that raise bees, and so on.]

Key Vocabulary:
- collect
- unload

Other similar titles:

 The Flight of the Honey Bee (Huber, 2015)

About the Book: Using a blend of narrative and informational text, Huber tells the story of Scout, the honey bee, who is on a perilous quest to find the last flowers off all. The narrative and informational text appear in different fonts. The back matter includes some additional facts about bees and an index. The main focus of this text is Scout's journey.

 Grandma Elephant's in Charge (Jenkins, 2003)

About the Book: Did you know that the most important member of the African elephant family is the grandma? In straightforward narrative nonfiction text, readers learn the vital role of the grandmother elephant. If interested, there are further facts about elephants on some of the pages in a smaller, boldface font. *Grandma Elephant's in Charge* could spark an inquiry experience to discover if any other animals' grandparents are essential to the survival of the group.

Learning Targets:

- I can explain what the book is mainly about.
- I can share details about the topic.
- I can notice how baby animals are similar to and different from their parents.

Notice Similarities and Differences

Book Title: *Wolf Pups Join the Pack* (American Museum of Natural History, 2017)

About the Book: Stunning photographs and straightforward text trace a litter of wolf pups from birth until they are young wolves.

To find a book like this one, look for the following:

- Accessible facts and supportive illustrations
- Informational texts about baby animals

Comprehension Conversation:

Before Reading

Notice the Cover Illustration:

- How do you suppose the American Museum of Natural History made this cover? Do you think the illustrators drew it, painted it, or took a picture with a camera? How can you tell?

- What do you already know about wolf pups? Tell your neighbor. Remember to listen carefully, and then ask your friend what he or she already knows.

Set a Purpose:

- When reading an informational text like this one, it is helpful to figure out what the book is mainly about. Do you have any ideas before we even start reading? What clues helped you to predict the main topic?

- I'm going to give you a challenge. As I'm reading aloud, ponder how wolf pups are similar to and different from their parents.

During Reading

- *On a sunny spring day, a litter of baby wolves is born.* page: A *litter* is a group of young animals born at the same time.

- *But wolf pups can't roam very far on their own.* page: What do wolf pups need from their parents? [Elicit students' responses.] Yes, they rely on their parents for food and protection. Does that remind you of anyone you know?

- *The parents of wolf pups leave the pack to go hunting.* page: So, what is the main topic of this book so far? Let's turn back and see how many times the author repeats the words *wolf pups* or *pups*. One way to figure out the main topic is to notice the author's words. Often, you will find words related to the main topic repeated in the text.

- *A wolf pup hears the call and answers with a howl of his own.* page: Turn and tell your friend three facts you've learned about wolf pups so far.

- *They curl up in a ball.* page: What are some of the differences between wolf pups and young wolves? [young wolves have large feet and sharp claws, they don't rely on others for food, they hunt with the pack]

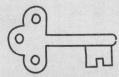
After Reading

- What was the main topic you learned about in this book? [wolf pups]

- What questions about wolves do you still have? How might you go about answering those questions?

Extend the Experience:

- To compare and contrast wolf pups and their parents, you can choose to either have students complete *H-Chart Reproducible Response Page* located on the companion website or complete together on a chart or interactive whiteboard document (See example below.)

- Pick a baby animal other than a wolf pup. Find out how that animal baby is the same as or different from its parent. Share your new learning with the class.

Key Vocabulary:

- protection

- rely

- useful

Other similar titles:

Born in the Wild: **Baby Mammals and Their Parents (Judge, 2014)**

About the Book: Writer and illustrator Lita Judge has skillfully captured the playfulness of 26 wild baby mammals and their parents. Following a pattern, the first two-page spread highlights a trait that baby animals share, and then the following spread features a paragraph about three different baby mammals and how they exemplify that trait. A glossary of terms and additional facts about each mammal are provided in the end notes.

Dolphin Baby! **(Davies, 2011)**

About the Book: A baby dolphin "POPS out into the blue" and swims up to take his first breath. From there, readers join the calf and his mother as he learns to nurse, meets the other members of his group, makes friends, and plays. We tag along until the dolphin baby catches his first fish and whistles his own "sound-name."

Wolf Pups	Both	Wolf Parents
small		big
need protection	need food	give protection to pups
drink mother's milk	member of pack	give food to pups
need help	howl	help pups
stay behind	look the same	run with pack
get food from parents		hunt for food

Name _____

H-Chart Comparing Wolf Pups and Wolf Parents

Download this form at resources.corwin.com/rampedup-readaloud

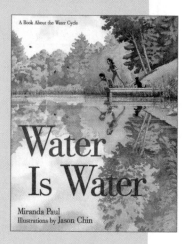

A Book about the Water Cycle

Water Is Water

Miranda Paul
Illustrations by Jason Chin

online resources

View song link at
resources.corwin.com/
rampedup-readaloud

Learning Targets:

- I can explain what the book is mainly about.
- I can share details about the topic.
- I can notice interesting ways authors share information.

Notice How Authors Share Facts and Details

Book Title: *Water Is Water* (Paul, 2015)

About the Book: The book begins, "Water is water unless it heats up." This pattern continues as water turns to fog, clouds, rain, ice, snow, and mud showing that water is constantly moving and changing. In the back matter, there is a brief description of the water cycle and Miranda Paul shares, "This story shows only some of the creative ways that water moves and changes over the seasons" providing a springboard for an inquiry into other ways water moves.

To find a book like this one, look for the following:

- Explains a scientific phenomenon in a distinctive way
- Main topic relates to water or the water cycle

Comprehension Conversation:

Before Reading

Notice the Cover Illustration:

- Look closely at Jason Chin's paintings on the front and back cover. Do you see anything on the cover that is made from water? [ponds, clouds, ice, snow]
- What do you already know about water?
- How many different forms of water do you think we will find in this book?
- Title page: It looks like their mom is calling to them. I wonder why. [Guide students to infer from the dark clouds that a storm is coming.]

Set a Purpose: As nonfiction readers, it is helpful to figure out what the book or text you are reading is mainly about. I bet after looking at the cover and reading the title you already have a sense of the main topic of this book. As we learn more about water, let's read like writers to notice the techniques Miranda Paul used in *Water Is Water*.

During Reading

- *they form low.* page: What form of water do you see on this page? [Fog. If needed, discuss students' experiences with fog.] What is the boy doing? [He is trying to catch a snake.]
- *puddles freeze.* page: Compare this page to the title page. What do you see? [It is the same pond, now it is frozen water.]
- *Creep. Seep.* page: What have you noticed about the boy? [He's always catching animals.]
- *there are roots.* page: What do you think happens to the water puddled under the tree? [Water will seep underground and the roots of the garden plants will absorb the water to help them grow.]

After Reading

- Miranda Paul chose to teach us about water in a unique way. What did you notice about this book?

- How might you use what you've noticed in your own writing?

Extend the Experience:

- On this index card, write two words that tell what this book is mainly about. This is called the *Two-Word Strategy*. You can use it to help you remember and retell the key ideas of a text (Hoyt, 1999, p. 4). (See example below.)

- [After reading aloud the "Water is . . . important!" paragraph in the back matter of the book, ask] What are ways we can conserve water at school or at home? Make a sign to remind either your friends or family what to do. [Hang signs around school in appropriate places.]

Key Vocabulary:

- [Introduce or review onomatopoeias such as *drip*, *patter*, *splatter*, *slosh*, *splash*, *smack*.]

Other similar titles:

All the Water in the World (Lyon, 2011)

About the Book: George Ella Lyon's poetic language along with Katherine Tillotson's stunning digital illustrations make this book about the water cycle a must read. The text provides opportunities for students to ponder statements like "Water doesn't come. It goes. Around." The innovative page layouts, creative use of fonts, text placement, and more make every page turn a delight. *All the Water in the World* ends with a message to keep the water and our Earth clean. So, you could also read it when celebrating Earth Day.

Water Can Be (Salas, 2014)

About the Book: Similar to the book *Water Is Water* (Paul, 2015), this book begins "Water is water." Then, with rhyming phrases, explains the different functions that water performs such as "garden soaker" and "valley cloaker." The phrases offer opportunities for students to infer which form of water the author is highlighting on the page. The back matter includes more detailed information about water.

Water Dance (Locker, 1997)

About the Book: Thomas Locker's stunning oil paintings accompany riddles about water in its different forms. The back matter contains added information about the water cycle. Use the riddle format as a mentor text for students who want to write their own riddles about a scientific topic. It also works well for a review of the water cycle in a Reader's Theater style. To do this, provide each pair of students with a riddle to perform while the other students try to guess the answer.

Two-Word Response Work Samples

A BOOK OF BRIDGES
HERE TO THERE
AND ME TO YOU

Written by Cheryl Keely
Illustrated by Celia Krampien

Learning Targets:

- I can explain what the book is mainly about.

- I can share details about the topic.

- I can think beyond the text and infer the big ideas.

Think Beyond the Main Topic

Book Title: *A Book of Bridges: Here to There and Me to You* (Keely, 2017)

About the Book: Blending brief, bouncy text and informational paragraphs, Cheryl Keely shares information about bridges in a multilevel fashion. Emerging learners can gain information from the central narrative, while bridge enthusiasts can dig into the factual paragraphs. Going a step further, she explores the metaphorical idea of bridges bringing people together.

To find a book like this one, look for the following:

- Informational text about one main topic

- Clear text and supportive illustrations

- Author's purpose goes beyond simply sharing facts about a topic

Comprehension Conversation:

Before Reading

Notice the Cover Illustration:

- Observers, take a minute to study the cover illustration. How many bridges do you see?

- The illustrator, Celia Krampien, drew a lot of different kinds of bridges on the cover.

- Have you ever seen a bridge like ones pictured here? Tell your neighbor one thing about your experience.

Set a Purpose: As nonfiction readers, it is helpful to figure out what the book or text you are reading is mainly about. I bet after looking at the cover and reading the title and subtitle you already have a sense of the main topic of this book. To grow our brains a little more, let's think beyond the text about the big ideas in the book.

During Reading

- *Bridges do more than connect one place to another.* page: Ponder what Cheryl Keely is saying here. Do you agree that bridges bring the whole world together? I'm thinking that as we continue reading we'll find out more about this big idea.

- *or in London, falling down.* page: Notice the way the author chose to write these words. [It looks like the words are falling down.] Does the use of creative conventions help you to remember something about this bridge in London?

- *Bridges just for animals help them find new homes, new friends, and plenty of food.* page: How is Cheryl Keely helping us to learn more about bridges? [She has a paragraph of facts on every page.] Turn and tell your neighbor something you remember about wildlife bridges. Say, "I remember _____." [I learned this

strategy from Linda Hoyt's (2002) book *Make It Real: Strategies for Success with Informational Texts*.]

- [As you continue reading and learning about bridges, use Linda Hoyt's "I Remember!" strategy to prompt children as they share their learning with their classmates.]

After Reading

- What did the author and illustrator teach us about? [bridges] So, this book was mainly about bridges. What details do you remember about bridges?

- I want you to dig a little deeper. What else did you learn about people and our world? What are the big ideas? [Bridges connect us to other people, bridges connect us to new places, and so on.]

- [If you turn back to the first page and look closely, you will see the three kids who were also on the last page!]

Extend the Experience:

- Why do we have bridges? Draw or write to explain your thinking.

- Next time you are walking or driving around with your family look for bridges. If you see one, take a picture of it, print it, and bring it to school. You can also have your parents e-mail it to me at school.

Other similar titles:

 ***Home* (Ellis, 2015)**

About the Book: Though this book has elements of nonfiction, it is not entirely factual. Readers see a variety of homes from an apartment to the old woman's shoe from nursery rhyme fame. Like *A Book of Bridges*, this text explores the big idea of what home means.

 ***Just Ducks!* (Davies, 2012)**

About the Book: From Candlewick's Read and Wonder series comes a book about an animal many of your students have probably seen—a mallard duck. As a girl goes through her daily activities, she informs readers about ducks based on what she's learned from observing them. Accompanying facts are included on each page in a different font than the running narrative. The back matter includes an index and a bit of additional information. The big idea in this book is that we can learn about the natural world through experience and observation.

Key Vocabulary:

- connect
- moveable
- swaying

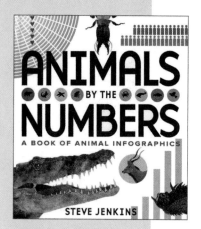

STEVE JENKINS

Learning Targets:

- I can ask and answer questions about key details in the text.

- I can use the text features to help me better understand information.

Use Text Features to Learn Key Details

Book Title: *Animals by the Numbers: A Book of Animal Infographics* (Jenkins, 2016)

About the Book: Children have a lot of questions about animals. In this book, Steve Jenkins answers many questions about animals using bright, accessible infographics.

To find a book like this one, look for the following:

- Informational books with interesting animal facts
- Nonfiction books with text features that enhance meaning

 ## Comprehension Conversation:

Before Reading

Notice the Cover Illustration:

- Steve Jenkins designed an interesting cover. What do you notice on the cover? His illustrations are easy to spot because he uses torn and cut-paper collage to create them.

- Do you have any questions about what you see on the cover?

Set a Purpose:

- Asking questions helps to focus your reading. As we read, we can try to answer some of your questions, and of course, you can continue to ask more questions.

- Notice that the subtitle of this book is *A Book of Animal Infographics*. An infographic is a visual image like a chart or a diagram that gives us information or data. We can look at it quickly and learn a lot of facts or details about the animals.

During Reading

- *Numbers help us understand our world.* page: Wow! Numbers help us a lot. Turn and ask your neighbor, "What did Steve Jenkins say numbers can help us do?" [understand our world; measure; compare; explain the past; predict the future; tell how big, fast, or loud something is]

- *In this book . . .* page: Look at the infographic on the facing page. It is a pie chart showing us how many times different animals appear in the book. Why do you suppose it is called a pie chart? Which animals appear the most? Where is the evidence for that? Which animals appear the least amount of times? Can you prove your answer using the infographic?

- *Contents* page: **Maria's Thinking:** Before reading aloud a nonfiction book with a table of contents, I have a conversation with my learners about the different ways in which they might go about reading the text and how reading nonfiction differs from reading fiction. Then, I read them the chapter or section titles and ask, "What would you like to learn about today?" I usually conclude

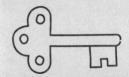

the read-aloud experience after a chapter/section or two, and then I continue in the same fashion for a few more days. Basically, reading the text bit-by-bit, the same way I would read a chapter book. If we don't finish the book during our read-aloud experiences, I place it in our classroom library for further exploration. As you'll see in the conversation that follows, one infographic can take quite a while to discuss.

- *Size* page: [little and big section] Okay, you wanted to learn more about animal sizes today. Let's see what we can figure out and learn by reading this infographic. We should start by reading the title and explanation below the title. Beneath that we find a key. The key tells us that the animals pictured in black are alive today and the animals shown in gray are extinct. Tell your friend how many of the animals in this infographic are extinct. How can you be sure? Now we can find out which animal is the largest.

- *Size* page: [giants section] To better understand how large these animals are, we will read about the scale. The text says that the animals are shown at the same scale as this human. That means if a human were that size (about the size of a dime), the animal would be that much bigger compared to the human pictured on this page. Why couldn't Steve Jenkins draw them as their actual size? [Because they are too big to fit!]

- *Size* page: [life-size section] These animals are small enough that Steve Jenkins *could* show them on the page at their actual size. Which numbered animal is the smallest? Yes! Number two, let's read the key. Number two is a dwarf goby. Have you ever heard of that animal? We might have to do some research to find out more about the dwarf goby.

- [Continue in a similar manner with other infographics based on your students' interest. It might be helpful to project the images using a document camera.]

After Reading

- How did the infographics help you learn interesting details about animals?

- Nonfiction writers, look at the infographic on the back flap! Here Steve Jenkins broke down how much time he spent researching, writing, and creating the illustrations for this book!

Extend the Experience:

- [For this response, I'm going to model how children might go about creating an infographic. I chose to use hair color, but you can choose any type of data that makes sense for your kids and matches your curriculum.] Today, I'm going to show you how to create an infographic about the different hair colors of the kids in our class.

  o Step 1: Divide a piece of paper into four sections and label each section with the words *mostly black*, *mostly brown*, *mostly blonde*, *mostly red*. On the back, label one section *other*.

  o Step 2: Ask each of your classmates what color hair they have. Make a tally mark in the correct box for each of their answers.

Key Vocabulary:

- Will vary depending on which infographics you and your students choose to read.

- Step 3: To create your infographic, draw one circle to stand for each child in our class. Color the circles to match your data. For example, if 12 kids have mostly black hair, then you will color 12 circles black.

  - Label your infographic and add a key.

- Nonfiction writers, next time you are researching and writing, think about making an infographic to display data that you want to share with your readers. (See work sample below.)

Other similar titles:

 Apex Predators: The World's Deadliest Hunters, Past and Present (Jenkins, 2017)

About the Book: Learn about the animals at the top of the food chain in their particular habitats. Those who dominate their territory because they were (or are) too dangerous, too big, and/or have their own deadly weapons. The nonfiction features in this book include pronunciation guides for obscure animal names, comparison diagrams for each apex predator, headings, and bold print.

 Weird and Wild Animal Facts (Loy, 2015)

About the Book: In this photo-essay, Loy shares fascinating facts and traits of fourteen different animals. Each two-page spread contains four to six facts along with photographs. In each fact, key words are highlighted in a colored font. Includes a table of contents, making it easy to read one animal at a time when you have a few free minutes.

Pie Chart Work Sample

My Favorite Informational Texts to Read Aloud

Draw Diagrams to Remember Key Details

Book Title: *Giant Squid* (Fleming, 2016)

About the Book: Readers dive deep into the murky ocean to learn facts about the mysterious and elusive giant squid. With each page turn, children will discover facts and learn about the unanswered questions that still surround this creature. Use this book when introducing the concept of inquiry or asking questions in science or as a stunning mentor text for nonfiction writing.

To find a book like this one, look for the following:

- Informational books about animals that intrigue your students
- Nonfiction books that include diagrams

Comprehension Conversation:

Before Reading

Notice the Cover Illustration:

- Notice how Eric Rohmann's full-color paintings wrap around the front and back cover. Why do you think he chose to do that?

Set a Purpose: I can't wait to open the book and learn more details about this strange-looking creature. As you learn more about what a giant squid looks like, see if you can make a mental diagram to help you remember.

During Reading

- When you reach the title page: Hmmm! We've already read five pages and we are just getting to the title page. That's unusual. Can you think of other books where the story/information begins before the title page? [*Yes Day!* (Rosenthal, 2009); *Shark vs. Train* (Barton, 2010)]

- *Here are its tentacles, two, curling and twisting . . .* (2 pages): What did Candace Fleming teach us about the tentacles?

- *The beak.* page: Yikes! I didn't know giant squids had beaks. Turn and tell your neighbor something you learned about the beak.

- *In the murk . . . an eye!* page: Wait! Let me reread these sentences, "Some as big as soccer balls. The biggest eyes on the planet." How did Candace help us understand the size of a giant squid's eyes? [comparison]

After Reading

- Wow! What an ending! Turn and talk. Tell your neighbor what you are thinking or wondering. Ask your neighbor what he or she is thinking and wondering.

Learning Targets:

- I can ask and answer questions about key details in the text.

- I can use the illustrations and text features to help me better understand information.

- I can create my own diagrams to help me remember and describe key details.

Extend the Experience:

- Work with a partner and draw a diagram of a giant squid and label the parts. When we write or draw after reading, it helps our brain better remember the details we learned.

- 3, 2, 1 Strategy (Zygouris-Coe, Wiggins, & Smith, 2004): Write and/or draw three facts you learned about this creature, two questions you still have, and one thing you will never forget about this book.

Key Vocabulary:

- creatures
- examine
- mystery

Other similar titles:

 ***Star of the Sea: A Day in the Life of a Starfish* (Halfmann, 2011)**

About the Book: Follow an ochre sea star through her day as she searches for food. Learn how she uses her tube feet to move and her traveling stomach to eat. See what happens when she loses one of her rays (arms) to a predator. Readers will find a diagram of the top and bottom of the starfish in the end notes.

 ***Surprising Sharks* (Davies, 2003)**

About the Book: With humor, creative use of text placement, and various fonts, Nicola Davies and illustrator James Croft surprise readers who might think all sharks are man eaters. Two double-page spread diagrams of a shark's inside and outside appear in the middle of the book.

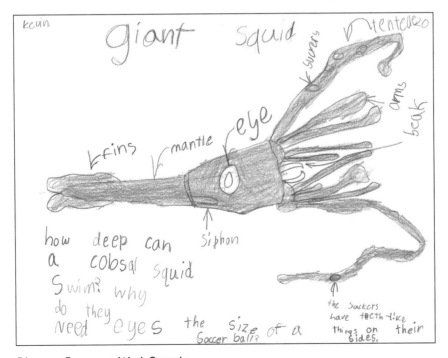

Diagram Response Work Sample

Learning Targets:

- I can ask and answer questions about key details in the text.

- I can use the illustrations to help me better understand information.

- I can draw during reading to help me remember and describe key details.

Draw During Reading to Remember Key Details

Book Title: *Squirrels Leap, Squirrels Sleep* (Sayre, 2016)

About the Book: With rhyming text and Steve Jenkins's signature collage illustrations, readers learn the habits and behaviors of squirrels. In the back matter, you'll find additional information about squirrels and their trees.

To find a book like this one, look for the following:

- Informational books about topics that are familiar to your students
- Accessible facts and supportive illustrations
- Rhyming text

 ## Comprehension Conversation:

- [To prepare for this read-aloud experience, invite students to bring a piece of paper divided into four sections to your read-aloud area. When I do this, I have the children secure the paper to a clipboard and sit on the clipboard until it's time to draw. If students are adept at sketching on a device, that is another option.]

Before Reading

Notice the Cover Illustration:

- Steve Jenkins is another illustrator who uses cut- and torn-paper collage for his illustrations. He has illustrated a lot of interesting nonfiction books. From the cover you can probably figure out what the main topic is for this book—squirrels. What do you already know about squirrels?

Set a Purpose: As nonfiction readers, we want to remember the key ideas and details about the topic. Today I'm going to pause at different points in the book so you can draw a quick sketch to help you remember the key details in *Squirrels Leap, Squirrels Sleep*.

During Reading

- *Squirrels wrestle.* page: I noticed that Steve Jenkins has created a picture to match each of the activities squirrels do on this page. How does the illustration help you as a nonfiction reader? Let's notice if he does that on every page.

- *Meet the squirrels: Gray. Fox. Red.* page: In box one, draw your favorite kind of squirrel. [My guess is that most kids will draw the flying squirrel!]

- *Paws for climbing.* page: Let's go back and reread the last three pages. What are they teaching us about? [The different parts of a squirrel's body.] In box two, draw a quick sketch showing one of the parts of a squirrel's body that you just learned about.

- *Squirrels stretch.* page: In box three, draw a sketch of what the last two pages were mostly about. [acorns]

After Reading

- In box four, draw a sketch of one thing squirrels do.

- Use your sketches to tell a friend what you learned about squirrels.

- Did sketching during this book help you to better remember the details you learned about squirrels? Do you think this strategy would be helpful to you when you were reading other nonfiction books? Why or why not?

Extend the Experience:

- Write a sentence to go with each of your sketches to tell your family what you learned about squirrels today.

- [If your school is in an area where you can observe squirrels, take children outside to watch their behavior. Then, discuss what they noticed that can add to the facts they learned about in the book. Another option is watching a video of school behavior on YouTube (after you've previewed the clip without children present!)]

Key Vocabulary:

- gather
- store (verb)

Other similar titles:

 ***Up, Down, and Around* (Ayers, 2007)**

About the Book: With bouncy, rhyming text, readers learn about garden vegetables that grow above the ground, below the earth, and those that wind around the garden. Pair this nonfiction book with the story *Tops and Bottoms* (Stevens, 1995). If you choose to have students sketch while you read this book, invite them to divide their paper into three sections and label the sections *Up*, *Down*, and *Around*. Then, children can record which plants from the book belong in each section.

 ***Woodpecker Wham!* (Sayre, 2015)**

About the Book: What do woodpeckers do? They send messages, drill holes for nesting, hide from hawks, spread seeds, feed their chicks, and much more. In addition to the facts found in the rhyming text and collage illustrations, readers can learn more by reading the coordinating paragraphs in the back matter entitled "Woodpecker World."

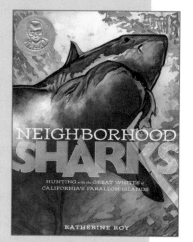

View more information about *Neighborhood Sharks* at resources.corwin.com/rampedup-readaloud

Learning Targets:

- I can ask and answer questions about key details in the text.

- I can use the text features to help me better understand information.

- I can draw or write during reading to help me remember and describe key details.

Draw or Write During Reading to Remember Key Details

Book Title: *Neighborhood Sharks: Hunting With the Great Whites of California's Farallon Islands* (Roy, 2014)

About the Book: Roy's suspenseful narrative introduction leads us into the world of the great white sharks who hunt elephant seals a mere 30 miles off the coast of San Francisco. Once readers are hooked by the two-page spread where the shark attacks the seal, she slows down the pace and dives into detailed factual pages about the characteristics of a shark. Although this book may take you a few read-aloud experiences to complete, it is worth every minute!

To find a book like this one, look for the following:

- Informational books about the characteristics of animals that are familiar to your students

- Accessible text, supportive illustrations, and text features

 ## Comprehension Conversation:

- [To prepare for this read-aloud experience, invite students to bring a piece of paper divided into six sections to your read-aloud area. When I do this, I have the children put the paper on a clipboard and sit on the clipboard until it's time to draw or write. If students are adept at sketching on a device, that is another option.]

Before Reading

Notice the Cover Illustration:

- I'll open the wrap-around cover so that you can get a full view of Katherine Roy's painting of the shark. Do you notice any other details in the illustration besides the shark?

- Front end papers: Do you remember the bottom of the boat we saw on the cover? I wonder if this the same boat? This bridge is a famous bridge in San Francisco, California, called the Golden Gate Bridge. Let me show you where San Francisco is on this map.

Set a Purpose: As nonfiction readers, we want to remember the key ideas and details about the topic. Today, I'm going to pause at different points in the book so you can draw a quick sketch or write some notes to help you remember the key details in *Neighborhood Sharks*.

During Reading

- *Every September the great white sharks return to San Francisco.* page: Katherine Roy doesn't tell us what the sharks' favorite meal is yet, but can you infer from the illustration what it might be?

- Two-page spread of shark attacking the elephant seal page: Yikes! I think we have a better idea what the great whites like to eat.

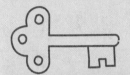

- *HOT LUNCH* page: Draw or write something you remember to remind you why elephant seals are a good meal for hungry white sharks.

- [The next five pages include details about each of the sharks' five hunting weapons: the perfect body, warm blood, sensitive vision, sharp teeth, and projectile jaws. I would suggest reading just a page or two more and providing time for learners to jot or sketch something they remember. Then, at a later time, pick up where you left off. The second half of the book, beginning with the *BUT NOT SO FAST!* page, highlights scientists who study the sharks and some of their discoveries. So, this is also a nice place to pause again, if needed.]

Key Vocabulary:

- survive

- unsuspecting

After Reading

- Great white shark experts, what did you learn today that surprised or amazed you?

- How did Katherine Roy's words, pictures, and text features help you better understand _____. [Fill in the blank with whatever information you read about that day.]

Extend the Experience:

- Use your sketches and your notes to teach your neighbor something you learned.

- Did sketching help you remember the details? Why or why not? If not, what strategy might work better for you?

Other similar titles:

 Eye to Eye: How Animals See the World **(Jenkins, 2014)**

About the Book: Jenkins's signature eye-popping illustrations introduce readers to animal eyes of all shapes and sizes. The cover has an array of different eyes providing students an opportunity to guess which animals match the eyes (the answers are on the back cover). In addition, the front and back end papers look like an eye chart. After an introduction about why sight is important to animals and the different categories of eyes, readers learn about more than 20 different animal's eyes. The back matter includes diagrams and descriptions of the evolution of the eye, facts about each animal including size, habitat, and diet, and a glossary of terms. Like *Neighborhood Sharks*, this book is complex and will take a few days to read.

 Feathers: Not Just for Flying **(Stewart, 2014)**

About the Book: Melissa Stewart uses similes to compare the characteristics of feathers to everyday objects. Science enthusiasts learn the function of the feathers from 16 different birds. The illustrations resemble a scrapbook or science journal.

TRAPPED!
A WHALE'S RESCUE

ROBERT BURLEIGH   PAINTINGS BY WENDELL MINOR

Learning Targets:

- I can wonder and ask questions before, during, and after reading.
- I can figure out different ways to answer my own questions about the world.

Research to Answer Lingering Questions

Book Title: *Trapped! A Whale's Rescue* (Burleigh, 2015)

About the Book: Based on a true story, a humpback whale gets ensnared in fishing nets. Brave rescue divers work to free the whale. In the back matter, readers can learn more about the actual event, rescuing whales, and humpback whales.

To find a book like this one, look for the following:

- Plots based on true events
- Books that lead to more questions

Comprehension Conversation:

Before Reading

Notice the Cover Illustration:

- Let's look at the wrap-around cover and ponder the title of this book *Trapped! A Whale's Rescue*. What do you think is happening on the cover? Share what you notice and think with a partner. Now, what are you wondering?

- Notice it says "Paintings by Wendell Minor." Inside, you can read that he uses a special kind of paint called gouache (gwash) to create his illustrations. Gouache paint is not see-through (or transparent) like watercolor paint.

- The painting on the title page really helps you see how small a human is compared to a whale, doesn't it?

Set a Purpose: As we read, we'll see if the book answers some of your before-reading questions and if we have more questions as we read and after we're done.

During Reading

- *The huge humpback whale dips and dives.* page: I'm wondering what the words *spyhop* and *lobtail* mean. Maybe if I look in the back of the book I can find out. Right here in the "Did You Know" section, it says when whales pop their heads above the water to look around it is called *spyhopping*, and when they slap their tails on top of the water it's called *lobtailing*. Sometimes readers wonder about words when they're reading.

- *But wait—danger haunts these waters.* page: What do you think is going to happen? Did we see evidence for your predictions earlier in the book? [Turn back to the cover illustration to show that the whale is trapped in the net.] What are you wondering?

- *The chug-chug of the motor fills the air.* page: What are you wondering? I'm remembering back to the title page and thinking about how immense a whale is compared to a human. I'm wondering if it is safe to try to rescue a whale.

After Reading

- As readers, we wondered about many things as we read. We wondered about words, about what might happen next, and about whether rescuing a whale is safe. Often, nonfiction books leave us with more questions. Do you have any lingering questions?

- How did asking questions as we read help you as a reader?

Extend the Experience:

- In this book, we can find some answers in the back matter (the information authors add at the back of a book). How else could we find the answers?

- [If students have lingering questions, invite them to form a research group to find the answers to their question and share their new learning with the class.]

Key Vocabulary:

- immense
- rescue
- struggle

Other similar titles:

 Elizabeth, Queen of the Seas (Cox, 2014)

About the Book: Named after the Queen of England, Elizabeth the elephant seal was happiest when swimming in and basking near the Avon River in Christchurch, New Zealand. One of her favorite spots to nap was a two-lane road near the river. After a near miss with a car, the townspeople towed her back to the ocean. But she returned. After two more attempts, the second a hundred miles away, Elizabeth returned to *her* river and stayed there until her death in 1985.

 Ivan: The Remarkable True Story of the Shopping Mall Gorilla (Applegate, 2014)

About the Book: The touching tale of Ivan, a western lowland gorilla, who was captured and held captive for 27 years at the B & I Circus Store in Tacoma, Washington, until 1994 when he was moved to Zoo Atlanta.

How to find answers to our questions . . .
- Read a book
- Visit a zoo, museum, or park
- Observe
- Ask an expert
- Research on the computer

Notice Where Questions Lead

Book Title: *Margaret and the Moon: How Margaret Hamilton Saved the First Lunar Landing* (Robbins, 2017)

About the Book: Margaret asked a lot of questions, studied hard in school, and developed innovative solutions. This mindset helped her to become one of the only female computer scientists in the 1950s and 1960s. In 1969, Margaret's computer programming helped Apollo 11 land safely on the moon.

To find a book like this one, look for the following:

- Plots based on true events
- Books that lead to more questions
- Biographies about inspiring individuals whose questions lead to innovations

Learning Targets:

- I can wonder and ask questions before, during, and after reading.
- I can figure out different ways to answer my own questions about the world.
- I can notice where questions lead.

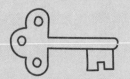

Key Vocabulary:

- convinced
- gazed
- solution

Comprehension Conversation:

Before Reading

Notice the Cover Illustration:

- Notice Margaret's face on the cover. When you see someone with their hand on their chin like that what do you think that person is doing? [thinking, wondering, pondering]
- The subtitle reads *How Margaret Hamilton Saved the First Lunar Landing*. Do you have any before-reading questions? Are there any puzzling words in that subtitle? [If children aren't familiar with the word *lunar*, explain that it means the same thing as moon.]
- Based on the cover and title, do you think this will be a fiction or nonfiction book? Talk with your partner about that.

Set a Purpose: I'm noticing that Margaret is wondering about something. Wondering and asking questions helps us to figure out what is happening in a story, and when we find the answers to our questions we often learn new things. Let's turn the page and find out what is making her ponder and if her questions lead to new learning.

During Reading

- *WHY WERE THERE ONLY DADDY LONGLEGS?* page: Margaret sure asks a lot of questions. That's just like us! She must know that asking questions and finding solutions helps your brain grow. What were some of her solutions?
- *SHE GAZED AT THE NIGHT SKY IN WONDER.* page: What do you notice in the sky? [constellations]
- *AND THEN SHE DISCOVERED COMPUTERS!* page: Hmmm! I'm wondering if Margaret's story happened recently or long ago. What do you think? Talk about that with your neighbor.
- *THE EAGLE'S COMPUTER STARTED* . . . page: What are you thinking? What are you wondering?

After Reading

- How did asking questions and wondering shape Margaret's life? Where did her questions lead?

- How can you take what you learned from Margaret and use it in your own life?

- [Notice that the back end papers have real photographs of Margaret. The photo of her with the standing next to the stack of code is depicted in the book!]

Extend the Experience:

- What happens when you are curious and ask questions? Let's write a few of your ideas down. (See example.)

- Create a "Wonder Center" (Heard & McDonough, 2009) by placing a large piece of chart paper and some sticky notes in a center. Invite children to write down their questions and post them on the chart. Then, provide children with age-appropriate resources to research and answer their questions. (See photo.)

Wonder Center

Other similar titles:

***Ben Franklin's Big Splash: The Mostly True Story of His First Invention* (Rosenstock, 2014)**

About the Book: Unlike most people in Colonial Boston, young Ben Franklin loved to swim. As he swam, he asked himself questions which led to his first invention—swim fins. Filled with alliterative verbs, all starting with the letter *s*, *Ben Franklin's Big Splash* will spark conversations about how scientists ask questions, solve problems, and learn from their mistakes.

***On a Beam of Light: A Story of Albert Einstein* (Berne, 2013)**

About the Book: Albert didn't speak until the age of three, but once he started talking he asked a barrage of questions. He read, studied, and continued to wonder. When Albert began sending his discoveries to science magazines, people began to notice. Then, he spent the rest of his life "imagining, wondering, figuring, and thinking." The book ends with an invitation to readers to seek out the answers to their own questions.

What happens when you are curious and ask questions?
- Invent something
- Discover new ideas
- Solve problems
- Learn something new

Question to Determine the Author's Purpose

Book Title: *Tree of Wonder: The Many Marvelous Lives of a Rainforest Tree* (Messner, 2015)

About the Book: Messner invites readers into an almendro tree, also known in Latin America as the *tree of life*. At each page turn, learners meet the creatures that inhabit and depend on the tree. The number of creatures doubles each time you turn the page starting with two macaws and concluding with 1,024 leafcutter ants.

To find a book like this one, look for the following:

- Books that lead to more questions
- Accessible facts and supportive illustrations for young learners
- Theme of conservation

Learning Targets:

- I can wonder and ask questions before, during, and after reading.
- I can figure out different ways to answer my own questions about the world.
- I can ponder the author's purpose for writing the book.

Comprehension Conversation:

Before Reading

Notice the Cover Illustration:

- Simona Mulazzani used paint and pencil to make her illustration of the tree and the animals in it. As you look at the cover, think about the title and subtitle. Why do you suppose Kate Messner called this rainforest tree a "Tree of Wonder"? What do you think she means by "The Many Marvelous Lives" of this tree?

- End Papers: What do you notice on the end papers? Were some of the same animals on the cover? Let's check.

Set a Purpose: After looking at the cover, we already have a lot of unanswered questions. What is the best way to answer our questions? [READ!] Smart thinking! It's also smart to continue asking questions as we read. Afterward, let's think and talk together about why Kate Messner might have written this book.

During Reading

- *Deep in the forest, in the warm-wet . . .* page: After hearing this page, do you have any questions? Are there any puzzling words I can help you to figure out? I'm wondering what Kate Messner means when she says, "A whole hidden world bustles and thrives [in this tree]." Can you spot any animals hidden on this page?

- *Look up—way up!* page: Oh! Now I'm wondering if this is going to be a counting book. Since the first page had one tree and this page has two macaws. Any other questions before we continue?

- *Who's hungry?* page: Wait! That doesn't make sense. I thought the next page would have three animals on it, and it has four. See if you and your partner can put your heads together and figure out what is going on. [Each page doubles the number of animals.]

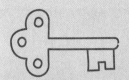
- *What's that growly, roaring sound?* page: Did this page with eight howler monkeys confirm your thinking?

- [Continue inviting listeners to notice, question, and discuss the happenings in the book.]

After Reading

- Now that we've read the book, talk about why you think Kate Messner called this rainforest tree a "Tree of Wonder"? What did she mean by "The Many Marvelous Lives" of this tree?

- Why do you think Kate Messner wrote this book? What do you think she wanted us to learn and remember? How do the title and subtitle connect to her purpose?

Extend the Experience:

- If Kate Messner wrote this book to remind us to take care of our rainforests, I think it would be smart to learn more about the rainforest. What questions do you have about the rainforest? [Record students' questions. As a class, categorize the questions into groups such as rainforest animals, rainforest plants, rainforest locations, rainforest characteristics. Then, divide your class into small groups to do a bit of research and report back their findings.]

- [In the back matter, Kate includes word problems at different levels. Select a problem or two that match the level of your students and see if students can complete the problem and explain their process.] Now that we've solved the word problems that Kate wrote, I'm going to show you a page in the book. Create your own word problem for your friends to solve.

Key Vocabulary:

- bustles

- hauling

- lurk

Other similar titles:

Animal Ark: Celebrating Our Wild World in Poetry and Pictures (Alexander, 2017)

About the Book: Through poetry and stunning photographs, readers tour the animal kingdom meeting endangered and threatened animals from around the world. In the author's note, Kwame invites readers to look at the photographs and create their own haiku poems.

The Great Kapok Tree: A Tale of the Amazon Rainforest (Cherry, 1990)

About the Book: A man who is tasked with the job of cutting down the kapok tree, gets tired of chopping and falls asleep. While he sleeps, the rainforest animals visit him and plead with him to leave it standing. When he wakes up, he comes face-to-face with the animals and leaves the rainforest without chopping the tree down.

Hello Hello (Wenzel, 2018)

About the Book: Using his signature multimedia illustrations, Wenzel introduces readers to 92 different animals. The back matter lists all of the animals along with their conservation status.

Wake Up!

Helen Frost and Rick Lieder

Learning Targets:

- I can wonder and ask questions before, during, and after reading.

- I can figure out different ways to answer my own questions about the world.

- I can think beyond the text to ponder big ideas.

Question to Ponder Big Ideas

Book Title: *Wake Up!* (Frost, 2017)

About the Book: Poetic text and intriguing photographs of baby animals prompt young readers to question and wonder about the natural world.

To find a book like this one, look for the following:

- Poetic texts

- Illustrations or photographs that highlight the natural world

Comprehension Conversation:

Before Reading

Notice the Cover Illustration:

- How do you suppose Rick Lieder created this picture on the cover? You're right; it is a photograph. He took this picture with a camera.

- Ponder the title *Wake Up!* Do you have any questions before we begin reading?

Set a Purpose: Wow! Let's read together to see if we can answer some of your questions and see if we can figure out the big ideas in this book.

During Reading

- *Sun says, Wake up—come out and explore.* page: I wonder what kind of bird is in this photograph. Sometimes in nonfiction books the authors include extra information in the back of the book. I'm going to check. It says in the back that the bird is a sandhill crane chick that is only one week old. Isn't it cute? I wonder if all of the photographs are going to be about baby animals. Let's keep reading to find out.

- [Continue consulting the back matter of the book to help answer your students' queries about the photographs.]

- *Who's inside these eggs?* page: Carefully examine this photograph. Do you see anything unusual about the nest? [It is lined with feathers.]

After Reading

- I'm going to reread the whole poem again without stopping. As I'm reading, see if you can figure out what the author and illustrator are saying to us as readers.

- What do you think the big ideas are in this book? [pay attention to what is around you, notice animals]

Extend the Experience:

- What is one way you can *Wake Up!* and experience the world around you? Let's make a list. [Some possibilities include go to the park, look in a tree, dig in the dirt, go for a walk in the woods, look at the sky, examine a bug] Then, you can make a sign to hang in the hallway that says Wake Up! _____.

- [Gather a collection of baby animal resources. Books, photographs, and/or kid-appropriate websites or databases.] What is your favorite baby animal? Find a photograph or illustration of it to share with the class. Tell/or write what the baby animal is doing in the photograph. This baby animal is _____.

Other similar titles:

 Life (Rylant, 2017)

About the Book: "Life begins small," and then it grows. In this tribute to life and the wonders of the natural world, Rylant explores the joys, ups, and downs of living. Notice all the hidden animals in Brendan Wenzel's illustrations. The big ideas might include enjoy life, protect animals, things change, living things grow and change.

 Now (Portis, 2017)

About the Book: A young girl shares her favorite things. She points out that they are her favorite because she is experiencing them *now*. Although this book is not nonfiction, it lends itself to a big ideas conversation about living in the moment and enjoying what you are doing right now.

Key Vocabulary:

- exploding
- explore
- snuggles

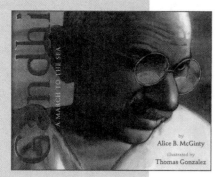

View the book trailer at
resources.corwin.com/
rampedup-readaloud

Learning Targets:

- I can notice the connections among ideas and events in a biography.

- I can share important details about a person's life.

Connect Important Events

Book Title: *Gandhi: A March to the Sea* (McGinty, 2013)

About the Book: You can almost hear their footsteps in the rhythm of McGinty's words as you travel with Gandhi and his fellow protestors on their March to the Sea. This partial biography depicts Gandhi's non-violent Salt March that took place in 1930. The march received international press coverage and became a step forward in trying to free India from British rule. It took until 1947 for India to finally be free.

To find a book like this one, look for the following:

- A biography that highlights a major accomplishment in a person's life or informational book about one historical event

- A book about peaceful protests

Comprehension Conversation:

Before Reading

Notice the Cover Illustration:

- [If possible, print or display a photograph of Gandhi] Compare this photograph to Thomas Gonzalez's illustration on the cover. What do you think? Does the picture he created using paints, colored pencils, and ink look like the photograph?

- What do you already know about Gandhi? [Record any prior knowledge on a chart or interactive whiteboard document.]

- Before we read this book about one important event in Gandhi's life, I'll read you the introduction. In a partial biography such as this one, an introduction is like when you first meet someone and they tell you a little bit about themselves. Alice McGinty did this to help you better connect the event in this book to the rest of Gandhi's life.

Set a Purpose: As we read this biography, think about how the March to the Sea was important in Gandhi's life and in the lives of the people of India.

During Reading

- *JUST BEFORE SUNRISE, a small, brown-skinned man . . .* page: How do you suppose it would feel to be marching with Gandhi?

- *Gandhi takes the lead . . .* page: Here it says the road was *risky*, which means it was dangerous. Why do you think the marchers were willing to walk the risky road? Would you be willing to walk the risky road? Talk about that with the person next to you.

- *Each law broken, every stride, every garment . . .* page: I notice the words, "One more step toward freedom" look different than the other words on the page. They

are written in italics; see how the letters look like they are leaning to one side. I wonder why Alice McGinty chose to do that.

- *Each law broken, every stride, every garment* . . . page: Here are the words in italics again. Did you notice anything about the words? [Alice McGinty has used repeated sentences. This repeated section appears again on the last page of the book with the last line changed. Discuss why kids think Alice McGinty chose to repeat this section in her book.]

Key Vocabulary:

- gaze
- risky
- unfair

After Reading

- What was Gandhi trying to accomplish with this march? How do you think the march connected to Gandhi's goals?

- Did you learn something important about Gandhi or about the country of India that you didn't already know? Share your new learning with a friend.

- Do you have any lingering questions?

Maria's Thinking: I believe it is important to ask the question, "Do you have any lingering questions?" and then follow up with a conversation about the various ways students could go about finding their own answers. For example, if applicable, you can show learners the back matter of the book containing more information. In addition, showcase the different databases you have available in your classroom or school like *PebbleGo: The Emergent Reader Research Solution* (Capstone) and *Kids InfoBits* (Gale). Encourage children who choose to do further research to bring their new learning in to share with the class.

Extend the Experience:

- Let's go back and look at [the chart/interactive whiteboard document] to see what you already knew about Gandhi before we started reading. What is your new learning about Gandhi's life? Record one important detail you learned about Gandhi on this sticky note, and we'll add it to the bottom of the chart. It is amazing to see how much we can learn from reading one book!

- Using the *Inspiring Individuals Reproducible Response Page* located on the companion website (adapted from Walther & Phillips, 2012), why was Gandhi an important historical figure? What did you learn about him that you can use in your own life?

_____

I learned about _____.

This person is important because _____

_____

Reading biographies about him/her taught me _____

_____

Name _____

Inspiring Individuals Reproducible Response Page

Download this form at resources.corwin.com/rampedup-readaloud

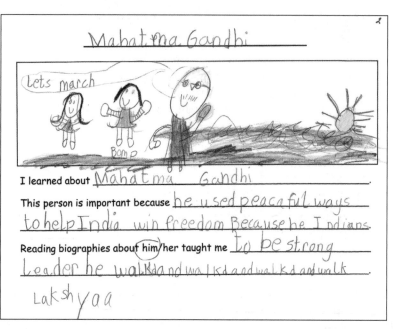

Inspiring Individuals Work Sample

....

Other similar titles:

Maya Lin: Artist-Architect of Light and Lines (Harvey, 2017)

About the Book: Budding artists and architects will enjoy hearing the biography of Maya Lin, designer of the Vietnam Veterans Memorial. As a child, she grew up with art. When she went to college she decided to be an architect. In her senior year, she entered the contest to design the memorial and won. Many were surprised by her young age and did not like her design, but it was finally approved.

We March (Evans, 2012)
[a book about peaceful protests]

About the Book: A family joins the March on Washington on August 28, 1963. Evans' tells the story with few words and simple yet compelling illustrations. It would be helpful if children had a bit of background knowledge about the march to fully appreciate this powerful text.

My Favorite Picture Book Biographies to Read Aloud

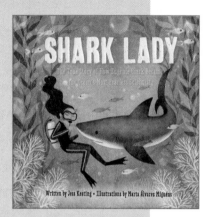

View the book trailer at resources.corwin.com/ rampedup-readaloud

Learning Targets:

- I can notice the connections among ideas and events in a biography.

- I can share important details about a person's life.

- I can talk, write, or draw about the person's character traits.

Connect Character Traits to Text

Book Title: *Shark Lady: The True Story of How Eugenie Clark Became the Ocean's Most Fearless Scientist* (Keating, 2017)

About the Book: The biography of Dr. Eugenie Clark (1922–2015) who followed her dreams and became a respected zoologist who specialized in sharks. Jess Keating did a magnificent job of keeping the text concise, interesting, and accessible to young learners.

To find a book like this one, look for the following:

- Biographies that include information about the person's childhood

- Biographies that are accessible and interesting to young learners

Comprehension Conversation:

Before Reading

Notice the Cover Illustration:

- Wow! Do you think you would be brave enough to dive with a shark? Let's open the book so that we can compare the front cover to the back cover. What do you notice? [On the back cover we see Eugenie as a young girl, on the front cover she's grown up.] I'll read you the back cover blurb.

Set a Purpose: As we read about the Shark Lady, I want you to think about what steps she had to take to become "the ocean's most fearless scientist" and what we notice about the way Eugenie thinks and acts.

During Reading

- [As you're reading, notice how Jess Keating used multiple meaning water words like *dove*, *plunged*, and *fished*.]

- *Eugenie pretended she was walking on the bottom of the sea.* page: How does the illustrator show you that Eugenie is pretending? What does this tell us about her? [She used her imagination.] I'm wondering how using her imagination might help her in the future.

- *The salt stung her eyes, but she didn't want to miss a single fish.* page: What is Eugenie imagining she is on this page? [a shark] Where did all of her imagining about sharks lead her?

- *Despite all of the people . . .* page: Here it says that people still doubted her. That means the people still weren't sure that she could be a scientist. Can you find someone on this page who is not sure. Do you remember who he is? [her teacher] Even with people doubting her, she continued to study sharks. What does that show us about her character? [she followed her dream, she studied hard, she became the smartest student, she didn't give up]

- *Sharks were not mindless killers.* page: Talk to your neighbor about what you notice on this page. [Eugenie is looking at a little girl who likes sharks the same way she

did when she was a young child.] How did her feelings and actions as a little girl connect to who she ended up being as an adult?

After Reading

- What steps did Eugenie have to take to become a scientist? Notice how each step was connected to the one before it.

- What do her actions reveal about her character?

Extend the Experience:

- What traits or characteristics did you notice about Eugenie as we read this book? Let's list them on a web.

- In a biography such as this, authors often add extra information. Let's see what is in the back matter of the book. [Share a few "Shark Bites" and the Time Line of Eugenie's life.]

....

Other similar titles:

 Malala's Magic Pencil (Yousafzai, 2017)

About the Book: When Malala was little, she dreamed she had a magic pencil, one that solves any problem. As she grows up, she realizes that it is words and ideas, not magic, that fosters change.

 Tito Puente, Mambo King/Tito Puente, Rey del Mambo (Brown, 2013)

About the Book: In this vibrant bilingual biography, readers meet salsa drummer Tito Puente. As a child, Tito was already making music by banging pot and spoons. Fueled by his love for music, he pursued his dream of becoming a band leader. Your students will enjoy chiming in on the refrain, "¡Tum Tica! / ¡Tac Tic! / ¡Tum Tic! / ¡Tom Tom!"

Who Says Women Can't Be Doctors? The Story of Elizabeth Blackwell (Stone, 2013)

About the Book: The kid-friendly biography of Elizabeth Blackwell (1821–1910) who became the first woman doctor despite the skepticism and ridicule she encountered.

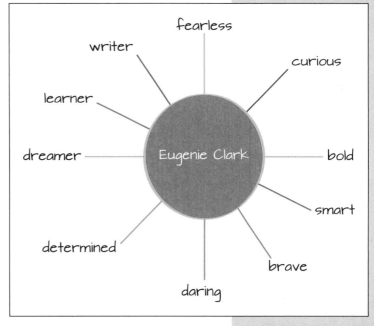

Character Traits of Eugenie Clark Chart

Connect Character Traits to Life Lessons

Book Title: *I Am Abraham Lincoln* (Meltzer, 2014)

About the Book: This is one of the biographies in the Ordinary People Change the World series. These books are ideal for young readers because they are told in an engaging manner that connects with children, while also clearly illustrating the lasting importance of the accomplishments of each individual. Notice that the illustrator hid Brad Meltzer (the author) in the picture where Lincoln is marching arm in arm after he gave the Gettysburg Address.

To find a book like this one, look for the following:

- Biographies that highlight the character of the inspiring individual
- Biographies that appeal to young readers

Learning Targets:

- I can notice the connections among ideas and events in a biography.
- I can share important details about a person's life.
- I can think beyond the text to ponder life lessons.

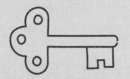

Key Vocabulary:

- avoided
- preferred
- reveal

Comprehension Conversation:

Before Reading

Notice the Cover Illustration:

- Do you recognize the person on the cover? Yes! That is Abraham Lincoln. Does Abe look a bit different than he does in other pictures you've seen of him? What do you notice? [He kind of looks like a kid.] Why do you think the illustrator, Christopher Eliopoulos, chose to draw him in that way? [If you have other books in this series, you can show the covers of those books to compare.]

- End Papers: Hmmmm! I wonder why there are turtles on the end papers. We'll have to see if we can figure out how turtles are important to the story of Lincoln's life.

Set a Purpose: Today as we learn more about Lincoln's life, I challenge you to think about what Lincoln's actions show you about his personality and what lessons we can learn from the way Lincoln acted.

During Reading

- *In that moment, I could have just walked away.* page: What is important to remember about the turtle story? [Abe did the right thing, he stood up for the turtle and told the boys to stop hurting it.]

- *When it came to learning, my best teachers . . .* page: What do we know so far about Abe's personality? Turn and share his traits with your partner. [He liked to learn, he loved books, he taught himself to read and write, he thought it was wrong to hurt animals]

- *Sometimes, the hardest fights . . .* page: Let's think about what Brad Meltzer is telling us about Lincoln on this page. He says, "Sometimes, the hardest fights don't reveal a winner—but they do reveal character." In this sentence the word *reveal* means the same as *show or tell*. So what did the fight with the bullies show you about Lincoln's character or personality? Turn and tell your neighbor, "It revealed he _____." [He stands up for what he believes in.]

- *If I had turned my head and looked away, I would've avoided the fight.* page: This page also reveals something about Lincoln's character. See if you can figure it out with your friend. [Help others, when someone needs help, stand up for them, and so on.]

After Reading

Life Lessons We Learned

- Read to learn new things
- Do the right thing
- Protect animals
- Fight for what you believe in
- Fight for what's right
- Stand up for other people who need you
- Stand up and say what you want to say

- When we read a biography like this one, we can learn facts and details about the person's life. We can also learn more about how that person's character or how that person acted in various situations. First, let's share some facts and details. Then, we'll think about life lessons that we learned from Lincoln's actions.

Extend the Experience:

- Brad Meltzer chose to focus on parts of Lincoln's life that revealed something about his character and helped us to learn some lessons to think about in our lives. Let's write down some of those life lessons. (See example above.)

- Using the *Take Action! Reproducible Response Page* located on the companion website, take one of the lessons you learned from this book and tell how you might use that lesson at school or at home.

Name _____

Take Action!

I learned this _____	So I will do this _____

Take Action! Reproducible Response Page

Download this form at resources.corwin.com/rampedup-readaloud

Other similar titles:

 I Am Amelia Earhart (Meltzer, 2014)

About the Book: From the time she was a little girl, Amelia Earhart was drawn to *unladylike* adventures. From building a roller coaster in her backyard to flying with pilot Frank Hawks when she was 23, she was determined to fly. After saving her money for flying lessons, Amelia bought her first plane named *Canary*. From there, she went on to break many records.

 Rosa Parks (Kaiser, 2017)

About the Book: From the Little People, Big Dreams series, this is an ideal biography for our youngest readers. Highlighting the important events in Rosa Parks' life, this introduction can lead to further inquiry about her life. The back matter contains real photographs and more details.

Learning Targets:

- I can notice the connections among ideas and events in a biography.
- I can share important details about a person's life.
- I can connect an inspiring individual's life choices to my life choices.

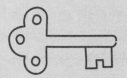

Key Vocabulary:

- cherished
- curious
- observed

Connect Character Traits to Future Plans

Book Title: *Me . . . Jane* **(McDonnell, 2011)**

About the Book: Young Jane Goodall loved the outdoors. She was curious, observant, and a dreamer. Together, these traits, along with persistence, helped her forge a new path for women in science. This book is an engaging introduction to the early life of Jane Goodall. If your students are curious, you can follow up by reading the other biographies listed below or learn more about Jane via the Jane Goodall Institute website. Your kids might also enjoy listening to the song "Jane Jane" by Raffi.

To find a book like this one, look for the following:

- Biographies that include information about the person's childhood
- Biographies that are accessible and interesting to young learners

Comprehension Conversation:

Before Reading

Notice the Cover Illustration:

- This is a book about a real person named Jane Goodall. Have you ever heard of her?
- Look carefully at the cover illustration that Patrick McDonnell created, notice that it looks like a photo album or scrapbook. I wonder why he chose to do this.
- Title page: Look! This is a real photograph of Jane Goodall when she was about your age. Let's compare it to the cover illustration and see what we notice.

Set a Purpose: As we read about Jane, I want you to think about what kind of kid she was. What did she like to do? How did she spend her time?

During Reading

- *She cherished Jubilee and took him everywhere she went.* page: Can you figure out what the word *cherished* means? [Cherished means to love or care about something very much.] Tell your neighbor something that you cherish. Say, "I cherish _____." Then, ask your neighbor what he or she cherishes.
- *The Alligator Society* page: If you turn to the "Art Notes" in the back of the book, you find out that these are copies of drawings and puzzles that Jane created when she was a young girl. Isn't that cool?
- *One day, curious Jane wondered where eggs came from.* page: Hmmm! What does it mean to be *curious*? [Curious people want to know or learn more about something.] What are you curious about?
- *to awake one day . . .* page: Let's go back a page. What do you notice about these two illustrations? [on the "and fall asleep . . ." page Jane is a little girl sleeping in her bedroom, and on the "to awake one day" page she is grown up and sleeping in a tent]

After Reading

- What was Jane's *dream come true*?

- Think about Jane as a little girl. What did she like and what did she do that helped her to accomplish her dream?

- In many books about famous people, the authors include more information in the back matter. If we turn the page, we find more information about Jane Goodall and a note from Jane herself!

Extend the Experience:

- Using the *Connect Character Traits to Future Plans Reproducible Response Page* located on the companion website, ask the following: What did Jane care about and dream? What steps did she take to make her dreams come true? After you've completed your page, talk with a friend about what steps might you have to take to make your dreams come true?

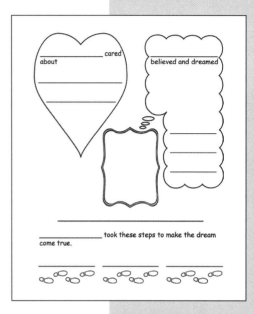

Connect Character Traits to Future Plans Reproducible Page

Download this form at resources.corwin.com/rampedup-readaloud

View more information about Jane Goodall at resources.corwin.com/rampedup-readaloud

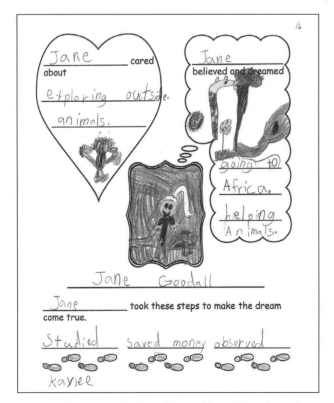

Connect Character Traits to Future Plans Work Sample

Maria's Thinking: I learned this idea from a presentation I attended with Jan Burkins and Kim Yaris, at CCIRA in 2016. The authors of *Reading Wellness: Lesson in Independence and Proficiency* (Burkin & Yaris, 2014) shared that it is important to help children think about how childhood passions can turn into possibilities.

- What traits or characteristics did you notice about Jane as we read this book? Let's list them on a web. (See example below.)

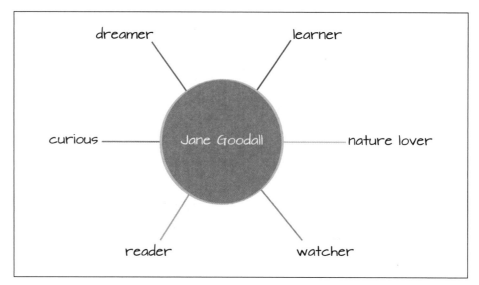

Character Traits of Jane Goodall Chart

Other similar titles:

 I Am Jane Goodall **(Meltzer, 2016)**

About the Book: In this full and lengthy biography of Jane Goodall's life, readers learn details about Jane's journey to become the first woman to study chimpanzees in the wild. This book is part of the Ordinary People Change the World series. For young listeners, plan on reading this biography over a few read-aloud experiences.

 The Watcher **(Winter, 2011)**

About the Book: From the time she was a little girl, Jane was a *watcher* and always dreamed of living in Africa. Through determination, bravery, and hard work, this dream was fulfilled.

Notes

"Aw shucks," said Russell.

"All I've ever wanted was to work with words, like you."

"You do seem to have a talent for it." Lexie admitted.

—*Lexie the Word Wrangler* by
Rebecca Van Slyke and Jessie Hartland

Build Foundational and Language Skills

Working With Words

Certainly the read-aloud experiences in this chapter are not intended to replace your current foundational and language skills curriculum. Instead, they are designed to extend what you're already doing and create word wonder. To do this, I have woven together what I've learned from my teaching experiences and from experts in the word-study field like Pat Cunningham and Tim Rasinski. When it comes to effective instruction in word identification, we know that teaching words taken from authentic texts and playfully practicing words are two proven research-endorsed methods. To develop fluency, research tells us to model fluent reading, encourage students to engage in rereading, and offer plentiful opportunities for wide reading (Rasinski, 2017). In keeping with these findings, in Chapter 5, you'll find books and experiences that focus on the following:

- Sing, Chant, and Rhyme: Strengthen Phonemic Awareness
- Understand Parts of Speech
- Play With Words
- Build Fluency

On the next page, you will find the concepts you will introduce or review while strengthening students' foundational and language skills. As you introduce the concepts to your learners, use the kid-friendly definitions to clarify their understanding. "Foundational and language standards do not exist in a vacuum. Our young learners need to develop these skills and strategies so they can effectively comprehend text and communicate with others" (Walther, 2015, p. 92). By developing each child's talent to work with words, we set them on a path toward successful reading and writing experiences.

Use and Explain Key Comprehension Strategies

Compare and Contrast: To think about how two people, characters, objects, or other things are the alike (compare) and different (contrast).

Predict: Think ahead of your reading by using clues from the pictures and text to think about what might happen next in the story.

Read Fluently: Read like you talk with expression. To do this, readers use the author's punctuation as a signal. For example, when there is an exclamation mark, you read the words with excitement. If there is a question mark, you read the words like you ask a question.

Foster a Growth Mindset

Notice: Pay attention to what is happening in the world around you or in the words and pictures in a book.

Build Foundational and Language Skills

Develop Students' Social and Emotional Learning

Listen: Listening is important for learning. When you are listening to something your brain is thinking about what the person is saying. Also, by looking at the person and nodding your head or making comments when he or she is done, you are showing the person you care about what he or she has to say.

Join in: When we join in together to read a poem or sing a song, try to read at the same pace as the group. When we read or sing together, it should sound like one voice.

Sing: There is a difference among your talking voice, your outside voice, and your singing voice. When we sing together, try to make your voice match the tune and the other voices singing with you.

Teach Literary Language

Adjective: Describes a noun or pronoun. Usually answers one of these questions: Which one? What kind of? How many?

Expressive Words: Words that describe characters, their actions, sounds, emotions, and so on. These words could include adjectives, onomatopoeia, and interjections.

Interjection: A word or words that show how the author or the character is feeling. Most interjections end with an exclamation mark. Some interjections you've probably heard in books are *Yuck!, Yum!, Hooray!,* or *Uh-oh!*

Nursery Rhyme: A short, simple song or poem that was created just for children.

Onomatopoeia: A word like *Boom!, Bang!,* or *Crash!* that imitates a sound.

Poem: A special way to write about a topic using a small number of powerful words.

Rhyming Words: When a similar sound or sounds are repeated in more than one word. Rhyming words usually sound the same at the end of a word.

Verb: Tells the action of the sentence.

Chapter 5 Concepts, Terms, and Kid-Friendly Definitions

My Favorite Read Alouds for Foundational and Language Skills

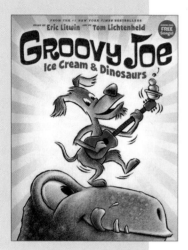

View the book trailer at resources.corwin.com/rampedup-readaloud

Learning Targets:

- I can notice how characters change from the beginning to the end of a story.

- I can think about the events that caused the change.

- I can talk, write, or draw about how characters' change.

Listen for Rhymes as You Sing Along

Book Title: *Groovy Joe: Ice Cream and Dinosaurs* (Litwin, 2016)

About the Book: If your students enjoy Eric Litwin's *Pete the Cat* books, they'll flip over his latest character Groovy Joe. In the first book about sharing, Joe divvies up his ice cream with increasingly larger dinosaurs until there is none left. What will happen next? Begin or end your day in a joyful way with this song picture book.

To find a book like this one, look for the following:

- Rhyming songs, poems, or song picture books
- Catchy tunes that entice listeners to sing along

 ## Comprehension Conversation:

Before Reading

Notice the Cover Illustration:

- Think about the title of the book and take a careful look at Tom Lichtenheld's cover illustration. What do you infer the dinosaur is thinking? [He either wants to eat Groovy Joe, or he wants to eat the ice cream.] What clues in the illustration help you to infer that? Tom always adds interesting details in his illustrations. Do you notice any here or on the back cover? [Front cover: dinosaur spit; Back cover: bird singing, city of Chicago skyline]

Set a Purpose: Since Groovy Joe has a guitar, I'm thinking we should sing along with him. I'll play the music so you can help me read and sing along. As we're reading and singing together, listen carefully to the words. We'll talk about what we've noticed after we've finished rockin' with Groovy Joe.

During Reading

Maria's Thinking: Since this is a song, I would suggest reading/singing it one time through without stopping. Then, the second time you can *sing* it without the music, pause on the second word in a rhyming word pair to let children fill in the missing word, and have the following conversations.

- What did you notice about the words in this book? [They rhyme.] This time, let's sing the book without the music and you can help me fill in the missing words.

- *Groovy Joe saw something yummy.* page: Notice the words on the truck. It reads "Häagen Dogs®" Doggy Ice Cream. This is a joke because there is real ice cream named Häagan-Dazs®.

- *ROAR!! OH NO!! A LITTLE dinosaur stomped into the room.* page: After the little dinosaur enters the room, he *glared* at Groovy Joe. Look at the illustration to see if you can figure out what the word *glared* means on this page.

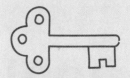
- *ROAR!! OH NO!!! A HUGE dinosaur smashed into the room.* page: Why do you think Eric Litwin chose to use the word *smashed* on this page? Let's go back to see what words he used for the other dinosaurs. [Little dinosaur stomped; Big dinosaur burst.]

After Reading

- What did you notice about this rhyming song book?

- Do you think Eric Litwin wrote this for a reason? What do you think he is trying to teach us? [It's awesome to share!]

Extend the Experience:

- As we reread the book, see if you can find the rhyming word pairs that you heard. [yummy/tummy, dream/cream, chair/share, through/who] Let's write down the rhyming words and see what we notice. [Point out that some pairs have the same spelling pattern, while others have different spelling patterns.] When words have the same spelling pattern like *dream* and *cream*, we sometimes call those words a *word family*. Words in the same family can help us spell other words. Let's try it. Using the spelling pattern from *dream*, how would you spell *beam, team, steam, stream,* or *scream*?

- If you were going to write another Groovy Joe book, what would it be about? Make a book cover with a title and illustration to show your idea. When you're finished, I'll take a picture of your book covers and send them [via social media] to show Eric and Tom your unique ideas.

Key Vocabulary:

- burst
- glared
- rose (verb)

Other similar titles:

 ***Footloose* (Loggins, 2016)**

About the Book: When his first granddaughter was born, Kenny Loggins decided to adapt the song *Footloose* for children. In the updated version, zookeeper Big Jack and all of his animal friends "cut Footloose!" The picture book includes a CD recording of the song performed by Kenny Loggins.

 ***Groovy Joe: Dance Party Countdown* (Litwin, 2017)**

About the Book: Groovy Joe is back at it again. This time, he is singing and dancing about double facts (1 + 1 = 2, 2 + 2 = 4). The message of *Groovy Joe: Dance Party Countdown* is that "There's always room for more."

 ***Octopus's Garden* (Starr, 2014)**

About the Book: Illustrator Ben Cort takes singers on a magical journey when a boy imagines himself under the sea with all of his friends. If you're a Beatles fan, then you'll want to add *Octopus's Garden* to your song picture book collection! Includes a CD recording of the song (not the Beatles' version!).

Chime In and Rhyme

Book Title: *Doris the Bookasaurus* (Murray, 2017)

About the Book: Dinosaur Doris thinks books are "mega-dino-tastic," but her brothers don't agree. They beg Doris to stop reading and play with them; however, she is having too much fun in the world of books. After Doris entices them to read with a shark book, they're finally hooked. Later, she wants to play, but her brothers are too busy reading!

To find a book like this one, look for the following:

- Rhyming text
- Engaging storyline

Comprehension Conversation:

Before Reading

Notice the Cover Illustration:

- Yuyi Chen drew the pictures in this book with pencil, and then she colored them on a computer. Zoom in on the first word in the title. What do you notice? [The name Doris is made out of books.]

- If Doris is a *bookasaurus*, what do you suppose that tells you about Doris? Look at the cover again; can you figure out which one is Doris?

Set a Purpose: As I read this book aloud to you, I'm going to leave out words, pause, and point at you. See if you can figure out the word that is missing and say it when I pause.

During Reading

- *Yes, I always need some more.* page: [Pause and point when you get to the word ROAR! to see if children can use the rhyming pattern to fill in the missing word.] How did you know the missing word was *ROAR*!? [Discuss how they used context clues and the rhyming pattern to predict the missing word.]

- [Continue doing this now and then without interrupting the flow of the story.]

- *while lounging in my boulder bed . . .* page: Did you hear a made-up word on this page? [mega-dino-tastic] One of the joys of being a writer is that you can create your own unique words.

- *Max and T.J. make a fuss.* page: What do we know about the main character, Doris? [She loves books. She reads books all the time.]

- *Max and T.J. stop and stare.* page: It seems like something is about to change on this page. Predict what you think might happen next.

- *I'm all revved up from head to toe.* page: Now Doris is ready to play. What do you predict her brothers are doing?

After Reading

- Did your prediction match Diana Murray's thinking?
- Have you ever lost yourself in a story?

Learning Targets:

- I can predict the words that come next in a rhyming text.
- I can think and talk about pairs of rhyming words.

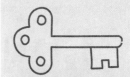
- I'm going to turn back to the copyright (verso) page because I want to read you something. Remember how we talked about the © symbol means that you can't copy the words and pictures in this book. The author wrote a little poem to remind you about that! [Read poem aloud.]

Extend the Experience:

- [To prepare for this response, an adaptation of *Rounding up the Rhymes* (Cunningham, 2017), write down a few pairs of rhyming words from the book, some that have the same spelling pattern and some that do not, such as the following: *more/roar, land/sand, bed/head, hot/spot, toe/go, say/day, high/cry, look/book.* If writing them on a chart paper or an interactive whiteboard document, write each pair of words one word above the other. If writing on index cards, put words in pocket chart one above the other.]

  o Today we heard a lot of rhyming word pairs in this book. I wrote a few of them down. Look at and say each pair and see what you notice.

  o Now I'll underline all of the letters after the first consonant to see which words have the same spelling pattern.

  o [Cross out, tear up, or throw away the ones with different spelling patterns.]

  o [Discuss how rhyming words that have the same spelling pattern like *land, hot, say,* and *look* can help them read and spell a lot of other words.]

  o [Brainstorm a few more words for each pair.]

- [The goal of this extension is to make and discuss a bar graph. You will need one sticky note for each child. At the bottom of your board or a piece of chart paper, write the three types of books Doris read: joke books, fact (nonfiction) books, adventure books.] Doris read different kinds of books. I'm curious to find out which of those books you prefer. We're going to make a bar graph to collect the data. Write your name on this sticky note. When I call your name, place your sticky note above the type of book you prefer. [Call students up to place their sticky note above one of the three choices.] When we're done, we'll discuss what the bar graph shows us about the readers in our class.

Key Vocabulary:
- lounging
- rowdy
- stomping

. . . .

Other similar titles:

The Gruffalo (Donaldson, 1999)

About the Book: As mouse walks through the woods, he meets a fox, an owl, and a snake that want to eat him. To make sure they don't, he tells each animal that the Gruffalo is coming and that his favorite meals are fox, owl, and snake. When the real Gruffalo actually shows up, mouse outsmarts him too by saying he is the "scariest creature in this wood." If your students like this rhyming book, Julia Donaldson has written many others that they may enjoy.

One Big Pair of Underwear (Gehl, 2014)

About the Book: A rhyming book that begins with a giant pair of underwear is sure to be a hit in your classroom. When two bears try to share the underwear, one bear is left out (2 - 1 = 1). Then three yaks only have two salty snacks, so one yak doesn't get any (3 - 2 = 1). The book continues in this fashion until twenty pigs figure out how to go down ten twisty slides, piggy back, of course. The rest of the animals follow suit and decide to share with each other.

ELLI WOOLLARD · BENJI DAVIES

THE GIANT OF JUM

online resources

View the book trailer at resources.corwin.com/rampedup-readaloud

Learning Targets:

- I can predict the words that come next in a rhyming text.

- I can think and talk about pairs of rhyming words.

- I can use rhymes to help me predict what might happen next in a story.

Use Rhymes to Predict

Book Title: *The Giant of Jum* (Woollard, 2015)

About the Book: The Giant of Jum is pining for children to eat. After remembering a story his brother told him about young Jack, he sets off in search of Jack for a snack. Along the way, he helps children fetch their ball from a fountain and rescue their cat from a tree. When he finally meets Jack, the children convince the giant that he is too kind to eat a child. Instead, he should eat cake.

To find a book like this one, look for the following:

- Rhyming text
- Engaging storyline

Comprehension Conversation:

Before Reading

Notice the Cover Illustration:

- This book is called *The Giant of Jum.* Do you know any other stories about giants? [If your students are not familiar with the tale of *Jack and the Beanstalk* you could read them Steven Kellogg's (1991) version with the creepy (and a little bit scary) ogre and his shrunken-head-necklace wearing wife.] What do you notice about Benji Davies's illustration of the giant? Do you think he notices the children running alongside him?

- Back Cover Blurb: Hmmmm! These words, "Fee Fi Fo Fum!" sound familiar. Perhaps this story is just like *Jack and the Beanstalk.*

- Title Page: Look at all of the animals. Can you infer how they are feeling? [scared, nervous] What is the giant holding in his hand? [It appears to be a tree!]

Set a Purpose: Listeners, as I read this book aloud to you, I may leave out a word here or there to see if you can predict what is missing. Doing this may also help you to predict what might happen next in the story. I'm excited to find out more about *The Giant of Jum.*

During Reading

- *He thought of a tale . . .* page: Oh! His brother told him the story of *Jack and the Beanstalk.* What do you know about the giant so far? [He's grumpy; he wants to eat children.]

- *But the children said, "What a magnificent man!"* page: Look at the giant's face. It seems like he's a little confused. Anyone else see that differently?

- *The giant said, "Well, I suppose it won't hurt, but soon, have no fear, I'll be back."* page: Oh, I see. He didn't eat these kids because he's trying to find Jack. Do you think the giant will find Jack? Turn and chat with your neighbor.

- *The giant said, "Well, I suppose I don't mind," and he lifted the boy to his back.* page: [Before you read the name Jack, have the children predict his name based on the rhyme.] What name would rhyme with *back*? Yikes! What do you predict he's going to do with Jack?

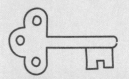
- *But the children said, "Oh no, you wouldn't! We think that you've made a mistake."* page: What might the giant eat that rhymes with the word *mistake*?

After Reading

- Hmmmm! This story was different than I expected. Does anyone else feel that way? Let's talk about it.

- How did listening to the rhyming word pairs help you predict what might come next?

Extend the Experience:

- As readers, we used rhyming word pairs to predict what might come next. We can use the same idea as writers. I've written some "Roses are red" poems. See if you can predict this missing word using what you've learned about rhymes. [After children have practiced filling in the missing rhymes, you might want to write a few poems together. Following this shared demonstration, invite children to write their own "Roses are red" poems.]

Roses are red.

Grass is green.

At first, the giant

Was very
_____. [mean]

Roses are red.

Coal is black.

The Giant of Jum

Wants to eat
_____.
[Jack]

Roses are red.

Cats eat mice.

The kids helped the giant

Learn to be
_____. [nice]

Roses are red.

I like to bake.

The Giant of Jum

Loves to eat
_____.
[cake]

Roses Are Red Poems

- How was *The Giant of Jum* the same as *Jack and the Beanstalk*, and how was it different? We can compare and contrast using an H-Chart. [The *H-Chart Reproducible Response Page* is located on the companion website.]

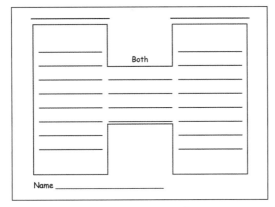

H-Chart Reproducible Response Page

Download this form at resources.corwin.com/rampedup-readaloud

---

Key Vocabulary:

- fetch
- gobble
- tale

Other similar titles:

 Frog on a Log? (Gray, 2015)

About the Book: Cat demands that Frog sits on a log, but Frog doesn't want to sit on an uncomfortable log. Instead, Frog would rather sit other places, but cats sit on mats, and hares sit on chairs. In the end, Frog asks where dogs sit. You guess it, they sit on Frogs. Which leads to the sequel entitled *Dog on a Frog?* (2017). To encourage children to predict using rhymes, read the place that Frog would rather sit (without showing the picture) and then ask, "What animal rhymes with _____ and might sit there?" After listening to a few predictions, show the illustration.

 Mighty, Mighty Construction Site (Rinker, 2017)

About the Book: It's dawn at the construction site and five trucks wake up, ready to work. Once they see the massive job expected of them, Cement Mixer puts out a call. Many of the trucks that join them work in pairs, and eventually the structure gets completed. Teamwork was the key to their success.

My Favorite Rhyming Read Alouds

Notice and Use Vivid Verbs

Book Title: *Some Pets* (DiTerlizzi, 2016)

About the Book: A girl and her chinchilla visit a pet show in the park. At the show, readers meet all different kinds of active pets. Notice that all the pets pictured on the title page appear in the story! Also, there is a two-page spread in the back of the book naming all of the different kinds of pets.

To find a book like this one, look for the following:

- Books brimming with vivid verbs
- Books organized using a list structure

Maria's Thinking: Before engaging in this read-aloud experience, I would have introduced the terms noun, verb, and adjective and helped students develop an understanding of how the parts of speech work together in a sentence. The purpose of this read-aloud experience is to review and reinforce the understandings students have already gained from previous grammar mini-lessons.

Learning Targets:

- I can notice how the author uses interesting verbs.
- I can use what I've learned about verbs from this story in my own reading, writing, and conversations.

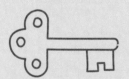

Key Vocabulary:

- bound
- nibble
- scurry

Comprehension Conversation:

Before Reading

Notice the Cover Illustration:

- On the copyright page, it says that "The illustrations for this book were rendered (that means created) in almost everything imaginable."
- I'll open the wrap-around cover. What animals do you see? [Illustrator Brendan Wenzel also wrote and illustrated the 2017 Caldecott Honor book *They All Saw a Cat* featured on page 90.]

Set a Purpose: Animals do a lot of different things. Notice the words Angela DiTerlizzi used to tell what they do. Thinking about words can help us be even better readers and writers.

During Reading

- *Some Pets* page: What does the sign say?
- Title Page: There are a lot of kids and pets at the show. I wonder if we'll see some of the same pets we see here on the inside the pages of the book.
- *Some pets SLITHER.* page: I remember seeing this playground on the title page. [Turn back to the title page.] I wonder if you can find all of the places on the title page on the inside pages of the book. After we read, I'll put this in the reading center so you can do some detective work and find out.
- *Some pets SQUEAL.* page: What do you notice about the three verbs on this page? [They all begin with an *SQU*.]
- *Whether . . .* page: What kinds of words are these? [adjectives]

After Reading

- What kind of words did Angela DiTerlizzi use to tell what pets do? [verbs] That's right, verbs are action words.

- I made a list of all of the verbs Angela DiTerlizzi chose to use in this book. Can you add another verb you might use to tell other things pets do?

Extend the Experience:

- I'm wondering if you could use Angela DiTerlizzi's pattern to make a similar little book about a different topic. Why don't we brainstorm a list of possible topics to get you started? Then, you can use the verbs we found in the book and those we added to write about all the different actions of your person or creature.

- **Action Charades:** On this index card, write your name and an action that you like to do on the playground, at school, or at home. I'll collect them. During the next few days, I'll choose an action and have you act it out for the class to see if they can guess your action!

Topics for our own books
babies
kids
teachers
principals
sharks
dinosaurs
dragons

Other similar titles:

 The Perfect Dog **(O'Malley, 2016) [organized using a list structure]**

About the Book: With permission from her parents, a girl tries to pick a perfect dog. This book uses the repeated sentence stem "A perfect dog should be . . ." and superlatives as readers join the girl in her search for the perfect dog.

 Some Bugs **(DiTerlizzi, 2014)**

About the Book: Bugs are busy critters. Read about all the things they do in *Some Bugs*. Brendan Wenzel's illustrations add visual interest to the story. Notice the cat and the ladybug on the title page. The cat reappears in the beginning, middle, and end. The ladybug appears on every page. On the "and find SOME BUGS in your backyard!" two-page spread, you can locate every animal in the book (except the mole, unless I missed it!).

Verbs found in *Some Pets*		
sit	scurry	squeeze
stay	squeal	nuzzle
fetch	squawk	lick
play	squeak	cuddle
slither	nibble	
bound	drool	

View the making of *Bug Zoo* at resources.corwin.com/rampedup-readaloud

Learning Targets:

- I can notice how the author uses adjectives to describe characters, places, and things.

- I can use what I've learned about adjectives from this story in my own reading, writing, and conversations.

Key Vocabulary:

- folks
- main
- spied

Notice and Use Imaginative Adjectives

Book Title: *Bug Zoo* (Harkness, 2016)

About the Book: Ben loves bugs and wants to open a bug zoo. Sadly, no matter how many bugs he collects in his jars, no one visits his zoo. When he realizes that the bugs are dying, he releases them. Thinking creatively, Ben fills the empty jars with honey and opens a honey stand.

To find a book like this one, look for the following:

- A tale brimming with adjectives
- Books about bugs

Comprehension Conversation:

Before Reading

Notice the Cover Illustration:

- Andy Harkness made his illustrations in a unique way; he used clay. Can you tell that by looking at them? What parts of the cover illustration helped you to know that?

Set a Purpose: While we're reading *Bug Zoo*, let's notice the words the author uses to describe the bugs. Noticing an author's choice of words can help us as we read and write.

During Reading

- *Ben picked fresh leafy branches—one for each . . .* page: Wow! Look at all of the adjectives Andy Harkness used to describe Ben's bugs. Tell your neighbor your favorite adjective. Say, "My favorite adjective is _____."

- *The moth looked sad.* page: Why do you think the moth is sad? What do you think Ben should do?

- *Ben released each . . .* page: Were you surprised by what Ben did? I wonder what Ben is going to do next? Wait! Before we turn the page, did you notice all the adjectives? I'm going to read them again because I love the way they sound. You can join in.

- *. . . and in the grass.* page: What do you suppose Ben is going to put in all of those empty jars?

After Reading

- Did your prediction match the author's thinking? Were you surprised that Ben put honey in the jars?

Extend the Experience:

- [To extend the read-aloud experience, select a person, book character, place, or thing that makes sense with your curriculum. Some examples might include Rosa Parks, Tacky the Penguin, frogs, volcanos, and so forth. (See the examples on the facing page.)] Now that we've learned more about adjectives, let's use them to describe _____.

- If you have clay available, invite learners to create their own three-dimensional illustration using Andy Harkness's as inspiration. Another option is to show this book to your art teacher to see if he or she can help children create clay illustrations.

Adjectives Describing Rosa Parks Work Sample

Other similar titles:

 Fireflies (Brinckloe, 1985) [books about bugs]

About the Book: A boy and his friends catch hundreds of fireflies in jars. When the boy takes the jar of fireflies back to his room, he learns that sometimes you need to set something free in order to keep it alive.

 I Like Bugs (Brown, 1954/1982)

About the Book: Margaret Wise Brown's poem "I Like Bugs" is brought to life in this easy-reader book. She tells about many kinds of bugs including "Black bugs. Green bugs. Bad bugs. Mean bugs."

Adjectives Describing Tacky Chart

Penny Dale

Learning Targets:

- I can notice how the author uses adjectives to describe characters, places, and things.

- I can notice how the author uses onomatopoeias and interjections to spice up the writing.

Notice and Use Expressive Words

Book Title: *Dinosaur Rocket!* (Dale, 2015)

About the Book: In the fourth book of her dinosaur series, Penny Dale launches the dinosaurs into space. This bright and lively picture book is filled with adjectives and onomatopoeias.

To find a book like this one, look for the following:

- A story brimming with adjectives

- Expressive writing including onomatopoeias and interjections

Comprehension Conversation:

Before Reading

Notice the Cover Illustration:

- Penny Dale used watercolor and pencils to create her illustrations. What words would you use to describe her illustrations?

- Let's read the title and back cover blurb to see what the book in going to be about. [The back cover blurb is an ideal mentor text for when students are writing their own blurbs.]

Set a Purpose: What sounds would you expect to hear on a *Dinosaur Rocket*? How do you think you would write those sounds in a story? Let's read to find out how Penny Dale did it in her book.

During Reading

- *Brave dinosaurs climbing.* page: What kind of words does Penny Dale use to describe the sound the dinosaurs' feet make? [clank] The word *clank* is called an onomatopoeia or sound word. Let's see if we notice any other sound words in the book.

- *Dinosaur rocket roaring.* page: Do you hear any more sound words?

- *Hero dinosaurs splashing down.* page: Hmmmm! The word *hooray* is not a sound word. Does anyone know what kind of word it is? *Hooray* is called an interjection. Just like sound words, writers add interjections to make their stories more interesting. I bet you can try that out when you write today.

After Reading

- Let's go back and reread to see if we can find the words Penny Dale uses to describe the astronauts. [brave, nervous, excited, proud, laughing, quiet, happy] These words are called adjectives. They describe the noun.

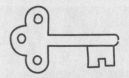
 ## Extend the Experience:

- To help us as writers, we'll make a chart of some of the onomatopoeias that Penny Dale used in case we want to use them in our own writing. Can you add any of your own to the chart? [Create an anchor chart of onomatopoeias or invite students to record them in their writers' notebooks.]

- Penny Dale used adjectives to describe the dinosaurs. Draw a picture of yourself and surround it with adjectives that describe you.

Key Vocabulary:
- final
- hero
- thundering (verb)

Other similar titles:

 ### Click! (Ebbeler, 2015) [onomatopoeia]

About the Book: A boy clicks off his bird-shaped bedside lamp and goes to sleep. Soon the boy is tossing and turning because of all of the noises in the house. Fortunately, the long-legged bird lamp is off to solve the problem. This noisy book is told in a graphic format using only onomatopoetic words.

 ### Snip Snap! What's That? (Bergman, 2005)

About the Book: On the title page, you see that the manhole cover is askew. The dedication page pictures a man running and some alligator tracks in the street. Next, the tip of the alligator's tail is shown as he walks up the stairs. As the shiny, spiked alligator with the tremendous tail snips, snaps, and slithers around the apartment, the children cower in fear until . . . they gather their courage and scare the alligator away.

Learning Targets:

- I can understand more about how words work.
- I can notice the difference between two similar words.
- I can use what I learned about words in my own writing and reading.

Compare and Contrast Words

Book Title: *Take Away the A* (Escoffier, 2014)

About the Book: On each page of this one-of-a-kind alphabet book, readers discover what happens when one letter is subtracted from a word. Every two-page spread includes an illustration that tells a story. Notice the little white mouse that appears now and then.

To find a book like this one, look for the following:

- Texts that include word play
- Books where readers have to differentiate between similar words

 Comprehension Conversation:

Before Reading

Notice the Cover Illustration:

- What is happening on the cover? [The beast is about to eat the letter *A*.] Does anyone have any questions about the cover? What else do you notice?

Set a Purpose: [This before-reading activity might be easier if students have an individual whiteboard and marker or pencil and paper handy.] How many of you have the letter *A* in your first name? What would your name look like and sound like if we took away the *A*? [Invite children with the letter A in their names to figure out and share.] How is your original name different than your name without the letter A. Look carefully at the words in this book called *Take Away the A*.

During Reading

- *Without the A* page: Chat with your neighbor about what happened on this page. Did you notice that when you take the letter *A* out of the word *beast* it becomes *best*? Did you or your partner notice anything interesting in the illustrations? [The beast came in 1st place because he was the "Scariest and Hairiest." The duck earned 2nd place, and the fish finished in 3rd place.]

- *Without the B* page: What happened to the word *bride* when you take away the letter *B*? What letter do you suppose will come next? What kind of book is this? [an alphabet book]

- [Continue noticing the difference between the two words and all the details in the illustrations. You may need to split this book into a few read-aloud experiences.]

After Reading

- That was such an original idea for an alphabet book. I don't think I've ever read one like this before. What did you think of it? Show me with your thumbs. [thumbs up = liked the book, thumbs in the middle = OK book, thumbs down = not my favorite book] What made you feel that way? [Invite a few children to share the reasons behind their opinion.]

Extend the Experience:

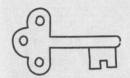

- [Invite children to take out a piece of paper or individual whiteboard and marker.] I'm going to teach you how to play a "Take Away the Letter" game. See below for an example and other groups of words to get you started.

- [Gather enough alphabet books so that each child in your class can read one with a partner. Invite each pair to choose an alphabet book to read.] Today we are going to have an alphabet book read-in. See what you notice about the book you and your partner are reading. After you're done reading, practice what you want to tell us about your book. [Provide time for pairs to share their "book commercials." Then, place the alphabet books in a place where children can read them during independent reading.]

Key Vocabulary:

- foes

- hails

Other similar titles:

 Red Sled (Thomas, 2008)

About the Book: Pairs of rhyming words tell the tale of a boy and his father who go sledding to change their moods from sad to happy.

 There's a Bear on My Chair (Collins, 2015)

About the Book: Mouse finds a bear on his chair and tries everything he can think of to get him off. In the end, Bear goes home to find a mouse in his house. The book is created with words that rhyme with *bear* and *chair*. After reading, children could compare and contrast the rhyming words by noticing words have the same spelling pattern as *bear*, others that have the same pattern as *chair*, and those that have a different spelling pattern than either *bear* or *chair*.

How to Play	Other Groups of Words to Use			
Write the word:	stop	meet	chat	bite
spine	top	met	cat	bit
Take away the e. What word do you have?	to	me	at	it
spin				
Take away the s.				
What word do you have?	they	this	share	bone
pin	the	his	hare	one
Take away the p.	he	is	are	on
What word do you have?				
in				

Take Away the Letter Game

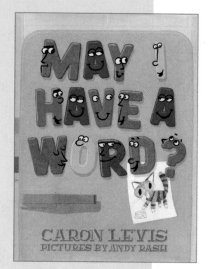

CARON LEVIS
PICTURES BY ANDY RASH

Learning Targets:

- I can understand more about how words work.
- I can use what I learned about words in my own writing and reading.

Notice How Letters Work

Book Title: *May I Have a Word?* (Levis, 2017)

About the Book: The magnetic letters on the refrigerator want to create a story, but the letters K and C can't agree on who should get the starring role. Retreating to opposite sides of the fridge, the other letters worry what life (and words) will be like without C and K. In an effort to coax them back, the letter N encourages K to join in creating a new tale (using "kn" words). In the end, K apologizes to C and all of the letters cooperate.

To find a book like this one, look for the following:

- Plots that include word play
- Books where letters are missing from words

 ## Comprehension Conversation:

Before Reading

Notice the Cover Illustration:

- Can you figure out where we are in this illustration on the cover? Maybe if we open the wrap-around cover and look at it all together, it will help. [in a kitchen, looking at the refrigerator]

Set a Purpose: Have you ever used magnetic letters like these before? What did you do with the magnetic letters? I'm wondering what is going to happen to the letter magnets in this book. Maybe they will teach us more about how words work!

During Reading

- *Once upon a refrigerator, the letters of the alphabet . . .* page: What did the author choose to write instead of "Once upon a time"?

- *"What about a crab?" said C.* page: What do you already know about the letters C and K? [sometimes they stand for the same sound]

- *C and K stormed off to separate sides of the refrigerator.* page: Look at the letters' faces. Can you tell by their expressions what the word cranky means? What is another word for *cranky*? [crabby, grouchy, grumpy]

- *The other letters were worried.* page: What is missing from *all* of these words? [the letters "ck"]

- *KNICKERS!* page: Can you infer what *knickers* is another name for? [underwear!]

After Reading

- Wasn't that book fun? Caron Levis did a lot of interesting things with words in this book. What did she do? [The letters talked, made words, and had faces. She showed what words would look like with missing letters and so on.]

- I wonder if there will be a sequel. What might happen in a sequel?

Extend the Experience:

- [Place a set or two of refrigerator magnetic letters in a literacy center for students to manipulate.]

- In this book, we read a lot of *C* and *K* words. To help us remember which words begin with C and which begin with K, we'll make a chart to hang by our word wall.

Key Vocabulary:
- cooperate
- cranky
- exclaimed

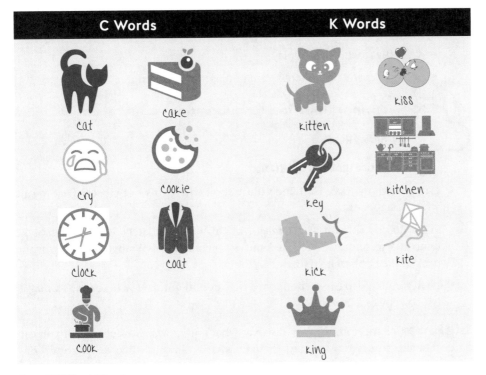

C and K Word Chart

Other similar titles:

 E-mergency **(Lichtenheld & Fields-Meyer, 2011)**

About the Book: When the letter E gets injured, the alphabet decides to have O take his place. So, the words in the illustrations and those spoken by the characters all have O instead of E with humorous results. Only the narrator continues to use E until the letters make him stop.

 Tyrannosaurus Rex vs. Edna the Very First Chicken **(Rees, 2017)**

About the Book: Unlike the other dinosaurs, Edna, the chicken, is not afraid to stand up to the breakfast-hunting Tyrannosaurus. Edna uses her mighty beak, flapping wings, pointy claws, and feathers to escape from the dinosaur's mouth. As Edna fights for her freedom, Tyrannosaurus's roars come out a new way—with letters missing!

online resources

View the book trailer at resources.corwin.com/rampedup-readaloud

Learning Targets:

- I can understand more about how words work.

- I can rearrange letters to make new words.

- I can use what I learned about words in my own writing and reading.

Manipulate Letters to Make Words

Book Title: *Lexie the Word Wrangler* (Van Slyke, 2017)

About the Book: Lexie was living happily on her ranch tying, mixing, and herding words together into sentences and stories. Then, Lexie noticed someone causing mayhem by stealing and adding letter and words. Once she catches him, Lexie takes the rustler under her wing, and they work together to wrestle and wrangle words.

To find a book like this one, look for the following:

- Plots that include word play

- Characters who are interested in and use words in unique ways

Comprehension Conversation:

Before Reading

Notice the Cover Illustration:

- Can you tell by Jessie Hartland's illustration where this story is set? That means where it happens.

- What do you think a *word wrangler* might be? Fortunately, Rebecca Van Slyke (who is a second-grade teacher) put a "Dictionary of Wrangler Words" in the back of the book to help us.

- I will turn back to the dictionary so we can find out. It says here that a *wrangler* is a cowboy or a cowgirl.

Set a Purpose: As we read, we may discover what a *word wrangler* does. See if you can figure it out because it may help us to better understand words when we read and write.

During Reading

- *Like all wranglers, Lexie could ride . . .* page: Hmmm! The word *cantankerous* is a puzzling word for me. I'll look it up in the "Dictionary of Wrangler Words" in the back. It says *cantankerous* means bad-tempered or ornery. *Bad-tempered* and *ornery* are other words for mean, stubborn, grumpy, or grouchy. Tell your friend about a time when you've felt cantankerous. Say, "I felt cantankerous when . . ."

- [Continue using the "Dictionary of Wrangler Words" as needed throughout the story.]

- [As you continue reading, pause and notice all the different things Lexie is doing with the letters and words.]

- *Nearly everyone, that is.* page: Look at Lexie's face. Can you tell by her face that something different is going on in the story? Something has changed.

- *She looked at Russell.* page: Lexie sees that Russell has *talent*. That means he has a special skill or ability to wrangle words like Lexie does.

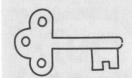

After Reading

- What different ways did Lexie *wrangle* words in that book? [She put two words together to make a compound word. She watched small words grow into bigger words. She mixed up letters to make new words. She used words to make sentences and stories.]

Extend the Experience:

- Are you ready to be word wranglers? I challenge you to see how many words you can make out of the word WRANGLER. Possible answers appear in the chart below.

- On this sticky note, write down your five favorite words. Share your most favorite word with the class and explain why it is your favorite.

Key Vocabulary:
- annoying
- ordinary
- talent

2 Letter Words	3 Letter Words	4 Letter Words	5 Letter Words	6 Letter Words
an	ran, wag, rag, lag, ear, law, raw, leg, age	gear, near, wear, glen, wren, read, rang, real, lean, wage, lane, rage	angle, glare, large, wager, range, anger	ranger

Little Words Made From the Big Word WRANGLER

Other similar titles:

 Max's Words (Banks, 2006)

About the Book: Max's brother Benjamin collects stamps. His other brother, Karl, collects coins. So, Max decides to gather a collection of his own—words. As Max builds up his bank of words, he realizes that, unlike his brothers' collections, when he puts his words together he can create thoughts and stories.

 The Word Wizard (Falwell, 1998)

About the Book: While eating breakfast, Anna notices that when she stirs the cereal letters with her magic spoon they make different words. With her magic spoon in hand, she helps a lost boy find his home by changing words. I always read this book to my students before our first word study lesson.

Word Wrangler

Little words made from the big word _____

2-Letter Words	3-Letter Words	4-Letter Words	5-Letter Words	6-Letter Words

Name _____

Word Wrangler Reproducible Response Page

Download this form at resources.corwin.com/rampedup-readaloud

Join In on Repeated Words

Book Title: *OUT!* (Chung, 2017)

About the Book: A boy and a dog are pals and love playing together (see front end papers). Then, when dad puts the boy in his crib, he screams, "OUT!" Eventually, the baby gets himself out of the crib, and he and Jo Jo the dog resume their adventures. The story doesn't end until you *read* the illustrations on the back end papers and the back cover.

To find a book like this one, look for the following:

- A nearly wordless picture book with a small number of repeated words
- Engaging storyline that encourages readers to chime in

Comprehension Conversation:

Before Reading

Notice the Cover Illustration:

- Arree Chung used paint, paper, and the computer to make the illustrations for this book. What is the title? [OUT!] What do you suppose is happening on the cover? [Maybe the baby boy is telling the dog to get out, or maybe the baby wants help getting out of the crib.]

Set a Purpose: I can't wait to turn the page to find out what is going to happen. Readers, I'm going to need your help reading some of words in this book, so get your voices ready! Let's notice the clues the author gives us to help us understand how to read his words with expression. Some of those clues might be punctuation marks such as periods, exclamation marks, or question marks.

During Reading

- Front end papers: This story begins on the front end papers. See how the boy and the dog are playing. Turn and tell your partner what you see them doing. What happens over here? [Point to the picture where the arms are lifting the child.]

- Title page: Now the end paper picture makes sense. The dad put the baby in his crib. What is he saying? [OUT!] Read that part the way you think he would say it. What clues helped you to know that? [all capital letters, bold text, exclamation mark]

- *Out.* page: How do you suppose the boy and dog are feeling? What makes you think that?

- *Woof! Woof! Woof!* page: Who is saying "Out!" on this page? [the parents] Say it the way they would.

Learning Targets:

- I can join in on repeated words of a story, song, or poem.

- I can use the punctuation and other text clues to help me read with fluency and expression.

- *Woof?* page: Look at the punctuation marks after the words "Woof!" on these two pages? Why do they change from a question mark to an exclamation mark? Read them aloud the way you think the author wants them to sound. Sometimes we have to reread when we notice clues to make sure our voice matches the signals the author is giving us. Rereading helps us to be more fluent.

- Jo Jo, the dog, is carrying the boy back to his crib. page: Do you think the parents notice them walking by? Why not? [They are dancing.]

- *OUT!* page: Look! The boy got the dog out of his crate. I'm going to turn to the end papers because the story continues here. [Notice how Jo Jo carries the boy into the parents' bed. Then, on the back cover you see them all sleeping there.]

After Reading

- What surprised you in this book? What was your favorite part? Why?

- How did the signals the author gave (all capital letters, big and bold words, and ending marks) help you to know how to read the words?

Extend the Experience:

- [Divide a plain piece of copy paper into four squares.] Writers, now it is your turn. Write a short comic like Arree Chung's using just one or two words. Remember to give your readers a signal to show them how to read your words.

- What might Jo Jo and the boy do the next day? Write your prediction on a sticky note. Once you are finished, we will share them with a friend.

Other similar titles:

 Ball (Sullivan, 2013)

About the Book: Using only one word, *ball*, the illustrations in this book clearly depict the dog's feelings and dreams as he waits patiently for his ball-throwing companion to get home from school.

 Look! (Mack, 2015)

About the Book: He's done it again! Jeff Mack, author of AH HA! (2013), has created another two-word masterpiece. This one, using the words *look* and *out*, is about a gorilla, a boy, and the power of books.

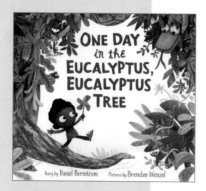

online resources

View the book trailer at resources.corwin.com/rampedup-readaloud

Learning Targets:

- I can join in on repeated parts of a story, song, or poem.

- I can use the punctuation and other text clues to help me read with fluency and expression.

Join In on Repeated Parts

Book Title: *One Day in the Eucalyptus, Eucalyptus Tree* (Bernstrom, 2016)

About the Book: In this rhythmic, rhyming, cumulative tale, a snake hiding in the eucalyptus tree slides down and eats a boy. The clever boy tricks the snake into gobbling down more and more until his belly is so full that he spits out all of the contents and ends up with a "crummy tummyache."

To find a book like this one, look for the following:

- Repetitive text that invites listeners to join in

- Punctuation and other text clues that signal readers to adjust the speed and volume of their reading

Comprehension Conversation:

Before Reading

Notice the Cover Illustration:

- On the copyright page it says that "the artist used everything imaginable to create digital illustrations for this book." When you look at the cover what kinds of artist's tools might Brendan Wenzel have used? [collage, maybe chalk on the trunk, maybe colored pencils for the lines on the leaves and snake]

- Do you see any animals hiding in the eucalyptus tree? Ask your neighbor if they have any predictions about what might happen in this book?

Set a Purpose: Have you noticed that when I read aloud to you my voice changes as I read. Sometimes it slows down during suspenseful parts and other times it speeds up. Sometimes I read quietly and other times I read VERY LOUDLY! When I do this, it helps me to better comprehend or understand what is happening in the book. Today, I'm going to show you how to do the same while you are reading so that you can get even better at comprehending.

Maria's Thinking: Tim Rasinski (2004) stresses the link between fluency and comprehension. The dimension of fluency that this read-aloud experience focuses on is *prosidy* or the reader's ability to parse the text into syntactically and semantically appropriate phrases. Rasinski cautions, "If readers read quickly and accurately but with no expression in their voices, if they place equal emphasis on every word and have no sense of phrasing, and if they ignore most punctuation, blowing through periods and other markers that indicate pauses, then it is unlikely that they will fully understand the text" (p. 46). Thus, if we teach readers from an early age, the importance of phrasing, punctuation, and expression, we can help them to better comprehend.

During Reading

- *and gobbled up the boy . . .* page: Did you notice any words on this page that sound familiar? [The words in the title are repeated on this page.] As we

continue reading, join in on this repeated line, "One day in the eucalyptus, eucalyptus tree." Notice how the word *eucalyptus* is darker. This is called bold print. That means the author wants us to emphasize or read that word a little louder. Ready, here we go!

- [As the story continues, invite the children to join in with you on this repeated refrain. Point out the punctuation and other text clues that support reading with expression.]

- *"I'll bet," said the boy, in the belly dark and deep.* page: Where is the boy in this picture? [in the snake's belly] Hmmm! Why do you think the boy wants him to eat more? Repeat the boy's part together with me. How might he say that?

- [Notice that the part of the page with the boy in the snake's belly gets bigger and bigger as the story progresses.]

- *Slurp, buuuuurrrrp! came a belch from the leaves of the tree.* page: Look at how the author stretched out the word burp. Let's slow down and read it the way he has signaled us to read it.

- *Buzz, buzz hummed a noise from the leaves of the tree.* page: Do you notice anything different about the illustration on this page? [We are no longer looking inside the snake's belly.]

- *Gurgle-gurgle came a blurble from that belly deep and full.* page: Oh my goodness! What are you thinking? Look at the words "STRETCH, STRETCH, STRETCH." They get bigger and bigger. That is a signal to read them louder and louder. Let's read them the way the author wrote them.

After Reading

- Look at the very last page! [The boy is sitting by the tree and a crocodile is looking at him.] Do you have any predictions?

- I'm going to go back and point to some different parts of the story that we read together so you can tell me what signals helped you to know how to read the words.

- Does this story remind you of any other stories you've read? [If your students are familiar with *There Was an Old Lady Who Swallowed a Fly* there are some similar elements.]

Extend the Experience:

- [To quickly facilitate this response write each of the ten verbs (*whizzed, rolled, buzzed, ran, swung, slunk, dashed, flew, slimed, skipped*) on a separate index card or piece of paper and divide your kids into ten groups.] I'm going to reread the page where all of the animals come out of the snake's mouth. Daniel Bernstrom used ten different verbs to describe their movement. I'm going to put you in a group, and I want you to work together to act out the action the way you think the creature (or boy) would do it. Then, we'll perform them for the class as I read.

- Look at the very last page in the book, write or draw what you think might happen next.

Key Vocabulary:
- gobbled
- rare
- rustle

Other similar titles:

 There Was an Old Lady Who Swallowed a Fly (Taback, 1997)

About the Book: In Simms Taback's Caldecott-Honor retelling of the American folk poem, he uses die-cut pages to allow reader to see inside the old woman's expanding stomach.

 There Was an Old Monster! (Emberley, Emberley, & Emberley, 2009)

About the Book: This is one of my kids' favorite song picture books. It's a lively version of the cumulative rhyme, "There Was an Old Lady Who Swallowed a Fly." In the downloadable song, when the old monster swallows some ants, the repeated refrain goes "man those ants had him dancing in his pants. Scritchy-scratch, Scritch, scritchy, scratch!" After listening, you'll be "scritchy-scratching" for the rest of the day.

My Favorite Read Alouds for Building Fluency

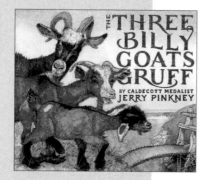

Think Beyond Fluency to Big Ideas

Book Title: *The Three Billy Goats Gruff* (Pinkney, 2017)

About the Book: In a fresh retelling of the tale, Jerry Pinkney chose to add a new character—a giant fish. This addition provides an opportunity for the troll to find out what it is like to be bullied. See artist's note in the back matter of the book for more details about his intentional decision to add the giant fish.

To find a book like this one, look for the following:

* Repetitive text that invites listeners to join in
* Dialogue with multiple voices allowing readers to vary their tone, pitch, volume

Comprehension Conversation:

Before Reading

Notice the Cover Illustration:

* Did you know that Jerry Pinkney won the Caldecott medal for his illustrations in the book *The Lion and the Mouse* (2009)? He's also received five Caldecott honors for his pictures. For this book, he used pencil and watercolors to create the gorgeous illustrations. What do you notice on the wrap-around cover? [If you can take the book jacket off, you can show your students the troll hiding on the book case.]

* Front End Papers: Look at where the goats are and where the troll is? What are the differences in the two places? Do you see the gate on the bridge? Why do you think it is there?

Set a Purpose: Since I'm guessing this is an *old favorite* book, I'd like you to join in when I invite you to help me read different parts. We'll work together to use a voice that fits the character. When we read like the character talks, we are reading with fluency and expression. Then, when we're finished, we're going to put our heads together to see if we can figure out the big ideas.

During Reading

* *The billy goats became so tempted . . .* page: I don't remember the part in this story where the water was full of fish. Do you? I wonder if Jerry Pinkney added this for a reason.

* *Trip, trap! Trip, trap!* page: Help me out on this part. How would the little billy goats' hoofs sound on the bridge?

* *"WHO's THAT TRIP-TRAPPING OVER MY BRIDGE?" roared the selfish troll.* page: Here it says that the selfish troll *roared* these words. Can you roar them in your meanest *troll* voice?

* [As the story unfolds, continue inviting children to join in on the same two parts, prompting them to vary their tone, pitch, and volume based on the clues in the text and illustrations.]

Learning Targets:

* I can read along using different voices for different characters.

* I can use the punctuation and other text clues to help me read with fluency and expression.

* I can figure out the lessons, morals, or big ideas.

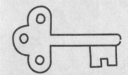
After Reading

- Why do you think Jerry Pinkney chose to add the fish to this version?

Extend the Experience:

- What do you think is the big idea, lesson, or moral of this story? Write your thinking on a sticky note.

- Look carefully at the back end papers. How are they different from the front end papers? What do you think happens next in this story? Draw, write, or act out your ending.

Other similar titles:

The Little Red Hen (Pinkney, 2006)

About the Book: In Jerry Pinkney's retelling of the traditional tale, he adds a few new details. First, when Hen asks the animals to help, she highlights a specific characteristic of one animal. For example, she asks dog to plant because he's good at digging. Second, each animal's name appears in a color that matches its feathers, fur, or hide.

Out of the Way! Out of the Way! (Krishnaswami, 2010) [repetitive text that invites listeners to join in]

About the Book: A boy finds a baby tree and sets out to protect it. As he, the tree, and the village in India grow, passersbys shout, "Out of the way! Out of the way!" Invite your children to join in on the repetitive phrase.

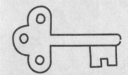

Key Vocabulary:
- greedy
- nasty
- selfish

"When you wake up in the morning,

open your eyes and open your window

and let your story out into the world.

It is a little gift from you to me."

—*Everywhere, Wonder*
by Matthew Swanson and Robbi Behr

Inspire Writers

Sharing the Gift of Writing

When I'm searching for mentor texts and authors to highlight the traits of compelling writing, I use what I've learned from my dear friend and "Trait Lady," Ruth Culham. Through her books and presentations, she has taught me how to intentionally weed through stacks of books to select the perfect ones for my budding writers, books that will highlight the specific aspects of writing I want my students to try out as they craft their own pieces. In her book *Dream Wakers* (2016), Ruth guides us with these wise words: "Books can be mentor texts only if we learn something about writing from them. And to make that learning accessible to students, we have to dig into the authors' words and note their moves" (pp. 6–7).

In Chapter 6, I will sit alongside you and the authors of the books as, together, we'll demonstrate how to do the following:

- Develop Ideas
- Explore Craft and Structure
- Discover Wonderful Words
- Hear the Voice

Then, when you are ready to immerse your students in a particular genre, turn to this section to find mentor texts for these genres:

- Narrative
- Opinion
- Poetry
- Informational

On the next page, you will find the concepts you will share as you strengthen your students' ability to make decisions as a writer. To support you in using these terms, I've included kid-friendly definitions. With each book you open and every author and illustrator you introduce to your budding writers, you present the wide array of craft techniques found in published books. With that knowledge, young authors can imagine how they might replicate those same techniques in their own books. When you invite children to try things out and celebrate their approximations, you give them to power to share their stories with the world. What a gift!

Use and Explain Key Writing Terms

Ideas: Clear, focused ideas are the key to a strong piece of writing. Ideas come from many places including your experiences, the books you read, and your imaginations.

Organization: Like puzzle pieces or Legos™, writers have to put their ideas together carefully, fitting each part in just the right spot so that their readers can see a complete picture.

Word Choice: Writers know there are many words from which to choose and they select their words carefully in order to clearly communicate their ideas to their reader.

Voice: Each writer has his or her own unique voice. When you are writing, try using your *talking voice*. Imagine that you are talking directly to your reader.

Foster a Growth Mindset

Create: To make something unique using your own original ideas or imagination.

Notice: Pay attention to what is happening in the world around you or in the words and pictures in a book.

Wonder: When we wonder, we are curious about something. Curiosity makes us smarter.

Inspire Writers

Develop Students' Social and Emotional Learning

Make Decisions: We make decisions in all parts of our lives. We decide what we want to eat for lunch and who we might play with at recess. To make a decision, we think about the different choices, gather information to make the best choice for the situation. Then, we take action. After making a decision, we can go back and review our decision to ponder how or why we might make the same or different decision next time.

Share Opinions: When you share your opinions with your friends you are telling them what you believe or think about something. Not everyone has the same opinion and that's okay.

Teach Literary Language

Cause and Effect: A cause is why something happened. An effect is what happens.

Circular Structure: When the stories ending leads back to the beginning.

Poetry: A special way to write about a topic using a small number of powerful words.

Question-Answer Structure: In a question-answer structure, a question is usually asked on one page, then on the next page, the answer appears.

See-Saw Structure: In a see-saw structure, the same words are used over and over again, back and forth. Sometimes the words are opposites such as in the book *Lost. Found.* (Arnold, 2015).

Chapter 6 Concepts, Terms, and Kid-Friendly Definitions

My Favorite Read Alouds for Inspiring Writers

Learning Targets:

- I can notice where writers get ideas.
- I can read, notice, and wonder to help me decide what to write.

Read, Notice, Wonder, and Write

Book Title: *Everywhere, Wonder* (Swanson, 2017)

About the Book: Through the magic of reading, a boy is transported to breathtaking locations around the world. Then, back in his neighborhood, he takes time to wonder about commonplace occurrences in his everyday life. In the end, the boy uses what he has read, noticed, and wondered about to draw and write his own stories.

To find a book like this one, look for the following:

- Invites readers to notice the world around them
- Demonstrates the reading-writing connection

 ## Comprehension Conversation:

Before Reading

Notice the Cover Illustration:

- Whoa! There is so much to notice on the cover of this book. Turn and tell your friend a few things you notice. Do you think we will see some of the pictures on the cover again on the inside pages of the book?

- Now, think about the title *Everywhere, Wonder* while I read you the back cover blurb. What are some things that you noticed on your way to school today? [If you have a hardcover edition, take the book jacket off and notice the difference between the book jacket and the book case.]

Set a Purpose: As we enjoy *Everywhere, Wonder* ponder what you learn about being a writer.

During Reading

- *The world is full of people and places and things, all of them interesting.* page: What do you think the author and illustrator are trying to show you here? What's happening? [The boy is reading a book and the book is *taking him* to new places.]

- *On the North Pole, there is a cold . . .* page: The boy's books took him to a lot of different places! Tell a friend which places you would like to visit and why.

- *Still, you notice him.* page: What do you think the author means when he says, "He walked off this page and into your head. Now he is part of your story"? [Help children to understand that the ideas you read about in books become part of your schema and can give you ideas for stories.]

- *Under the bridge . . .* page: I notice that the boy has a lot of questions. Do you ask yourself questions when you're looking around? Did you know that asking questions stretches your brain and helps it grow!

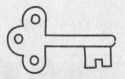
After Reading

- *Now my story is complete.* page: What do you think he means when he says your story is just beginning?

- *What did you learn about being a writer?* [Guide children to understand that ideas come from noticing . . . noticing when you read books, noticing things in your neighborhood. Then, using your imagination and asking questions about the things you noticed.]

Extend the Experience:

- [Take a noticing walk around the school/playground.] As we walk, I'll pause now and then so that you can draw or write down anything interesting you notice. When we get back to our classroom, you can think about if any of the ideas on your paper would be something you could write more about.

- Write down a few questions you have about the world. Keep them in your writing folder [writer's notebook]. Look back at these questions when you're stuck and can't think of what to write.

Key Vocabulary:

- notice
- unexpected
- wonders

Other similar titles:

 ***One Day, The End: Short, Very Short, Shorter-Than-Ever Stories* (Dotlich, 2015)**

About the Book: "For every story there is a beginning and an end, but what happens in between makes all the difference." So begins this one-of-a-kind book where the middle of each story is told solely with illustrations. You might consider showing each two-page spread using a document camera so that students can see the details and tell the story. This book is sure to spark ideas for writing.

 ***Someone Like Me* (MacLachlan, 2017)**

About the Book: Budding writers will enjoy hearing MacLachlan's gentle, semi-autobiographical book about the experiences she had as a child that made her the writer she is today. Use this book to launch a conversation about how writers are always listening, reading, imagining, and exploring.

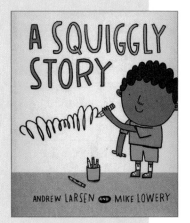

A SQUIGGLY STORY

ANDREW LARSEN *and* MIKE LOWERY

Learning Targets:

- I can notice where writers get ideas.

- I can read, notice, and wonder to help me decide what to write.

- I can make decisions about my writing.

Be the Boss of Your Story

Book Title: *A Squiggly Story* (Larsen, 2016)

About the Book: After watching his big sister read and write, the younger brother tries his hand at writing a story. With wise advice from his sister such as "Write what you know" and "It's your story. You're the BOSS," he creates his own imaginative tale. This book shows emergent writers that with just a few letters, words, and pictures, along with their imagination they, too, can write a story.

To find a book like this one, look for the following:

- Tales that inspire writers to trust in their own story

- Stories where friends and family offer story ideas and advice to the writer

Comprehension Conversation:

Before Reading

Notice the Cover Illustration:

- Hmmm! I'm thinking about the title *The Squiggly Story* and looking at Mike Lowery's illustrations on the front cover and back cover. What do you see?

- What character in the story do you think made all of those marks? Why do you think that?

Set a Purpose: Today as we're reading, let's think about what this boy learns about being a writer and how his discoveries can help us when we write books and stories.

During Reading

- *HOW?* page : What does the sister mean when she says, "Write what you KNOW"? How can this help you as a writer?

- *That's a good BEGINNING.* page: On this page, the sister tells him, "It's your story. You're the BOSS." When you are writing, you are the boss of your work. What does that mean to you? Turn and tell you neighbor what you're thinking.

- *And that's as far as I got.* page: When the boy's classmates offer suggestions to improve his story, what does he say? [It's his story and he doesn't want to add vampires.] Why do you think he says that?

After Reading

- What did you think of his ending? Would you have ended the story in a different way? Talk with your neighbor about your ideas.

- What did the boy learn about being a writer? [Elicit ideas such as these: *Write what you know. You're the boss of your story. Something has to happen in the middle of your story. My friends can give me ideas. When you're the author you can make your own decisions.*]

 Extend the Experience:

- The boy's friends offered suggestions to improve his story. Let's read one of our stories to a friend and see if he or she has any suggestions to make it even better. (Remember that you are the boss of your story so you don't have to include your friend's ideas.)

- What do you think will happen in the boy's next story? Divide your paper into three sections. Write and illustrate the beginning, the middle, and the end of his new story. On the other hand, if you prefer to write and illustrate a story of your own, you're the boss!

Key Vocabulary:

- offers
- single
- suggest

Other similar titles:

 ***Arthur Writes a Story* (Brown, 1996)**

About the Book: Arthur begins writing his story about how he got his puppy, Pal. After talking with his friends, he strays away from what he knows and ends up with a crazy, mixed-up song and dance. Mr. Ratburn helps Arthur understand the importance of writing about ideas that are close to his heart.

 ***The Best Story* (Spinelli, 2008)**

About the Book: A young writer tells readers all about her desire to win a writing contest. Each of her family members gives her writing advice, so she adds action, humor, and even romance to her story, but it just isn't right. Fortunately, her wise mother encourages her to write from her heart, she finally writes what she believes is *The Best Story*. Read this book to launch a discussion about writing from the heart.

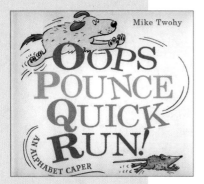

Mike Twohy

Organize Ideas Different Ways

Book Title: *Oops Pounce Quick Run!*
An Alphabet Caper (Twohy, 2016)

About the Book: Written in alphabetic words and phrases, we follow the lively action of a dog chasing a mouse around the house. In the end, the mouse gives the dog a present and they become friends.

To find a book like this one, look for the following:

* Ideas presented in unique ways
* Distinctive alphabet books

Comprehension Conversation:

Before Reading

Notice the Cover Illustration:

* Have you ever heard the word *caper* before? A caper is another way of saying a playful or silly adventure. You might have a caper at recess when you run and jump around as you are chasing your friends.
* Look at the illustration on the cover. How does Mike Twohy show there is a caper going on? [crooked letters, lines showing movement]

Set a Purpose: As writers, we can think about how authors organize their ideas. I wonder if this will be similar to other alphabet books we've read.

During Reading

* *Ball* page: Where do you think the ball came from?
* *Grrrr* page: What is the next letter of the alphabet? What do you predict will happen next? Whisper your prediction to a friend.
* *Oops* page: What letter comes after O? Turn and think about another prediction with a friend.

After Reading

* Did you like the ending of the caper? Why or why not?
* How did Mike Twohy choose to organize his story? [He used the alphabet.] What are some other ways or patterns you could use to organize a story? [counting books, days of the week books, see-saw structure, circular structure, cumulative structure.] (See the facing page for a chart showing different structures.)

Extend the Experience:

* Challenge yourself to try out the same structure Mike Twohy used in this book to create a mini-story.
* In this caper, the dog was chasing the mouse. What other animal pairs can you think of that might chase each other in a book? Work with a

Learning Targets:

* I can notice where writers get ideas.
* I can read, notice, and wonder to help me decide what to write.
* I can make decisions about my writing.
* I can notice different ways that authors organize their ideas.

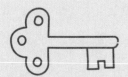

Key Vocabulary:

* caper
* pounce

partner to make a list of animal pairs. When we're done, we'll share and that will give us a lot of ideas for our own stories.

Other similar titles:

 AH HA! (Mack, 2013)

About the Book: Frog is relaxing in the pond (AAHH!) when he finds a rock (AH HA!). Close behind, there is a boy with a jar poised to catch him (AH HA!), and the chase begins. Using only four letters, Jeff Mack tells a rollicking tale. This story begins on the front end papers and ends on the back end papers.

The Little Red Cat Who Ran Away and
Learned His ABC's (the Hard Way) (McDonnell, 2017)

About the Book: In this nearly wordless alphabet caper, cat runs away and is being chased by an alligator, bear, chicken, dragon, and the chicken's egg. Readers have to infer what the letter on each page represents. Most answers are obvious, but in case they're not sure, there is an answer key in the back.

Pattern Books Chart

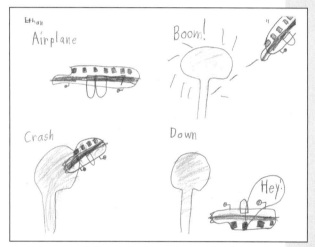

Oops Pounce Quick Run! Work Sample

Learning Targets:

- I can notice about where writers get ideas.
- I can read, notice, and wonder to help me decide what to write.
- I can make decisions about my writing.
- I can talk to my readers when I write.

Talk to Your Reader

Book Title: *This Is My Book!* **(Pett, 2016)**

About the Book: Author and illustrator Mark Pett wants to share the rules for writing a book, but Percy the Perfectly Polite Panda has his own ideas. In the end, they decide to finish the book together.

To find a book like this one, look for the following:

- Interactive picture books
- Characters who speak directly to the reader

Comprehension Conversation:

Before Reading

Notice the Cover Illustration:

- [Point out to students that Mark Pett created his illustrations using watercolor and ink.]
- I wonder why Mark Pett wrote the words "and no one else" in parentheses on the cover. What do you think?
- It looks like the man on the cover painted the title. Tell a neighbor who you think that man could be.
- What is the panda bear doing? [making hand prints] I wonder if the panda is going to be an important character in the book.

Set a Purpose: Some picture books are interactive. That means the author is *interacting* or having a conversation with you as the reader. This is a technique you might choose to use as a writer. Think about that as we read *This Is My Book* by Mark Pett.

During Reading

- *Look around at these spotless white pages.* page: Uh-oh! What is the panda doing now? [coloring in Mark Pett's book]
- *Did YOU do this?* page: Who does Mark Pett think colored in his book? [the reader] How do you know this?
- *Hey! I didn't say that!* page: Who is the panda referring to when he says, "they"? [the reader] What clues help you to know this?
- *Your book?* page: Who is the panda talking about when he says, "And it's their book, too?"

After Reading

- Did you like it when the author and the panda talked to you in the book? How might you do this when you're writing?
- Look at the author's note in the back of the book. What happened to it? [It appears that "Spike" the panda crossed out the information about Mark Pett and rewrote the author's note about himself.]

Extend the Experience:

- Let's think about how Mark Pett signaled that he was talking to us as readers. What did you notice? [Create an anchor chart like the one pictured below to support writers if they choose to use this technique.]

- [Gather a few more interactive picture books and place them in the classroom library or literacy center for children to explore. A few suggested titles appear below.]

Read These! Interactive Picture Books	
Don't Blink (Booth, 2017)	*I Want to Go First!* (Byrne, 2017)
The Happiest Book Ever (Shea, 2016)	*This Is a Ball: Books That Drive Kids Crazy* (Stanton & Stanton, 2015)

Other similar titles:

 Cat Secrets (Czekaj, 2011)

About the Book: If you are looking for an interactive read aloud to engage young learners, reach for this humorous book where three felines try to determine if their readers are cats so that they can reveal their "Cat Secrets."

 We Are in a Book! (Willems, 2010)

About the Book: Elephant and Piggie realize that they are in a book and have fun tricking their readers.

Tips for Talking to Your Readers

- Use the words <u>you</u> and <u>they</u>.
- Draw the characters facing forward looking out of the book.
- Draw characters pointing out at the reader.

Key Vocabulary:

- boring
- frustrating
- prefer

Lost. Found.

MARSHA DIANE ARNOLD
PICTURES BY
MATTHEW CORDELL

Learning Targets:

- I can notice the see-saw pattern or structure of the text.

- I can borrow the structures I learn to create my own texts.

Spot a See-Saw Structure

Book Title: *Lost. Found.* (Arnold, 2015)

About the Book: Bear's red scarf gets lost in the woods. Each woodland animal that finds the scarf uses it for a different purpose. In the end, the scarf is returned to Bear by his newfound friends.

To find a book like this one, look for the following:

- Structures that children can borrow for their own writing

- See-saw text structure

 Comprehension Conversation:

Before Reading

Notice the Cover Illustration:

- When I look at the wrap-around cover and think about the title, I'm wondering what might be lost. Turn and predict with a friend.

- Notice the bear's footprints in the snow. Matthew Cordell created these illustrations with pen, ink, and watercolors. I'm thinking he used watercolors for the footprints. What do you think?

- Title Page: What is Matthew Cordell showing you in this illustration? What kind of day is it?

Set a Purpose: Think about the title, *Lost. Found.* What kinds of words are lost and found? [opposites] After reading, we'll talk about how Matthew Cordell used these two opposite words in the story.

During Reading

- *Lost.* page: What is lost? Did your prediction match the author's thinking?

- *Found.* page: Why did the raccoons lose the scarf? [Continue to notice what the different animals do with the scarf when they find it and how they lose it again.]

- Two-page spread of animals surrounding scarf page: What do you suppose might happen next? Whisper your prediction to your neighbor.

- Knitting page: What are the animals doing? Why do you think they are working together to knit the scarf?

After Reading

- At the end of the story, what did bear find?

- Did you notice any patterns in this book? This pattern is called a see-saw structure. Say it with me: *Lost. Found. Lost. Found. Lost. Found.* [While saying these words, invite children to move their hands up and down like a see-saw.]

Extend the Experience:

- Think of other pairs of opposite words you could use to write a similar story or pattern book. I'll write them on a chart so you can use it for ideas during writing workshop. (See below.)

- Tell about a time you either lost or found something. How did you feel?

Opposite Words

asleep-awake

big-little

clean-dirty

down-up

fast-slow

happy-sad

high-low

long-short

night-day

on-off

Other similar titles:

 And Then Comes Summer (Brenner, 2017)

About the Book: Join a child, his family, and friends as they celebrate the sights and sounds of summer. *And Then Comes Summer's* "when-then" pattern provides a helpful structure for young writers. It would also be a splendid end-of-the-school-year read aloud!

 Good News, Bad News (Mack, 2012)

About the Book: If you are looking for another picture book with a see-saw pattern that mirrors the book *Fortunately* (Charlip, 1964), young readers will enjoy this tale of a rabbit and a mouse who, when trying to have a picnic, experience good news and bad news together.

Think About Cause and Effect

Book Title: *Because of an Acorn* (Schaefer & Schaefer, 2016)

About the Book: Richly textured illustrations and a repetitive cause-effect structure support young readers as they learn about the interdependence of a white oak forest ecosystem.

To find a book like this one, look for the following:

- Structures that children can borrow for their own writing
- Cause-effect text structure

Comprehension Conversation:

Learning Targets:

- I can notice the cause-and-effect pattern or structure of the text.
- I can borrow the structures I learn to create my own texts.

Before Reading

Notice the Cover Illustration:

- Let's open the book to look carefully at Frann Preston-Gannon's illustration on the cover. What other details do you see besides the acorn?
- How do you think she created these illustrations? [paint and ink textures that she arranged digitally]

Set a Purpose: As we read *Because of an Acorn*, notice the pattern or structure of the book. We'll stop and talk more about what you notice once you've had time to listen to a few pages.

During Reading

- [After each *Because of a . . .* page, ask "What do you think will come from the _____? Are there any clues on the page that helped you predict?"]
- *Because of a fruit* page: Now that we're about halfway through the book, talk to your neighbor about any patterns you notice. [Quickly pause here to discuss the cause-effect relationships in the book. Based on how much background knowledge your students have about ecosystems, you might want to offer a kid-friendly definition here.] The authors chose to use a cause-effect structure to show the interconnectedness of an ecosystem. In the back of the book the authors explain that an ecosystem is "a community of all of the plants, animals, and natural resources in one area and the relationship among them." Can you think of other ecosystems? [Guide children to share ecosystems they have studied, such as desert, lake, rainforest, or ocean.]

After Reading

- Why do you think the authors wrote this book? What did you learn from reading it?
- Can you think of other cause-effect relationships? What other plants come from a seed?

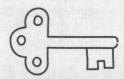

Extend the Experience:

- Let's create our own little books using the pattern we noticed in the book. Here are some ideas to get you started. (See below.)

- Draw a picture of the plants and animals you learned about in this book. Label your picture. Use your drawing to tell a friend about your new learning.

Because of a seed,	a pumpkin.	Because of a pumpkin,	a jack-o-lantern.
Because of a seed,	an apple.	Because of an apple,	a worm.
Because of a seed,	a tree.	Because of a tree,	a nest.

Ideas for Cause-Effect Books

Key Vocabulary:

- acorn
- ecosystem (appears in back matter)
- forest

Other similar titles:

● *First the Egg* **(Seeger, 2007)**

About the Book: The book begins, "First the EGG then the CHICKEN" [Note: There is no punctuation in the book and egg/chicken are in caps.] Then the book continues, to show first/then relationships including inanimate objects like *words* and *story*, *paint* and *picture*.

● *What Do You Do When Something Wants to Eat You?* **(Jenkins, 1997)**

About the Book: Readers discover the diverse ways that animals defend themselves, protect themselves, and escape from predators in this cause-effect structured nonfiction text. The book ends with the question, "What would *you* do if something wanted to eat *you*?" leading to an interesting conversation or written response.

by David Martin
pictures by Steve Johnson and Lou Fancher

Learning Targets:

- I can notice the circular pattern or structure of the text.

- I can borrow the structures I learn to create my own texts.

See the Circular Structure

Book Title: *Shh! Bears Sleeping* (Martin, 2016)

About the Book: Rhyming text and realistic oil paintings take you through a year with a mother American Black Bear and her two cubs. An informative author's note details the difference between true hibernators (toads, groundhogs, bats, and snakes) and the winter lethargy of bears.

To find a book like this one, look for the following:

- Structures that children can borrow for their own writing
- Books with rhyming text and/or a circular story structure
- Nonfiction narratives about bears' winter sleep

Comprehension Conversation:

Before Reading

Notice the Cover Illustration:

- Look closely at the illustrators' oil paintings. Do the bears in this book look real or make-believe? Do you think this book will be a fiction or nonfiction book?

Set a Purpose: We are going to read like writers to notice how David Martin chose to share bear facts and then ponder how we might borrow the structure for our own writing.

During Reading

- *Shh, bears sleeping . . .* page: What season comes after winter? What do you think bears do in the spring? Whisper your answer to a friend.

- *Skinny bears . . .* page: Look at your friend and take turns telling each other something that bears eat. [If needed, prompt children to remember the following: berries, honey, bees, bugs, grubs.]

- *Cubs frolic . . .* Look at the picture clue and think about the word *frolic*. What do you suppose that word could mean? What would make sense here? The word frolic means the same as having fun or being playful. Where do you like to *frolic*?

- *Follow momma* page: What do you notice about the words in this book? [rhyming text]

After Reading

- What did you notice about the way this book was written? [It started and ended in the spring so it is a circular story structure; it was written with rhyming text.]

Extend the Experience:

- What other plants or animals could you write about in a circular story? Let's make a list of ideas. (See below.)

- If we want to learn more about bears, we can read the pages at the end entitled "Shh, Bear Facts." Does someone want to work with a partner to read the pages and teach us more about bears?

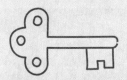

Key Vocabulary:

- beneath
- frolic
- gobble

Circular Story Ideas

Flutter! Butterflies Flying

Hop! Frogs Jumping

Crack! Chicks Hatching

Watch! Seasons Changing

Drip! Drop! Rain Falling

Other similar titles:

 Bear Has a Story to Tell **(Stead, 2012) [fiction]**

About the Book: In this circular story, Bear is anxious to tell his story to his animal friends, but they are all too busy getting ready for their winter sleep. In the spring, they gather to hear his story, but he has forgotten what it is. So, he begins again.

 Time to Sleep **(Fleming, 1997) [fiction]**

About the Book: Bear smells winter in the air, but before he can sleep he has to tell Snail. Then, Snail tells Skunk and Skunk tells Turtle and so on. In the end, Ladybug tells Bear, but he is already asleep.

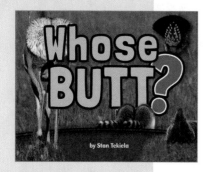

by Stan Tekiela

Learning Targets:

- I can notice the question-answer pattern or structure of the text.

- I can borrow the structures I learn to create my own texts.

Notice Question-Answer Structures

Book Title: *Whose Butt?* (Tekiela, 2012)

About the Book: In the introduction of the book, Stan Tekiela, a wildlife photographer explains that when you try to take pictures of animals, they often run or fly away. So, he's put together these photographs of animal butts to see if readers can guess the animal by looking at its rear end. If your students love the word *butt* as much as mine do, they will enjoy this question-answer book! For a humorous pairing you could also read the book *Chicken Cheeks* (Black, 2009).

To find a book like this one, look for the following:

- Structures that children can borrow for their own writing

- Informational books with a question-answer pattern

- Informational books that include humor and facts

Comprehension Conversation:

Before Reading

Notice the Cover Illustration:

- This is an interesting book cover. What did the photographer choose to put on his cover? [animal rear ends]

- I noticed that the title is a question. Perhaps the author is going to be asking us questions in this book. What do you think?

- Do you think this book will be a fiction book or a nonfiction book? What are the reasons behind your thinking?

Set a Purpose: I think it is a good idea to begin reading so that we can answer all of our questions!

During Reading

- *It's the Photographer!* page: Here Stan Tekiela answered one of our questions. Now I understand why he wrote this book.

- *This may look like an ordinary animal butt* . . . page: What do you suppose happens when this animal *dashes* away. When an animal *dashes*, it moves very fast or rushes away. Turn and share your thinking with your friend.

- *It's a Deer!* page: So, now what do you think? Is this a fiction or nonfiction book? Explain your reasons.

- *It's a Wolf!* page: What did you learn about the gray wolf? Turn and tell your neighbor something you remember about the gray wolf. Say, "I remember _____." [I learned this strategy from Linda Hoyt's book *Make It Real: Strategies for Success with Informational Texts* (2002).]

- [As you continue reading this question-answer format book, use Linda Hoyt's "I Remember!" strategy to prompt children to share their learning.]

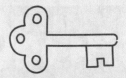
After Reading

- What did you notice about the structure or pattern of this book?
- Could you use the question-answer format in your own writing?

Extend the Experience:

- When you are working on books during writing workshop, try out the question-answer pattern.

- [Animal Memory Game: To prepare this activity, print two sets of 12–15 images of animals. For set one, print the whole animal. For set two, crop the image so that only one part of the animal is showing such as the animal's nose, ear, tail, eye, and so forth. Place the cards in a center so that children can play animal memory with the images.]

Key Vocabulary:

- communicate
- dashes (verb)

Other similar titles:

 Creature Features: 25 Animals Explain Why They Look the Way They Do (Jenkins & Page, 2014)

About the Book: Discover why thorny devils are spiny and sun bears have long tongues in this distinctive nonfiction picture book. The text is written in a *Dear Animal* format where each of the creatures is asked about one of their features and the answer is written from the creature's point of view.

 What Do You Do With a Tail Like This? (Jenkins & Page, 2003)

About the Book: Readers learn more about what different animals do with their tails, noses, ears, eyes, mouths, and feet. For each body part, the book asks the question, "What do you do with a [body part] like this?" On the *question* spread, readers see five different animals' body parts. Invite your students to guess which animal belongs to which part. On the pages that follow, Jenkins and Page give a brief description of how each animal uses that particular body part. Use this book as a mentor text for nonfiction writing using a question-answer format.

Notice and Use Striking Words in Stories

Book Title: *The Great AAA-OOO!* (Lambert, 2016)

About the Book: Mouse is on his way home when he hears a "horrible howl." Thinking it's a monster, Mouse and his fellow tree dwellers rescue a wolf cub from the ground. When the tree and all the animals come crashing to the ground, they realize the awful sound was coming from the scared little wolf.

To find a book like this one, look for the following:

- Fiction text where words are used in interesting and different ways
- Unique word choices that children can borrow for their own writing

Learning Targets:

- I can notice how an author uses words in different ways.
- I can think about my word choice when I'm writing stories.

Comprehension Conversation:

Before Reading

Notice the Cover Illustration:

- Look at the animals on the tree limb. Are those all animals you would usually find in a tree? The title of the book is *The Great AAA-OOO!* Why do you think the animals are in the tree? Think about it and share your thinking with your neighbor.
- Back Cover Blurb: Now I'll read the back cover blurb. Does that tell you more about what might happen in this book?

Set a Purpose: We're going to read like writers today and notice the kinds of words Jonny Lambert chose to use in this book.

During Reading

- *Bear grumbled up the tree, disturbed from his slumber by the hullabaloo.* page: Did you hear any words on this page that are fun to say? I heard the word hullabaloo. Let's say it together. It means a noisy and confusing situation. The author could have used the word *noise*, but I think *hullabaloo* is so much more interesting. Don't you? Recess is sometimes a hullabaloo isn't it?
- *KNOCK, SMACK, THWAK, Moose banged on the tree.* page: When moose is banging on the tree, what noises does he make? [If your kids are not familiar with the term *onomatopoeia* take a moment to explain that they are words that stand for a sound. Continue noticing the onomatopoeia found in the story.]
- *"A pie?" roared Bear.* page: Yikes! What do you predict will happen next? Turn and ask your friend what he or she thinks.
- *The animals came crashing . . .* page: Wait! What noises did you hear on this page? Who was making the AAA-OOO! noise?

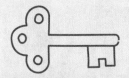

After Reading

- Were you surprised to find out which animal was making the noise?

- What did you notice about the words Jonny Lambert chose to use? [Guide children to notice that he used a lot of sound words or onomatopoeias. Return to the text so that students can expressively reread the onomatopoeias.]

 ## Extend the Experience:

- Writers try not to use the same words over and over. One of those words is the word *said*. We can notice all the different words Jonny Lambert used when the animals are talking. I'm going to write them on this chart, so that you can record a few of your favorites in your writer's notebook [or other place your children keep ideas for writing.] (See below.)

Key Vocabulary:

- bellowed
- slumber
- startled

Words for "said" found in *The Great AAA-OOO!*

squeaked	grizzled	cried	whimpered
hooted	grunted	added	roared,
huffed	bellowed	growled	whined

- Using onomatopoeia adds pizzazz to your writing. I'm going to write down the ones we heard in this book, so that you can record a few of your favorites in your writer's notebook [or other place your children keep ideas for writing]. (See below.)

Onomatopoeia found in *The Great AAA-OOO!*

KNOCK	QUACK	CREAKED	CRACK
SMACK	HONK	SHUDDERED	
THWACK	COO	GROANED	

Other similar titles:

 ### *Doodleday* (Collins, 2011)

About the Book: It's Doodleday! Ignoring his mom's warning not to draw, Harvey's pictures come to life and take over his house and neighborhood. Luckily, his "Doodlemom" comes to the rescue. Notice the words Ross Collins uses to mark the characters' speech like *shrieked, asked, said, gasped, cried, yelled,* and *bellowed.*

 ### *One-Dog Sleigh* (Casanova, 2013)

About the Book: In the cumulative, rhyming sequel to *One-Dog Canoe* (2003), a little girl and her perky dog pack one animal after another into their sleigh until they encounter a blizzard. Mouse leads the way as they push the sleigh to the top of the hill, then fly down (until they hit a bump!). Notice the onomatopoeia sprinkled throughout.

Learning Targets:

- I can notice how an author uses words in unique ways.
- I can notice how author/illustrators use expressive words to enhance illustrations.
- I can think about my word choice when I'm writing stories.

Notice and Use Expressive Words to Enhance Illustrations

Book Title: *Not Friends* (Bender, 2017)

About the Book: Giraffe and Bird are definitely not friends. They invade each other's space, swat and peck at each other, and much more. After losing their patience, they part ways only to realize that although getting along is difficult, it is worth it.

To find a book like this one, look for the following:

- Fiction text where words are used in interesting and different ways
- Unique word choices that children can borrow for their own writing
- Illustrations that are enhanced with expressive words

Comprehension Conversation:

Before Reading

Notice the Cover Illustration:

- Look at the two characters on the cover. Read the title and talk to your friend about what you notice. [They look like they're mad or upset with each other.]
- Can you tell what media (art tool) Rebecca Bender used to make the cover illustration? [acrylic paint on textured board—you can clearly see the texture in the background]

Set a Purpose: Today we are going to see what we can learn from Rebecca Bender about being a writer and an illustrator. I'm anxious to begin reading and figure out why these two characters are *Not Friends*. Let's get started!

During Reading

- *And if the giraffe could tell you, he'd say he can't abide the bird.* page: The bird "can't stand" the giraffe and the giraffe "can't abide" the bird. What do you think *can't abide* means? [The same thing as can't stand.] Why do you think that? [Both phrases make sense in the sentence; they are both written in the same font, and the giraffe and bird are both looking away from each other.]

- *Frequently the giraffe makes loud noises . . .* page: What words do you notice in the illustrations? [smack, slllrrp] *Smack* is an onomatopoeia but *slllrrp* is a made-up sound word. If you wanted to write the word *slurp*, it would have the vowel *u* in it. You can use both kinds of words in your own illustrations.

- *The pecking makes the giraffe shake his head until they are both dizzy.* page: Can you infer what happened when they fell to the ground with a "THUDD!?" [Giraffe has a broken neck and bird has a broken leg—they both have casts on those body parts.]

- *One day, the giraffe loses his patience and shouts at the bird.* page: I'm noticing that this book has a see-saw pattern, first the giraffe says something, then the bird says something, and so forth.

- *That night, there is a seriously scary storm.* page: Wow! How did Rebecca Bender show you how loud and scary the storm is? [illustration shows lightning and wind blowing tree branches and telephone poles down; there are onomatopoetic words like "CRACK!"]

- [Notice on the two-page spread where they're having a fight, you see many of the onomatopoetic words that appeared earlier in the book.]

After Reading

- Turn to your partner and discuss the ending of this book. What did you think about it?

- As a writer and illustrator, what can you learn from Patricia Bender?

Extend the Experience:

- Draw your favorite part of the story. Include expressive words in your illustrations to help us better remember that part.

- What do you think Rebecca Bender is trying to teach us about friendship? Write your thinking on a sticky note and get ready to share with your friends.

Other similar titles:

How to Find a Friend (Costa, 2016)

About the Book: A blue squirrel and a red rabbit are both looking for friends but keep missing each other. Two helpful bugs, one blue and one red, try to help the animals find each other. To add visual interest to the illustrations, Maria Costa included interjections, onomatopoetic words, and humorous comments spoken by the two bugs.

Rodzilla (Sanders, 2017)

About the Book: "Wobble-Wobble-Wobble. Toddle-Clunk." A monster has invaded the city. There are a lot of clues along the way that the monster is really a toddler wreaking havoc in his house. It is not until the end that readers know this for certain making *Rodzilla* a perfect book for inferring. In addition, Dan Santat's expressive illustrations are exploding with onomatopoeias.

Key Vocabulary:

- difficult
- frequently
- glum

HIPPOS ARE HUGE!

READ AND WONDER

JONATHAN LONDON illustrated by MATTHEW TRUEMAN

Learning Targets:

- I can notice how an author uses words in unique ways.
- I can think about my word choice when I'm writing nonfiction texts.

Notice and Use Striking Words in Nonfiction Text

Book Title: *Hippos Are HUGE!* (London, 2015)

About the Book: Using big and bold words, interjections, and onomatopoeia, Jonathan London teaches readers about the second-largest land mammal. The gorgeous illustrations and fascinating facts will grab your students' attention.

To find a book like this one, look for the following:

- Nonfiction text where words are used in interesting and unique ways
- Text containing onomatopoeia, interjections, and more

Comprehension Conversation:

Before Reading

Notice the Cover Illustration:

- Matthew Trueman made this picture of a hippo using a mixed-media illustration. What art tools do you think he might have used? How does the illustration make you feel? Would you want to meet a hippo in the wild?
- Think about the title *Hippos Are Huge!* What do you suppose Jonathon London is going to teach us about in this book?

Set a Purpose: As we're learning more about hippos, notice the types of words Jonathan London uses and how they appear in the text. I'm going to stop once in a while so we can study the different kinds of words and phrases the author chose to use.

During Reading

- *Watch out!* page: I just learned something new! I didn't know that a hippo's yawn was a threat. Did you learn anything you didn't already know? Share a fact with your friend.
- *Would you believe that the hippo is the most dangerous animal in Africa?* page: I'm going to read you part of a sentence, listen to the words. "With their monstrous jaws and razor-sharp teeth . . ." Jonathon London could have chosen to write "With their big jaws and sharp teeth." Which words do you prefer? Why?
- *Next, she bounces . . .* page: Look at the word "gliiiiiiides." Why do you think it is written that way? [So we stretch it out when we read it.] You could use that technique in your writing too.
- *When Hippo isn't dancing along . . .* page: The word "Yum!" is an interjection. Interjections show the feelings or reactions of the author. Do you think eating food stuck between a hippo's teeth is really yummy? Perhaps the author is making a joke.
- *Just then, a great commotion erupts!* page. Ewwww! That's disgusting! See the words "SPLAT! SPLOP!" that the author used to describe the dung hitting the hippo. Do you remember what those words are called? [onomatopoeia or sound words]

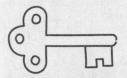
After Reading

- Tell your friend three facts you learned about hippos.

- Did Jonathan London's use of striking words make this book more interesting to you? Why or why not?

Extend the Experience:

- Draw a picture of a hippo and write some words around it to show some things you remember from this text.

- 3, 2, 1 Strategy (Zygouris-Coe, Wiggins & Smith, 2004): Write and/or draw three facts you learned about this creature, two questions you still have, and one thing you will never forget about this book.

Key Vocabulary:

- gracefully
- pounces
- threat

....

Other similar titles:

 ***I, Fly: The Buzz About Flies and How Awesome They Are* (Heos, 2015)**

About the Book: A fly attempts to convince a class of students, who are currently studying butterflies, why they should be studying flies instead. This lengthy text is written in first-person voice from the fly's point of view. You might consider reading it over a few read-aloud experiences.

 ***I'm Trying to Love Spiders. (It Isn't Easy)* (Barton, 2015)**

About the Book: A narrator debates whether she can like spiders or not. All the while, she invites readers to squish the spiders that are found in the book. There is much to notice about the words in this book such as when the author directly addresses the reader, the use of interjections, the way it is hand lettered with different sizes and colors, and more. This fact-filled text is sure to add laughter and learning to your read-aloud fare.

Notice and Use Striking Words in Poetic Text

Book Title: *Things to Do* (Magliaro, 2016)

About the Book: As a girl goes about her day, readers enjoy a short poem about everything she sees and does. Each wonder she encounters, whether it be natural like the dawn, sky, or a snail or man-made like scissors, is personified and its actions described.

To find a book like this one, look for the following:

- Poetic text where words are used in interesting and unique ways
- Words and ideas children could borrow for their own writing

 ## Comprehension Conversation:

Before Reading

 Notice the Cover Illustration:

- Look at Catia Chien's painting on the cover, what do you think the girl is doing? What are some things you like to do?

Set a Purpose: As we read *Things to Do,* let's read like a writer and notice the words that Elaine Magliaro uses. Think about what you can learn from her as a writer.

During Reading

- *Things to do if you are DAWN . . .* page: Hmmmm! I need to ponder for a moment. I know *dawn* is the morning time, and I also know that *dawn* **cannot** really do things. On this page, the author is using a technique called *personification.* That means she is giving human characteristics to non-living objects or ideas. Do you have any questions about that technique?

- *Things to do if you are BIRDS* page: Talk to your neighbor about this page. Are birds living creatures? Can they do the things in this poem?

- [As you continue reading the poems, point out those that where personification is used.]

- *Things to do if you are SCISSORS* page: Notice the words on this page. The poet did some interesting things. [Draw students' attention to the one-word sentences: *Open. Shut. Open. Shut.* and the onomatopoeia.]

After Reading

- What did you notice in that book?
- What did Elaine Magliaro do as a poet that you might be able to do in your own poems?

Learning Targets:

- I can notice how an author uses words in unique ways.
- I can think about my word choice when I'm writing poetry.

Extend the Experience:

- Let's challenge ourselves to use personification to describe the things a non-living object might do. We can write some ideas together to help you get started. (See below.)

- [Prior to this extension, give each child a sticky note and a pencil.] Which poem was your favorite? Let's go back and reread a few of your favorites and listen carefully for any words you like and might want to use in your own poems. If you hear an interesting word, raise your hand. Then, I'll pause so you can write it on your sticky note. After we're done, you can put your sticky notes in your writing folder/writer's notebook to use someday.

Key Vocabulary:

- nestled
- sprout
- vanish

> Things to do if you're a . . .
> - book
> - crayon
> - lunchbox
> - soccer ball
> - rainbow
> - train

Ideas for a "Things to Do" **Book**

Other similar titles:

 City Shapes (Murray, 2016)

About the Book: With kaleidoscope in hand, a little girl (Bryan Collier's daughter) leads us through the city in search of shapes. Murray's rhyming text captures the sights and sounds of the bustling urban environment.

 Drum Dream Girl: How One Girl's Courage Changed Music (Engle, 2015)

About the Book: Madeline Engle's poetic text is inspired by a Chinese-African-Cuban girl who performed in Cuba's first "all-girl dance band." Poets can notice the sensory language, rhythmic text, and repeated lines.

Notice Characters With Unique Voices

Book Title: *The Legend of Rock Paper Scissors* (Daywalt, 2017)

About the Book: Three great warriors, Rock, Paper, and Scissors, are looking for worthy opponents because they are growing weary of winning mismatched battles. At last, they find each other and have "the most massive and epic and three-way battle of all time."

Maria's Thinking: I chose this particular title to highlight the characteristic of voice because the various fonts provide learners with visual cues for reading with fluency. For example, when rock speaks, his text font is chunky and bold, prompting readers to read it in a *Rock* voice. The book also alternates between the voice of the narrator and the voices of the characters providing opportunities for readers to alter their tone, expression, and volume based on who is telling the story at a specific moment. Finally, young writers can apply many of the techniques that they notice in this book in their own writing.

View the book trailer at resources.corwin.com/rampedup-readaloud

Learning Targets:

- I can notice characters with unique voices.
- I can read along using different voices for different characters.

To find a book like this one, look for the following:

- Stories told by more than one character
- Fonts that change depending on which character is speaking
- Plots that include challenges or contests

Comprehension Conversation:

Before Reading

Notice the Cover Illustration:

- The title of this story is *The Legend of Rock Paper Scissors*. Do you already know something about legends? [If students are not already familiar with legends, share this kid-friendly definition: A *legend* is a story from long ago that is believed to be true but cannot be proven.]

- What do you notice about the characters Rock, Paper, and Scissors? [They are inanimate (non-living) objects yet they have faces!] After looking at this picture, do you think this legend is true?

Set a Purpose: As we're reading, I want you to notice how the author and illustrator help us to decide when to change our voices as we read different parts of the story.

During Reading

- *Long ago in an ancient and distant realm* . . . page: Who is talking on this page? [narrator] What kind of voice to you think the narrator should have? Let's read this page again with your *narrator* voice.

- *DROP THAT UNDERWEAR* . . . page: Who is saying "Drop that underwear . . . ?" What clues help you to know that? [bold, chunky font, and speech bubble] Let's reread this with our *Rock* voice.

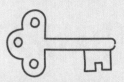
- *I gobble up the likes of you . . .* page: Who is the new warrior? [Paper] How can we tell when Paper is talking? [cursive font and speech bubble] Read what Paper is saying in a *Paper* voice.

- *Let us do battle, you tacky and vaguely round monstrosity!* page: Did you notice whether Scissors is a boy or girl? [girl] So, we have to read her words in a different kind of voice, don't we?

- [Continue to invite students to join you in reading the different parts with expression. They will enjoy reading the battle pages that all end with _____ is VICTORIOUS!]

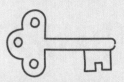

Key Vocabulary:

- foe
- unsatisfied
- victorious

After Reading

- How did you know to change your voice when reading different characters' parts? [The words looked different.]

- Did reading each character's parts in a unique voice help the story make sense? It also made it fun to read! When you're writing, think about how you can give signals to your readers to show them how to read the characters' different voices.

Extend the Experience:

- Using *Speech Bubble Response Page* located on the companion website, think of an animal. Write a sentence that you think that animal would say in the speech bubble. Remember to write it in a way that will tell your readers how you want it read. Then we'll read your speech bubbles and try to guess your animal. Let me show you some examples. If I were a snake I might say, "I'm llllloooonnnggg and thin. I hissssss when I'm in danger." If I were I lion I could say, "ROAR! I'm the king of the jungle!"

- Gather a collection of other legends for students to read and enjoy during independent reading time. Some might include: *Arrow to the Sun: A Pueblo Indian Tale* (McDermott, 1974); *Why Mosquitoes Buzz in People's Ears* (Aardema, 1975); *The Legend of the Indian Paintbrush* (dePaola, 1988).

Speech Bubble Reproducible Response Page

Download this form at resources.corwin.com/rampedup-readaloud

Other similar titles:

 Once Upon a Cool Motorcycle Dude (O'Malley, 2005)

About the Book: A girl and boy tell their favorite fairy tale to the class with two very distinct versions and voices. The font and illustrations are different depending on who is telling the tale. This book is ideal for performing with two different readers.

 Shark vs. Train (Barton, 2010) [plots that include challenges or contests]

About the Book: Who will win? Will it be shark or train? Well, that depends on what the competition entails. Enjoy reading this humorous, visually rich picture book again and again.

online resources

View the book trailer at resources.corwin.com/rampedup-readaloud

Learning Targets:

- I can notice how authors use their imagination to create stories.

- I can use original ideas and thinking in my own writing.

Find Original Ideas

Book Title: *Claymates* (Petty, 2017)

About the Book: A gray and a brown blob of clay sit waiting in an artist's studio. Soon, the sculptor enters and creates a wolf and an owl respectively. Once she leaves, the blobs of clay decide to have a little fun and transform themselves, and each other, into different creatures and objects. The character's dialogue appears as different colored pieces of paper making it easy to determine who is speaking. *Claymates* is playful, imaginative, and hilarious. Your students will want a blob of clay after reading this book.

To find a book like this one, look for the following:

- Unique idea or concept
- Inventive plot

Comprehension Conversation:

Before Reading

Notice the Cover Illustration:

- I think this title is a *play on words*. That means instead of the word *playmates*, Dev Petty and Lauren Eldridge chose to call their book *Claymates*. Get it? Look at the illustration on the cover. Why do you think they chose to do that?

Set a Purpose: When writers create stories, they think about new ideas and new ways to tell stories. They write in a way that makes you, as the reader, react. Think about how this book makes you feel. After reading, we'll talk about whether we have ever read a book like this one before.

During Reading

- [During the read aloud, when your students laugh, briefly pause to notice how the humor and visual jokes in this book make it fun to read.]

- *Finally! She's gone.* page: How can you figure out which character is talking? [The speech *papers* are written in the color that matches the character's color.]

- *You definitely shouldn't do that.* page: Can you infer how the owl is feeling right now? Isn't it amazing that Lauren Eldridge can make a piece of clay so expressive?!

- *Peanuts!* page: What do you predict gray blob is going to turn into now? Turn and tell your neighbor.

After Reading

- How did the author and illustrator choose to tell this story? [There was no narrator. They used only the dialogue, characters' words in speech *papers*, to tell the story.] Did you enjoy that technique? Could you do the same thing in your own books?

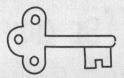
- Have you ever read a story like *Claymates* before? I know that I haven't. Instead of writing books like everyone else's, Dev Petty took a risk and did something new. That's what writers do!

Extend the Experience:

- Let's take a risk and create something new! In the book, gray clay wolf turns into a "pig-e-phant." Create and name your own imaginary animal(s). [Depending on availability of supplies, you can either have your students do this with clay, paper scraps, Legos, a drawing program on computer, or with paper and crayons.] For additional inspiration, see Jack Prelutsky's book *Behold the Bold Umbrellaphant and Other Poems* (2006) where he combines an animal and an inanimate object.

- [After students have created the character, invite them to write a few sentences to introduce their character to their friends. Then, use the Chatterpix Kid app (Duck Duck Moose, LLC) to record their voices and make their character come alive.]

Key Vocabulary:

- exhausted
- shock

....

Other similar titles:

 ***The Book With No Pictures* (Novak, 2014)**

About the Book: This book has no pictures, but it does have rules. "Everything the words say, the person reading the book *has to say*." Of course, from then on the reader has to read ridiculous words, including a friendly hippo's name, "BOO BOO BUTT." Your kids will be roaring by the end of this distinctive book.

 ***This Book Is Out of Control!* (Byrne, 2016)**

About the Book: Bella and Ben, the characters from *This Book Just Ate My Dog!* (2014) and *We're in the Wrong Book!* (2015), are back in another interactive story about a remote control toy that's on the fritz. When Ben presses the buttons, nothing happens to the fire truck, but it does control the dog, and then Bella and Ben. It's up to the reader to fix the problem.

Create Expressive Characters

Book Title: *Be Quiet!* **(Higgins, 2017)**

About the Book: Rupert, the mouse, wants to star in his own "artistic and visually stimulating" wordless book. Unfortunately, his friends Nibbs and Thistle find it impossible to stay quiet. Featuring characters from Higgins's other books *Mother Bruce* (2015) and *Hotel Bruce* (2016), this fresh and original title will have you and your students laughing aloud. A read-aloud experience for *Mother Bruce* can be found on page 72.

To find a book like this one, look for the following:

- Expressive text and illustrations
- Plot told entirely through dialogue
- Dialogue appears in speech bubbles

Learning Targets:

- I can notice how the author used words and illustrations to show me how the characters are feeling.

- I can use words and pictures to show my readers how characters are feeling.

Comprehension Conversation:

Before Reading

Notice the Cover Illustration:

- How would you read the title of this book? [loudly]

- How does Ryan Higgins show you to read it this way?

- Did you know that he hand-lettered all of the words in this book? That means instead of using a computer, he wrote them with a marker or pen.

- Front End Papers: [If you are able to take the book jacket off of the hardcover book, you can show students that Rupert first appears on the book case.] As readers, it is important to begin reading the pictures and words on the end paper and on the title page. Let's read what the mouse is saying.

- Title Page: Notice the title is on a banner pulled by the plane. Do you recognize the pilot from *Mother Bruce*? The title reads, "Rupert the Mouse Presents Be Quiet!" Now we know that the mouse with the glasses is named Rupert.

Set a Purpose: When authors write stories, they try to create characters that will connect with the reader. They write in a way that makes you, as the reader, react to the character. Think about how the characters in this book make you feel.

During Reading

- [During the read aloud, when your students laugh, briefly pause, to notice how the humor and jokes in this book make it fun to read.]

- *Please let me stay in the book.* page: How does Ryan Higgins want you to read Rupert's words on this page? What signals does he give you? [The words are big and bold.] Could you do the same thing in your own writing?

- *Is this more serious?* page: On this page, the author shows you how Rupert is feeling without using words. How did he do this? Could you use this illustration technique in your own books?

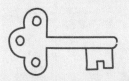
- *NO! NO! NO!* page: [If your students aren't familiar with the word onomatopoeia, pause here.] Do you know what *onomatopoeia* is? They are words that are imitations of sounds such as the ones on this page "POW," "BLAM," and "KABOOM!"

After Reading

- How did Ryan Higgins choose to tell this story? [There was no narrator. He used only the dialogue, characters' words in speech bubbles, to tell the story.] Did you enjoy that technique? Could you do something similar in your own books?

- What did you think about the characters Rupert, Nibbs, and Thistle? How did Ryan Higgins help you learn about their personalities? [facial expressions, dialogue, reactions to events]

Extend the Experience:

- Draw a picture of yourself. Put some details in the background and maybe a speech bubble or some other words to help us learn a little more about you.

- [Make a set of cards that contain either a word or image for the following moods: amazed, peaceful, scared, silly, angry, whiny, excited, tired. Pair your students with a voice pal. Show a card. Students talk to each other in that voice until you make a signal to stop. Show a different card. Repeat for a few minutes. Then, discuss how authors create different voices for their characters depending on their moods (Culham, 2005).]

. . . .

Other similar titles:

Any of the 25 Elephant and Piggie books by Mo Willems.

 Cookiesaurus Rex **(Dominy & Evans, 2017)**

About the Book: Cookiesaurus Rex wants to be decorated first, but when he notices his cookie friends getting fancier decorations than he has, he wants a do over. The decorator proceeds to frost him in different hysterical ways until he decides to take over.

Key Vocabulary:

- artistic

- onomatopoeia

- wordless

Create Unforgettable Characters

Book Title: *If You Ever Want to Bring a Circus to the Library, Don't!* (Parsley, 2017)

About the Book: The sign in the library reads, "You can do anything at the library." So, Magnolia figures it is fine to bring a circus. As she performs various acts for her friends, the library gets messier and noisier. Then the final act, "The Amazing Human Cannonball," puts an end to the circus. Notice, on the last page, when the kids are cleaning up, they are wearing parts of Magnolia's costumes.

To find a book like this one, look for the following:

- Expressive text and illustrations
- Distinctive characters
- Humorous plot

Comprehension Conversation:

Before Reading

Notice the Cover Illustration:

- Elise Parsley created these illustrations digitally. She drew them on a computer using one kind of software and painted them on a tablet using another kind of software. She even made her own font (that's the way the text looks) using her handwriting. Isn't that amazing?

- Do you notice any differences between the back cover illustration and the front cover illustration? [The side of the library on the back cover is neat and orderly (except for the popcorn). The side on the front cover is a disaster.]

- Do you think our librarian would let us bring a circus to the library?

Set a Purpose: When Elise Parsley wrote the books in this series, she created a character that connected to kid readers like you. As we read about Magnolia's latest adventure, think about what makes Magnolia an interesting character.

During Reading

- Title Page: Notice the boy sitting at the table, how do you think he is feeling? [He looks annoyed or angry because he's trying to study.]

- *You'll tell him that it's okay . . .* Do you think Magnolia can have a circus in the library and use an inside voice? Tell your neighbor why or why not.

- *You'll start by wowing the crowd as an acrobat.* page: How would you describe Magnolia on these two pages? [excited, proud, energetic]

- *And twirl!* page: Oh my goodness! Do you think the kids are using their inside voice on this page? What about Magnolia?

Learning Targets:

- I can notice how the author used words and illustrations to create an unforgettable character.

- I can use words and pictures to create characters my readers will remember.

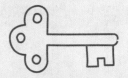
- *Well, here's what I would do . . .* Now that you know more about her personality, what do you predict Magnolia is going to do next?

- *Shhhhhh!* page: Who is saying, "Shhhhhh?" [the kid from the title page]

After Reading

- What words would you use to describe Magnolia? How did you figure that out?

- Compare the front and back end papers, see if you notice anything that is different.

 ## Extend the Experience:

- Do you think Magnolia is a memorable character? Why or why not? Does she remind you of any other book characters you know? Fold a piece of paper in half. On one side, draw a picture of Magnolia. On the other side, draw a picture of another of your favorite book characters. Compare the two characters by writing some adjectives that describe each character around your illustrations. Share your comparisons with a friend or two, to find out whether they think Magnolia was a memorable character or not.

- Magnolia showed a lot of different feelings or emotions in this story. As I show you the pictures again, we'll stop and talk about the clues that help us know how she is feeling so you can use some of those ideas in your own writing.

Other similar titles:

 ### *If You Ever Want to Bring an Alligator to School, Don't!* (Parsley, 2015)

About the Book: Magnolia brings an alligator to school for show and tell. The first time the alligator misbehaves, Magnolia's teacher writes her name on the board and it goes downhill from there. Finally, Magnolia scares the alligator away and thinks that maybe she won't have to go to the principal's office, but she's wrong! Don't forget to look at the front and back endpapers!

 ### *If You Ever Want to Bring a Piano to the Beach, Don't!* (Parsley, 2016)

About the Book: In the second book in the Magnolia Says Don't series, she chooses to take a piano to the beach. After it's covered with seagull droppings, Magnolia gives the piano a bath in the ocean. The piano floats out to sea and Magnolia goes home piano-less.

Key Vocabulary:
- audience
- dazzle
- distract

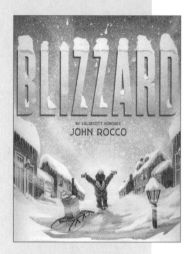

Learning Targets:

- I can notice how the author sequenced the events of a story.

- I can notice the techniques the author used to move the narrative through time.

- I can notice the way the author chose to end the narrative.

- I can use what I've learned as I write my own stories.

Sequence Your Story

Book Title: *Blizzard* (Rocco, 2014)

About the Book: Rocco recounts his experience as a ten-year-old boy in the New England snowstorm of 1978. On the fifth day, when the snowplows still haven't come, he sets off with tennis rackets strapped to his feet to get food for his family and for his neighbors. A gatefold spread shows his to journey to the store and back.

To find a book like this one, look for the following:

- A narrative told in first-person point of view

- An author who uses various craft techniques to draw the reader in, move the story along, and end in a compelling way

Comprehension Conversation:

Before Reading

Notice the Cover Illustration:

- My goodness! There is a lot of snow in this illustration.

- Look carefully at the cover. How does John Rocco show you how much snow has accumulated?

Set a Purpose: Today we are going to read like a writer to notice what John Rocco did as an author and illustrator to help move his story through time.

During Reading

- *The first flake fell right before recess.* page: Notice that the word *Monday* is written on the chalkboard. I wonder why John Rocco chose to do that?

- *The snow continued to fall through the night.* Notice the book on the boy's bed. It says, "Arctic Survival." Does anyone already know something about the Arctic? Why might that book come in handy?

- *The next morning . . .* page: Look, this time the word *Tuesday* is on the roof and it was made with the squirrel's footprints.

- [Continue noticing the days of the week cleverly hidden in the illustrations.]

- *On day five, I realized it was up to me to take action.* page: Why does he decide to take action? What do you predict he is going to do? Turn and tell your friend.

After Reading

- What was your favorite part of that story? What did John Rocco do as an author or illustrator to make you like that part?

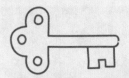
- Let's go back and notice the phrases he used to move the story through time. [the next morning; on the third day; by day four; on day five; at last; on the return trip; that night]

Extend the Experience:

- What interesting things did John Rocco do in his pictures and words? We can record them on a chart to remind us when we are writing.

- To help sequence your story, make a story board of an event in your life that you might want to write more about.

Key Vocabulary:

- continued
- journey
- prepared

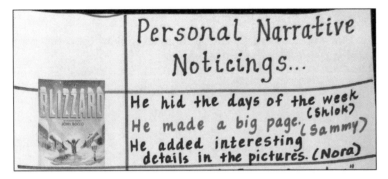

Blizzard Noticings Chart

Storyboard Work Sample

. . . .

Other similar titles:

 ***Picture Day Perfection* (Diesen, 2013)**

About the Book: His hair is messy, his shirt is wrinkly, and he's practiced the perfect scowl. Nothing is going to stop this boy from taking a *perfect* school picture—except a big smile! To move the story through time, the author uses transition phrases that will support your writers. I usually record them on an anchor chart for future reference.

 ***Saturdays and Teacakes* (Laminack, 2004)**

About the Book: Every Saturday, young Lester pedals his bicycle to visit his grandmother. Every Saturday, he and Mammaw spend the day together working, visiting, and making teacakes. Listen for the repeated phrase, *every Saturday*, and Lester's use of onomatopoeia, sensory language, and so much more!

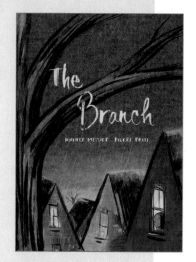

Learning Targets:

- I can notice how the author added interesting details to a narrative.

- I can notice the techniques the author used to help me better enjoy the story.

- I can use what I've learned as I write my own stories.

Key Vocabulary:

- concentrate
- potential

Add Interesting Details

Book Title: *The Branch* (Messier, 2016)

About the Book: After a winter ice storm, the narrator (a young girl) discovers that her favorite branch has fallen from the tree. Her neighbor, Mr. Frank, helps her see the potential in the downed branch. Together, they reshape the branch into a swing. You could also use this book as a jumping off point for discussing how to turn problems into possibilities.

To find a book like this one, look for the following:

- A narrative told in first-person point of view

- An author who uses various craft techniques to draw the reader in, move the story along, and end in a compelling way

Comprehension Conversation:

Before Reading

Notice the Cover Illustration:

- When we open the wrap-around cover, we can see what is happening in the girl's neighborhood. Tell me what you can infer from the cover about the setting of this story? [It's winter because there are no leaves on the trees. It's nighttime because the light is on in her room. It's raining outside.]

- Think about the title *The Branch* as you look at the cover. Do you have any ideas or thinking you want to share about the title? [Perhaps the branch came from the big tree on the cover.]

- Now let's look at the title page. Did that illustration add to or change your thinking about the title? [The girl is standing on a branch in the tree in the summer. Unlike the cover, we know it is summer in this illustration because of the green leaves.]

Set a Purpose: Today we are going to read like a writer to notice what details the author and illustrator added to help us enjoy his story.

During Reading

- *It's past my bedtime, but I can't sleep.* page: The author gives us some more clues on this page about the time of year this story is happening. Did you hear them? ["too excited for the holidays," "icy rain"]

- *Creak! Crack! Crash! Thud!* page: Yikes! What do you predict just happened? Ask a friend what he or she thinks and what clues led him or her to make that prediction.

- *Mom stands next to me at the window.* page: Can you infer how the girl is feeling? What clues in the illustrations and the words help you to know this? [She's upset. She rushes outside in her pajamas, and she looks sad. She says, "That was the branch I sat on, jumped from, played under . . ."]

- *Finally, Mr. Frank stops sawing . . .* page: Mr. Frank says her branch has *potential*. Why would the branch be worth keeping? What could she do with it?

- *Mom comes over, carrying mugs of hot chocolate.* page: Mr. Frank makes things with *salvaged* wood. Salvaged wood is wood he's saved from getting destroyed, such as wood from an old building or barn that's being torn down.

- *"No. It's even better!"* page: What do you suppose she and Mr. Frank are going to make from the branch? Ask your neighbor what he or she thinks.

- [As you continue reading, notice how the seasons change as they work on the project.]

After Reading

- What did her branch have the potential to turn into? [a swing]

- How did the girl's feelings change from after the storm to the end of the story?

- What details did the author and illustrator add to this story to make it more interesting? [onomatopoeia to describe the icy rain and the breaking branch; illustrations of the seasons changing as they worked on the swing]

Extend the Experience:

- I noticed that the author used sensory language to describe different events in the story. I'm going to reread some of those parts to see if you can tell me which senses you would use to better visualize what was happening. ["the entire neighborhood has been wrapped in a heavy blanket of diamonds"; "Mom touches the splintery part on the trunk where the branch used to be"; "Mr. Frank's workshop smells sweet, like Sunday breakfast."]

- What would you have made from the branch? Draw a picture showing your plans.

Other similar titles:

 ***All the Way to Havana* (Engle, 2017)**

About the Book: A boy and his family are driving to Havana to celebrate his cousin's birth. But first, he and his dad have to tinker with their beloved old car named *Cara Cara* to get it running. The blend of Margarita Engle's sensory language and Mike Curato's vivid illustrations make readers feel like they are riding right along.

 ***Building Our House* (Bean, 2013)**

About the Book: Told from his older sister's point of view, Jonathan Bean based this picture book on his parents' experience of building a house on an old farm field. Join his family as, together with relatives and friends, they build a house from the ground up. Your construction enthusiasts will enjoy all the details. You'll probably want to read this book in sections.

KING OF THE SKY

ILLUSTRATED BY LAURA CARLIN

NICOLA DAVIES

Learning Targets:

- I can notice how the author added descriptive words to a narrative.

- I can notice the techniques the author used to help me better enjoy the story.

- I can use what I've learned as I write my own stories.

Choose Descriptive Words

Book Title: *King of the Sky* (Davies, 2017)

About the Book: A young boy tells the story of his move from the city of Rome to a new home in a coal mining town in the hills. Feeling lost and lonely, he befriends Mr. Evans, a sickly former coal miner who races pigeons. As the man's health deteriorates, he and the boy race pigeon's together. When the boy's pigeon that he named "King of the Sky" finally makes it back from Rome, the boy realizes that both he and the bird are home.

To find a book like this one, look for the following:

- A narrative told in first-person point of view

- An author who uses descriptive words and phrases

- A story about immigration or refugees

Comprehension Conversation:

Before Reading

Notice the Cover Illustration:

- Look at the words on the cover of the book. How do you think Laura Carlin made them look like that? [She wrote them herself. In fact, she hand-lettered the entire book.] Notice how she made each of the letters a different color? You could do that when you are writing your own titles!

- Think about the title *King of the Sky*. What do you suppose the book might be about? Who might be the king of the sky?

Set a Purpose: Today we are going to read like a writer to notice what descriptive words the author and illustrator used to help us visualize the events happening in *King of the Sky*. We can use what we learn from the author in our own stories.

During Reading

- *It rained and rained.* page: Close your eyes. I'm going to reread this page. What do you imagine when you hear Nicola Davies's words? [smoking chimneys, streets smelling like coal dust and soup, clanging metal] Did you notice how Nicola Davies used sensory language to help you picture the setting? You can do the same when you're writing narratives!

- Two-page spread illustration of setting: Does this illustration look similar to what you visualized?

- *Just one thing reminded me . . .* page: What is different about his former home in Rome and his new home? Think and share your ideas with your partner.

- *Mr. Evans's face was crumpled . . .* page: What can you infer from Nicola Davies's description of Mr. Evans? [He's old; he loves his pigeons.]

- *Every day I came to see the pigeons.* page: Did you notice any descriptive language on this page? ["felt the small heart racing"; "head whiter than a splash of milk"] How did that help you as a reader?

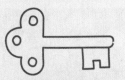
- *I smoothed his feathers, looked into his eye, and put him into the basket for the journey.* page: What do you think he means by, "A part of me was going with him." [He would miss the pigeon. He, too, wanted to go to Rome again, or other reasonable responses.]

After Reading

- How did the boy's feelings change from the beginning to the end of the story? What do you suppose caused the change?

Extend the Experience:

- Draw a picture of something you remember from the story. Label the objects in your picture using descriptive words or phrases.

- The boy in this story moved to a new place. He was lonely and sad. When someone moves to our school, they might be feeling the same way. How can we make new friends feel welcome when they join our classroom or school? (See chart below.)

Making New Friends Feel Welcome

- Make sure you know how to say your new friend's name the way he or she does.

- Smile at new friends!

- Ask new friends questions to learn more about them. Ask about their old schools, their families, and what they like to do.

- Help new friends learn the routines of our classroom.

- Invite new friends to sit by you at lunch.

- Ask new friends to join your games on the playground

Other similar titles:

 The Journey (Sanna, 2016)

About the Book: A visually striking tale of immigration. Told from a child's perspective, readers follow a family as they escape from a war-torn country and travel across many borders to safety.

 The Promise (Davies, 2013)

About the Book: A girl living in a "mean, hard, and ugly" city lives by stealing. One night as she is stealing a bag from an old woman, the woman says, "If you promise to plant them, I'll let go." The girl makes the promise and goes on to plant the acorns she finds in the bag. Little by little her city and her heart change.

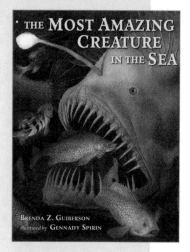

Learning Targets:

- I can form an opinion.
- I can share that opinion with my friends.
- I can use what I've learned in this book in my own writing.

Share Your Opinion

Book Title: *The Most Amazing Creature in the Sea* (Guiberson, 2015)

About the Book: Are your students fascinated by sea creatures? If so, they will be interested to hear thirteen different sea-dwelling creatures try to convince them that they are the most amazing animals in the sea.

To find a book like this one, look for the following:

- Informational book where creatures try to convince readers they are superior to other similar creatures
- Informational text with an opinion and supporting reasons

Comprehension Conversation:

Before Reading

Notice the Cover Illustration:

- Gennady Spirin's paintings look so real, don't you think? He used watercolor and tempera paint along with pencils to create the illustrations. Does anyone know the name of the sea creature on the cover? [It's an anglerfish, but if kids don't know, you can tell them that they will find out when you read the book.]

- I'm going to read you the back cover blurb. It sounds like we are going to have to decide which animal we think is the most amazing. Do you think we'll all agree? Probably not. We may all have different opinions and that's okay.

Set a Purpose: I wonder if the animal on the cover is the most amazing creature in the sea. Let's read to learn more about sea animals and share our own opinions about them.

During Reading

- [If you want your children to take notes or sketch to better remember each creature, make a page with 13 empty boxes on it (one for each animal).]

- *Who is the most amazing creature in the sea?* page: That is not the animal on the cover is it? Turn and tell your friend something amazing you learned about the box jellyfish. Draw a quick sketch or write a word or two to help you remember this animal.

- *I am a LEATHERBACK SEA TURTLE.* page: Which do you think is more amazing so far, the box jellyfish or the leatherback sea turtle? Ask your friend his or her opinion.

- *I am a MIMIC OCTOPUS.* page: There are a few words and phrases on this page that mean the same thing: mimic, disguise, take on many appearances, masquerade. What makes a mimic octopus amazing?

- *I am an ANGLERFISH.* page: It says that an anglerfish *lures* prey close to its mouth. That means its light attracts the fish close to its mouth. Of all the animals we've read about so far, which animal do you think is the most amazing and why? Share with your partner.

- [Continue to provide student with opportunities to share their opinion and facts they are learning by quickly sketching or jotting a few words to remember each animal. You may want to read this book over two or three read-aloud experiences to provide time for opinion conversations or note taking.]

After Reading

- Now that you've heard all of the sea creatures share what makes them amazing. Stand up and find a new friend to tell your opinion, and listen to his or her opinion. Then, find another friend and share.

Extend the Experience:

- Which creature did you think was the most amazing and why? Draw a picture of the creature and write a reason or two below your drawing.

- Pick a sea creature that is not in this book. Research the animal and find two or three reasons why you think it is the most amazing creature in the sea.

Other similar titles:

 The Deadliest Creature in the World (Guiberson, 2016)

About the Book: In the third book in the series, fourteen creatures from a golden poison dart frog to a Komodo dragon vie for the title of the deadliest creature in the world.

 The Greatest Dinosaur Ever (Guiberson, 2013)

About the Book: In first-person voice, each dinosaur argues why it was the greatest dinosaur of all. The pronunciation of each dinosaur's name is located directly underneath (helpful for those of us who are not dinosaur experts!).

Key Vocabulary:

- disappear
- disguise
- lure

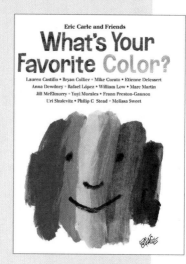

Learning Targets:

- I can form an opinion.
- I can give reasons for my opinion.
- I can share my opinion with others.
- I can use what I've learned in this book in my own writing.

Give Reasons for Your Opinion

Book Title: *What's Your Favorite Color?* (Carle, 2017)

About the Book: Eric Carle asks 15 different children's book artists "What is your favorite color?" Readers learn their 15 diverse opinions along with the reasons behind them. As you share this book with your learners, discuss the unique way each artist went about answering the question. Notice the different styles and genres of writing.

To find a book like this one, look for the following:

- Books where people share their opinions and the reasons behind that opinion

Comprehension Conversation:

Before Reading

Notice the Cover Illustration:

- Look at the way Eric Carle created the title. What do you notice? [The words are in different colors.]
- It's amazing that he could make the stripes of paint look like a face, isn't it?

Set a Purpose: Turn and ask your neighbor the question, "What's your favorite color?" Then ask, "Why is that your favorite color?" so that he or she can tell you the reason behind his or her opinion. Eric Carle asked 15 different picture book artists the same question. We can learn more about the various ways the authors and illustrators in the book share their opinions as we find out about their favorite colors.

During Reading

- *YELLOW Eric Carle . . .* page: What reason did Eric Carle give for liking yellow? [Because it's challenging for him when he tries to mix it with other colors.] That's such an interesting reason! You can tell he was thinking like an artist when he wrote his opinion.
- *BLUE Bryan Collier . . .* page: Bryan Collier gave a different reason for his favorite color, a reason from a happy memory. He was thinking like a dad when he wrote his opinion.
- *My favorite color is mint . . . Mike Curato . . .* page: Hmmm! Another different way of thinking about colors. Talk to a friend about Mike Curato's reason. [Mint chocolate chip ice cream is his favorite ice cream.] He was thinking about his favorite food.
- *BROWN William Low . . .* page: What do you notice about William Low's reason? [He was thinking about his favorite place.]
- [Continue reading and discussing the artists' different opinions and reasons. You may want to split this book in half and read seven or eight in one read-aloud experience and the rest in a second. This will give you more time to talk about the opinions.]

After Reading

- As a writer, what did you notice about the different ways the authors shared their opinions and reasons?

Extend the Experience:

- Now it's your turn. Write and draw about your favorite color. Think carefully about the reasons behind your opinion.

- Think of a different question you could ask your classmates such as, "What is your favorite food, sport, or book?" Fold a piece of paper in four sections. In the first section, write your question and your name. When everyone is ready, we're going to pass the paper to the person next to us so that they can write and draw their answer in the next box. Remember when you get the paper, write your name in the box. [Assist students in passing the paper to a classmate so that everyone gets a new paper. Then, continue in the same fashion until three different children answer the first child's question. Return the page to the first child so that he or she can cut on the folded lines and make a little book similar to Eric Carle's book.]

Another similar title:

 What's Your Favorite Animal? (Carle, 2014)

About the Book: In this companion book, Eric Carle asks 14 different children's book artists "What is your favorite animal?" and shares their responses in a variety of interesting ways.

 Why Did the Chicken Cross the Road? (Agee et al., 2006)

About the Book: Fourteen picture book illustrators offer their opinions in both pictures and words to the classic joke.

Learning Targets:

- I can notice how to give reasons to persuade or argue for something I want.

- I can use what I've learned in this book in my own writing.

Book Title: *One Word From Sophia* (Averbeck, 2015)

About the Book: Sophia's "one true desire" is to get a pet giraffe for her birthday. She presents compelling arguments to her mother (a judge), her father (a businessman), her uncle (a politician), and her grandma (who is strict). Each has the same advice—make it shorter. Finally, she uses one simple word—please!

To find a book like this one, look for the following:

- Characters who try to persuade or argue their case
- Plots about wanting a pet

Comprehension Conversation:

Before Reading

Notice the Cover Illustration:

- When you look at the cover, can you tell that Yasmeen Ismail used watercolor paints and colored pencils to create her illustrations?

- I'm wondering why the title is *One Word for Sophia*. What could the one word be?

Set a Purpose: Let's read to find out what Sophia's one word is and why that word is so important.

> **Maria's Thinking:** Although I usually draw students' attention to the learning target in the purpose statement, I chose not to for this book because there are no clues on the cover or blurb that Sophia is going to use compelling arguments to convince her parents she should have a giraffe as a pet. I try to make sure that the purpose statement doesn't reveal any of the surprise events that might occur in the book.

During Reading

- *The four problems were . . .* page: It says that her Uncle Conrad is a politician. A *politician* is someone who is elected to do a job in the government like a mayor, governor, or the president.

- *Her argument was accompanied by a compelling slideshow . . .* page: The word *compelling* means something that convinces you, or talks you into, doing something. What was the reason Sophia gave for wanting a giraffe? [It could take her to ballet class.]

- *"I'm sorry," said Mother . . .* page: I'm not sure what the words *quadrupeds* or *verbose* mean. Luckily, Jim Averbeck put a glossary in the back of the book. Let's read to find out what the glossary teaches us about those words.

- [Continue to use glossary, as needed, as the story progresses.]

- *So Sophia used fewer words with Father.* page: What reason did Sophia give on this page? [People would pay her for giraffe poop.]

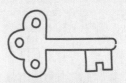
- *Sophie polled the other members of the household* . . . page: Let's turn the page and see what Sophie is doing. When you *poll* people, you ask their opinion about something.

After Reading

- What were some of the things Sophia included with her arguments when she was trying to persuade her family to get her a pet giraffe? [She drew pictures, made a graph, polled her family, made a pie chart, and gave grandma a foot rub.]

- Talk with a friend about whether you think this story is real or make-believe and why.

Extend the Experience:

- Do you think *One Word for Sophia* is a good title for this story? Why or why not? Explain your thinking in words and pictures.

- If you wanted a make-believe pet what would it be? Write a compelling argument to someone in your family about that pet. Don't forget to give some reasons why you want that pet. Perhaps you could also include a picture, graph, or pie chart just like Sophia did.

Key Vocabulary:

- argument
- compelling
- delighted

....

Other similar titles:

 How Do Dinosaurs Choose Their Pets?
(Yolen, 2017) [plots about wanting a pet]

About the Book: Dinosaur fanatics and children longing for a pet will enjoy the latest installment in the How Do Dinosaurs series by Jane Yolen and Mark Teague. In this book, a collection of unusual dinosaurs (named both on each page and on the endpapers) teach children how to find the perfect pet.

 ***I Wanna Iguana* (Orloff, 2004)**

About the Book: Alex really wants Mikey Gulligan's baby iguana, so he writes a series of letters to his mom. She responds to each letter with her own reasons for NOT getting an iguana as a pet. In the end, mom surprises Alex with the iguana.

 ***The Perfect Pet* (Palatini, 2003)**

About the Book: To satisfy Elizabeth who really, really wants a pet, her parents get her a cactus. Using various strategies such as "The Element of Surprise" and "Catch Them Off Guard," Elizabeth campaigns for a variety of pets until she finds Doug the Bug. Although, it is an unusual pet, her parents let her keep him.

Read Poetry All Year Long

Book Title: *When Green Becomes Tomatoes: Poems for All Seasons* (Fogliano, 2016)

About the Book: Beginning and ending on March 20, Julie Fogliano has penned a collection of poems to read throughout the year. Every poem is dated so you could mark your calendar and read each poem on its respective date.

To find a book like this one, look for the following:

- Poetry anthologies organized by season
- Poems that include various poetic devices

Comprehension Conversation:

Before Reading

Notice the Cover Illustration:

- On the copyright page, it says that Julie Morstad made her illustrations with paint and *pencil crayon*. She lives in a country called Canada. [If needed, locate Canada on a map.] In her country, colored pencils are called pencil crayons. That is new learning for me!

- Ponder the title of this book of poetry. It's called *When Green Becomes Tomatoes*. Has anyone grown tomatoes in a garden? What do you think Julie Fogliano means by *When Green Becomes Tomatoes?*

Set a Purpose: This year, we are going to be poets. Did you know that the best way to learn how to be a poet is to read poetry? I guess we'll be reading a lot of poetry this year! The poems in this book have dates on them, so I've marked the calendar and we will enjoy the different poems in this book on their special date. Let's begin!

During Reading

- [Below I will highlight just a few of the poems that appear in the book.]

- *September 10* page: Do you ever go out and look at the stars? Do you think her description, "more flicker glow than blinding," matches your image of stars? How would you describe stars?

- *September 22* page: Today is the first day of autumn or fall. It makes sense that this would be the first poem in the Fall section of the book, doesn't it? I'm noticing something about these poems. [show children the words] See the word *I* in these lines, what do we know about the word *I*? You're right! Writers always capitalize the word I. Why do you think Julie Fogliano chose not to in her poems?

- *October 31* page: Today is a special holiday for some of the children in our room—Halloween. What do you notice about the poem today? [She's repeated the word pumpkin on every line; it's about the life cycle of a pumpkin beginning and

Learning Targets:

- I talk, write, or draw about poems.
- I can think about how poems are organized.
- I can use what I learn about poetry to write my own poems.

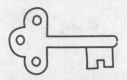
ending with pumpkin sprout.] I bet you could write a poem like this about a different plant. We can try one together! (See the example below.)

- [Continue reading and enjoying her poems throughout the seasons.]

After Reading

- How did Julie Fogliano choose to organize the poems in this book? What are some other ways you could organize poems?

Extend the Experience:

- Let's write to Julie Fogliano [via social media account] and ask her why she chose not to use punctuation or capital letters in her poems.

- Co-create a poem with your students using the technique found in the October 31st poem. (See below.)

Apple seed	Apple sauce
Apple tree	Apple pie
Apple blossom	Apple crunchy
Apple picking	Apple juicy

Co-Created Poem

Key Vocabulary:

- Will vary based on which poems you read aloud.

....

Other similar titles:

 ***One Big Rain: Poems for Every Season* (Gray, 2010)**

About the Book: How does rain change throughout the seasons? This question is answered though a variety of poetic forms including haiku. Some poetic techniques to notice include "The Mist and All" on Page 8, which begins and ends with the same words, and "Rain" on Page 20, which uses repeated words and onomatopoeia.

 ***The Year Comes Round: Haiku Through the Seasons* (Farrar, 2012)**

About the Book: Opening and concluding with winter, readers journey though the seasons with haiku poems. Poems provide opportunities to infer, ask questions, and expand vocabulary. Some of the words I would point out include *wily, parched, loll,* and *surrender.* In addition, the poems are not specifically marked by seasons, giving you the chance to ask children to decide when they think the poems change seasons. Another engaging seasonal Haiku title is *Guyku: A Year of Haiku for Boys* (Raczka, 2010).

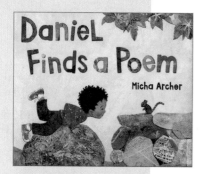

View Micha Archer's collage techniques at resources.corwin.com/rampedup-readaloud

Learning Targets:

- I can notice where poets get ideas.
- I can find sensory words or phrases in a poem or story.
- I can use what I learn about poetry to write my own poems.

Find Poetry in Your World

Book Title: *Daniel Finds a Poem* (Archer, 2016)

About the Book: After seeing a sign advertising a "Poetry in the Park" event, Daniel spends the week asking his animal friends, "What is poetry?" On Sunday, he combines all of their answers into his very own poem.

To find a book like this one, look for the following:

- If poetry is your focus—books that celebrate poetry
- If sensory language is your focus—an author who uses sensory language to describe events
- Main characters who are curious, asking questions, and exploring nature

Comprehension Conversation:

Before Reading

Notice the Cover Illustration:

- How do you think Micha Archer created this cover illustration? You're right! She used collage techniques; that means she created the illustrations by cutting out and carefully arranging different kinds of decorated papers.
- Do you know any other authors/illustrators who make collage illustrations? [Ezra Jack Keats, Leo Lionni, Eric Carle, Lois Ehlert, Steve Jenkins]
- Think about the title *Daniel Finds a Poem.* Where do you think he is going to go to find a poem?

Set a Purpose: I'm going to read the back cover blurb, "What is poetry? If you look and listen, it is all around you!" I want you to ponder what that means as we read together today.

During Reading

- *He looks up in surprise . . .* page: What sense did the spider use to describe poetry?
- [Continue noticing the sensory language the animals use as they describe what poetry means to them.]
- *On Sunday, the sun wakes up Daniel.* page: What do you think Daniel will write about in his poem?
- *Morning dew . . .* page: Where did Daniel get all of the ideas for his poem? [from the different animals]

After Reading

- What do you think Daniel learned about poetry?

Extend the Experience:

- Daniel found his poem by listening to the answers from the animals. How and where can you find ideas for your poems? Work with a partner to brainstorm different places and ways you can find ideas for poems.

- [Using the *What is Poetry? Interview Reproducible Response Page* located on the companion website: Go home and interview three people. Ask the question, "What is poetry?" Write down their answers and bring it back to share with the class.

Key Vocabulary:

- crisp
- silent
- reflecting

Other similar titles:

 All the World a Poem (Tibo, 2016) [poetry]

About the Book: Readers experience a wide variety of poetic forms as they read this child-focused tribute to reading, writing, and experiencing poetry.

 Finding Wild (Lloyd, 2016) [sensory language/curious characters]

About the Book: Celebrating the sights and sounds of nature, the book begins, "What is wild? And where can you find it?" Then, a girl and boy take a sensory journey through the wild.

Name _____

What Is Poetry?

Ask three people this question. "What is poetry?"
Write or draw their answers.

Name	Name	Name

What Is Poetry? Interview Reproducible Response Page

Download this form at resources.corwin.com/rampedup-readaloud

Learning Targets:

- I can notice the techniques poets use.

- I can use what I learn about poetry to write my own poems.

Notice Techniques Poets Use

Book Title: *Cricket in the Thicket: Poems About Bugs* (Murray, 2017)

About the Book: A collection of over 25 poems about bugs. Accompanying each poem is a short snippet with a few interesting facts about the bug. In the back matter, readers will find a paragraph of additional information about each creature.

To find a book like this one, look for the following:

- Short, kid-friendly poems about your students' favorite topics
- Poems that use various poetic devices

Comprehension Conversation:

Before Reading

Notice the Cover Illustration:

- There are so many bugs in Melissa Sweet's cover illustration. Do you see a favorite bug? I wonder if there will be a poem about each of these bugs?

Set a Purpose: Let's have some fun reading these poems about bugs and learn a few facts along the way! We can also read like a poet and learn from noticing the different techniques Carol Murray used in her poems.

During Reading

- [Below I will share some different options for reading this book. I would suggest only reading four or five poems in one read-aloud experience. Follow each poem with questions like, "What did you notice Carol Murray did as a poet?" or "Could you do that in your own poems?"]

- Option 1: Let's look at the table of contents. I'm going to read the names of the first few bug poems. [Read aloud the titles of the first five poems.] Which poem are you interested in hearing? [Continue in the same fashion until you've read four or five poems.]

- Option 2: Let's look at the cover. Do you see a bug you like? Let's read the poem about that bug. [Continue in the same fashion until you've read four or five poems.]

- Option 3: This book has 36 pages of bug poems. Pick a number between 6 and 36. We'll read the poem on that page. [Continue in the same fashion until you've read four or five poems.]

After Reading

- Which was your favorite bug poem today? What did you like about that poem?

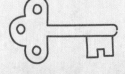

Extend the Experience:

- What did you notice as we were reading the poems? Let's make a list of the different techniques that poets use.

- [Here are some ideas to get you started: "Cricket's Alarm" on page 6, which shows how some poets use repeated words (cricket); "Trees and Knees and Bumblebees" on page 14, which shows how some poets use onomatopoeia (rumble); and "Daddy, What Long Legs You Have!" on page 23, which shows how some poets use alliteration (teeny, tiny torso).]

- Pick your favorite animal or bug and write a poem about it. Remember what you learned from reading poetry as you write your poems.

 Key Vocabulary:

- Will vary based on which poems you read aloud.

Other similar titles:

 Dreaming Up: A Celebration of Building (Hale, 2012)

About the Book: An anthology of concrete poems about building. The poem and an illustration of children building appear on the left-hand side of each spread. On the facing page, a photograph of a structure similar to what the children are making appears. In the back matter, readers learn more about the real structures and their respective architects. If you have a makerspace, you need this book!

Thunder Underground (Yolen, 2017)

About the Book: Kids who tunnel in the dirt and wonder about what lies below the surface will *dig* this poem book. Yolen has penned 21 poems about the subterranean world. The back matter includes "Notes on the Poems: Both Scientific and Personal." Some poems to notice include "Corny Conversations" on page 6, which shows how some poets use rhymes; "Thunder Underground" on page 10, which shows how some poets use onomatopoeia; and "Magma Pools" on page 26, which shows how some poets use repeated words.

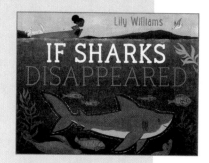

Learning Targets:

- I can notice how the author crafts a descriptive nonfiction text.

- I can notice the techniques an author and illustrator use to help me better understand the topic.

- I can use the techniques I learn in my own nonfiction pieces.

Describe Information

Book Title: *If Sharks Disappeared* (Williams, 2017)

About the Book: With a young girl as your guide, learn what will happen to the ocean ecosystem if sharks become extinct. Williams describes the grim reality with children but leaves them with a sense of hope and call to action. In the back matter, you will find a list of ways to help save the sharks.

To find a book like this one, look for the following:

- Informational texts about kid-appealing topics
- Informational texts written in unique and engaging ways

Comprehension Conversation:

Before Reading

Notice the Cover Illustration:

- When I open the wrap-around cover so that you can see both sides, what do you notice? [Maybe the girl in the boat is looking for sharks; she has binoculars. There is a dashed line around the shark on the cover, and there are sharks missing on the back cover.] Think about the title *If Sharks Disappeared*. Why do you suppose Lily Williams put a dashed line around the shark on the front cover?

- Look at the back cover. Turn and tell your friend what you are thinking. [Draw students' attention to the fact that there are only outlines of the sharks on the back cover—perhaps they are disappearing.]

Set a Purpose: As writers it is helpful to study the work of others to help us learn more about writing. Notice what Lily Williams did in this book to help you better understand what would happen *If Sharks Disappeared*.

During Reading

- *THIS IS A HEALTHY OCEAN.* page: Think about what Lily Williams is teaching us here. A healthy ocean needs to be balanced so animals can *thrive*. The word *thrive* means to grow strong and healthy. What do you need to thrive? Turn and share with a friend.

- *Sharks are apex predators, which means . . .* page: What is an apex predator? Why is an apex predator important to the ecosystem?

- *Today, roughly between one-fourth and one-third . . .* page: Think about the word *overfishing*. What do you suppose is happening to sharks? We can look in the glossary in the back to better understand this word. [People are fishing and catching sharks faster than the sharks can have babies, so there are less and less sharks.]

- *All species depend on one another . . .* page: What is Lily Williams showing you on this gatefold page? [a balanced ecosystem, thriving ocean animals, the creatures that live in different part of the ocean]

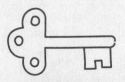
After Reading

- How did Lily Williams help you better understand the information in this book? [explaining what terms mean, including a glossary, using nonfiction features such as illustrations, a diagram with labels, and a map]

- What did you learn from this book that could help you as you write a nonfiction text?

Extend the Experience:

- [To prepare for this extension, divide children in small groups of three or four. Gather enough laptops or devices with access to Google Maps Treks for each group.] In the back of the book, the author tells us different things we can do to help save sharks. One of them is to "travel to or learn more about places that support shark education." As a learning team, travel to one of the spots using Google Maps Treks to see what you can notice and learn.

- Work with a partner to make a poster to hang in the hallway explaining why we need to save the sharks.

Key Vocabulary:

- balanced
- eventually
- thrive

Other similar titles:

 Pink Is for Blobfish: Discovering the World's Perfectly Pink Animals (Keating, 2016)

About the Book: The first book in Jess Keating's The World of Weird Animals series introduces animal enthusiasts to 17 different pink creatures including a South American primate called a red uakaris, pygmy seahorses, and the title animal—the blobfish. Because there is so much to learn and notice on each two-page spread, I recommend reading Jess Keating's descriptions of pink creatures one or two animals at a time.

 Who Was Here? Discovering Wild Animal Tracks (Posada, 2014)

About the Book: Clues about the animals along with their footprints appear with the question, "Who was here?" Then, readers turn the page to find an illustration and a one-paragraph description of each animal. Writers can easily adapt Posada's question-answer format when they share information.

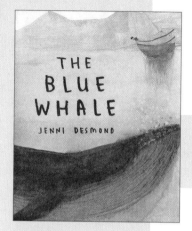

Learning Targets:

- I can notice how the author crafts a nonfiction text.

- I can notice how the author uses topic sentences to focus the reader.

- I can use the techniques I learn in my own nonfiction pieces.

Use Topic Sentences

Book Title: *The Blue Whale* (Desmond, 2015)

About the Book: A boy is reading a book about blue whales. Readers learn along with the boy as he discovers a wealth of facts about the blue whale.

Maria's Thinking: I chose this as a mentor text for informational writing because kids are interested in gigantic creatures like blue whales. Also, Jenni Desmond has done a number of things in her work that students can emulate in their own informational writing, including the following:

- Shares one characteristic about the blue whale on each page

- Begins each page with a topic sentence to focus the reader

- Uses comparison to help readers understand size, length, and weight

To find a book like this one, look for the following:

- Informational texts about kid-friendly topics

- Informational texts written in unique and engaging ways

 Comprehension Conversation:

Before Reading

Notice the Cover Illustration:

- We have to open this book and look at the whole wrap-around cover to see the blue whale! Why do you think Jenni Desmond chose to make it this big?

- She uses collage, paint, and colored pencils to create her illustrations and then she uses her computer to edit them so they are exactly the way she wants them to look.

Set a Purpose: Writers, today as we read a bit of Jenni Desmond's book, I want you to notice how it is organized and how she helps us to understand more about the size, length, and weight of the blue whale. [To keep your writing mini-lesson *mini*, I would suggest only reading 4 to 5 pages at a time over consecutive days.]

During Reading

- *A blue whale can measure up to 100 feet.* page: How did Jenni Desmond show us the length of the blue whale? [She compared it to a bunch of vehicles all lined up.] That's called *comparison*.

- Did her comparison help you to visualize the length of a blue whale? Turn and tell your neighbor something you learned about the length of a blue whale.

- *Blue whales are gray . . .* page: What was this page mostly about? [what a blue whale looks like] Let's go back and reread the first sentence. Did the author tell us in this sentence what the page was going to be about? This is called a topic sentence. As we read, we can see if she continues to begin each page with a topic sentence. Turn and tell your friend what a whale looks like.

- [As you learn more about blue whales, continue to notice the use of topic sentences, comparison, and other techniques Desmond uses as a nonfiction writer.]

After Reading

- What interesting facts did you learn about blue whales?
- Is there something you are still wondering about blue whales?

Extend the Experience:

- If we go back through this book and reread the topic sentences, we can create a summary of what we learned about blue whales. Let's work together, and I'll show you what I mean. [Guide students to take the important details from the topic sentences, reword them, and put them together into a summary. Your shared summary might start something like this: Blue whales are the largest living mammals. They mostly eat krill. Baby blue whales drink their mother's milk. Blue whales live about the same amount of time as humans.]

- Jenni Desmond used many comparisons in this book to help us better understand the information she was sharing about blue whales. As you work on your nonfiction pieces, think about how you can use comparisons. Also, as you are reading nonfiction texts, notice comparisons and mark them with a sticky note so we can all learn from them.

Key Vocabulary:

- colossal
- measure
- similar

· ·

Other similar titles:

 The Polar Bear (Desmond, 2016)

About the Book: A girl is reading a book about polar bears. Readers learn along with the girl as she discovers a wealth of facts about polar bears. Similar to *The Blue Whale*, this text includes topic sentences, comparison, and much more.

 Snakes (Bishop, 2012)

About the Book: Nic Bishop draws his readers into the world of snakes through stunning photographs and interesting, well-written information. I usually read his books a few pages at a time, like a chapter book, so we can enjoy the experience.

Learning Targets:

- I can notice how the author crafts a nonfiction text.

- I can notice how authors blend fiction and nonfiction elements in a text.

- I can use the techniques I learn in my own nonfiction pieces.

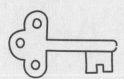

Key Vocabulary:

- challenge
- hover
- wisdom

Blend Fiction and Nonfiction

Book Title: *If You Were the Moon* (Salas, 2017)

About the Book: Blending brief, lyrical text and informational paragraphs, Laura Purdie Salas shares information about the moon in a multilevel fashion. Budding scientists can learn from the poetic text, while more advanced learners can dig into the factual paragraphs. The blending of the two types of texts helps cement important details in the minds of young learners.

To find a book like this one, look for the following:

- Informational texts about kid-friendly topics

- Texts that blend fiction and nonfiction elements

- Informational texts written in unique and engaging ways

Comprehension Conversation:

Before Reading

Notice the Cover Illustration:

- Look at Jaime Kim's painting on the cover. Do you think this book is going to be fiction or nonfiction? How will we decide?

Set a Purpose: As we begin reading see if you can figure out whether you are learning facts or hearing a story.

During Reading

- *But I do so many things, child.* page: Who is talking on this page? [the moon]

- *Hover near your mother.* page: The word *hover* means to stay near and watch closely. So, I'm inferring that the moon stays close to Earth because sometimes people call Earth *Mother Earth*. Wait! What are these words up in the corner? [Read fact paragraph.] Discuss with your partner whether you think this book is fiction or nonfiction now.

- *Hide in the shadows.* page: How are the author and illustrator working together to teach us facts about the moon? Do the illustrations help you to better understand and remember the facts?

Maria's Thinking: At this point, you can decide whether you want to read only the poetic text or read the fact paragraph that accompanies the lyrical text. If you are going to read both, I suggest splitting the book in half and stopping midway to recap the learning. Then, read the second half during another read-aloud experience.

After Reading

- What interesting facts did you learn about the moon?

- Is there something you are still wondering about the moon?

Extend the Experience:

- What things in nature have you already learned a lot about? Pick something in nature such as a cloud, a spider, a fish, or a volcano. Make a little book using the ideas you've learned from Laura Purdie Salas. First, let's make one together. (See example.)

- In the back matter of the book, the author shares a list of books we could read to learn more about the moon. Let's go to the school library and see if we can find some of the books she lists. Then, we can read the books together or you might choose to read one of them with a partner or on your own.

Other similar titles:

 Superbat (Carr, 2017)

About the Book: Pat the bat decides to be a superhero, but has trouble finding his superpowers. He discovers that all bats have super hearing, can fly, and use echolocation. Finally, when someone is in danger, he discovers his superpower—courage. Additional bat facts are located in the back matter.

 T. Rex (French, 2004)

About the Book: As they tour a dinosaur exhibit, a grandson asks his grandfather questions about dinosaurs. The dialogue is written in different sized fonts with facts in a third font size. The text includes a repeated line, bold print, ellipses, and more. Not only does this book have a lot for budding writers to notice, but it also leads to inquiry experiences and conversations about finding answers to scientific questions.

Example of Our Class Little Book: If You Were a Volcano

Resources

Professional Resources Cited

Beck, I. L., McKeown, M. G., & Kucan, L. (2002). *Bringing words to life: Robust vocabulary instruction*. New York, NY: Guilford Press.

Beck, I. L., McKeown, M. G., & Kucan, L. (2013). *Bringing words to life: Robust vocabulary instruction* (2nd ed.). New York, NY: Guilford.

Beers, K., & Probst, R. E. (2017). *Disrupting thinking: Why how we read matters.* New York, NY: Scholastic.

Burkins, J., & Yaris, K. (2014). *Reading wellness: Lessons in independence and proficiency.* Portland, ME: Stenhouse.

Cleaveland, L. B. (2016). *More about the authors: Authors and illustrators mentor our youngest writers.* Portsmouth, NH: Heinemann.

Culham, R. (2005). *6 + 1 traits of writing: The complete guide for the primary grades.* New York, NY: Scholastic.

Culham, R. (2016). *Dream wakers.* Portland, ME: Stenhouse.

Cunningham, A. E., & Zibulsky, J. (2014). *Book smart: How to develop and support successful, motivated readers.* New York, NY: Oxford University Press.

Cunningham, P. M. (2017). *Phonics they use: Words for reading and writing.* (7th ed.). Boston, MA: Pearson.

Duke, N. (2014). *Inside information: Developing powerful readers and writers of informational text through project-based instruction.* New York, NY: Scholastic.

Fletcher, R. (2017). *The writing teacher's companion: Embracing choice, voice, purpose, and play.* New York, NY: Scholastic.

Fuhler, C. J., & Walther, M. P. (2007). *Literature is back: Using the best books for teaching readers and writers across genres.* New York, NY: Scholastic.

Harvey, S., & Daniels, H. (2009). *Comprehension and collaboration: Inquiry circles in action.* Portsmouth, NH: Heinemann.

Heard, G., & McDonough, J. (2009). *A place for wonder: Reading and writing nonfiction in the primary grades.* Portland, ME: Stenhouse.

Hoyt, L. (1999). *Revisit, reflect, retell: Strategies for improving reading comprehension.* Portsmouth, NH: Heinemann.

Hoyt, L. (2002). *Make it real: Strategies for success with informational texts.* Portsmouth, NH: Heinemann.

Johnston, P. H. (2012). *Opening minds: Using language to change lives.* Portland, ME: Stenhouse.

Kesler, T. (2017). Celebrating poetic nonfiction picture books in classrooms. *The Reading Teacher, 70*(5), 619–628.

Layne, S. L. (2015). *In defense of read-aloud: Sustaining best practice.* Portland, ME: Stenhouse.

Nations, S., & Alonso, M. (2001). *Primary literacy centers: Making reading and writing STICK!* Gainesville, FL: Maupin House.

Rasinski, T. (2004). Creating fluent readers. *Educational Leadership, 61*(6), 46–51.

Rasinski, T. (2017). Readers who struggle: Why many struggle and a modest proposal for improving their reading. *The Reading Teacher, 70*(5), 519–524.

Walther, M. P. (2015). *Transforming literacy teaching in the era of higher standards.* New York, NY: Scholastic.

Walther, M. P., & Phillips, K. A. (2012). *Month-by-month reading instruction for the differentiated classroom.* New York, NY: Scholastic.

Yokota, J., & Teale, W. H. (2017). Striving for international understanding through literature. *The Reading Teacher, 70*(5), 629–633.

Zygouris-Coe, V., Wiggins, M.B., & Smith, L.H. (2004). Engaging students with text: The 3-2-1 strategy. *The Reading Teacher, 58*(4), 381–384.

Children's Literature Cited

Aardema, V. (1975). *Why mosquitoes buzz in people's ears.* (L. & D. Dillon, Illus.). New York, NY: Dial.

Agee, J., Arnold, T., Bliss, H., Catrow, D., Frazee, M., GrandPré, M. . . . Willems, M. (2006). *Why did the chicken cross the road?* New York, NY: Penguin.

Al Abdullah, R., & DiPucchio, K. (2010). *The sandwich swap.* New York, NY: Disney/Hyperion.

Alexander, K. (2017). *Animal ark: Celebrating our wild world in poetry and pictures.* (J. Sartore, Photographer). Washington, DC: National Geographic.

American Museum of Natural History. (2017). *Wolf pups join the pack.* Toronto, Ontario: Sterling.

Andros, C. (2017). *Charlotte the scientist is squished.* (B. Farley, Illus.). New York, NY: Clarion.

Applegate, K. (2014). *Ivan: The remarkable true story of the shopping mall gorilla.* Boston, MA: Clarion.

Archer, M. (2016). *Daniel finds a poem.* New York, NY: Penguin Random House.

Arnold, M. D. (2015). *Lost. Found.* (M. Cordell, Illus.). New York, NY: Roaring Brook.

Ashman, L. (2013). *Rain!* (C. Robinson, Illus.). Boston, MA: Houghton Mifflin.

Atkinson, C. (2016). *Explorers of the wild.* New York, NY: Disney/Hyperion.

Averbeck, J. (2015). *One word from Sophia.* (Y. Ismail, Illus.). New York, NY: Atheneum.

Ayers, K. (2007). *Up, down, and around.* (N. B. Westcott, Illus.). Somerville, MA: Candlewick.

Bania, M. (2004). *Kumak's fish.* Portland, OR: Alaska Northwest.

Banks, K. (2006). *Max's words.* (B. Kulikov, Illus.). New York, NY: Farrar Straus Giroux.

Banks, K. (2017). *How to find an elephant.* (B. Kulikov, Illus.). New York, NY: Farrar Straus Giroux.

Barnaby, H. (2017). *Garcia and Colette go exploring.* (A. Joyner, Illus.). New York, NY: Putnam.

Barnes, D. (2017). *Crown: Ode to a fresh cut.* (G. C. James, Illus.). Evanston, IL: Agate/Bolden.

Barnett, M. (2014). *Sam and Dave dig a hole.* (J. Klassen, Illus.). Somerville, MA: Candlewick.

Barton, B. (2015). *I'm trying to love spiders. (It isn't easy).* New York, NY: Viking.

Barton, C. (2010). *Shark vs. train.* (T. Lichtenheld, Illus.). New York, NY: Little, Brown.

Bean, J. (2013). *Building our house.* New York, NY: Farrar Straus Giroux.

Beaty, A. (2013). *Rosie Revere, Engineer.* (D. Roberts, Illus.). New York, NY: Abrams.

Bender, R. (2017). *Not friends.* Toronto, Ontario: Pajama.

Berger, S. (2017). *Monster's new undies.* (T. Carpenter, Illus.). New York, NY: Scholastic.

Bergman, M. (2005). *Snip snap! What's that?* (N. Maland, Illus.). New York, NY: Greenwillow.

Berne, J. (2013). *On a beam of light: A story of Albert Einstein.* (V. Radunsky, Illus.). San Francisco, CA: Chronicle.

Bernstrom, D. (2016). *One day in the eucalyptus, eucalyptus tree*. (B. Wenzel, Illus.). New York, NY: HarperCollins.

Berube, K. (2016). *Hannah and Sugar*. New York, NY: Abrams.

Biedrzycki, D. (2014). *Breaking news: Bear alert*. Watertown, MA: Charlesbridge.

Bishop, N. (2012). *Snakes*. New York, NY: Scholastic.

Bishop, P. (2017). *Bear's house of books*. (A. Edgson, Illus.). Wilton, CT: Tiger Tales.

Black, M. I. (2009). *Chicken cheeks*. (K. Hawkes, Illus.). New York, NY: Simon & Schuster.

Boelts, M. (2007). *Those shoes*. (N. Z. Jones, Illus.). Cambridge, MA: Candlewick.

Boelts, M. (2016). *A bike like Sergio's*. (N. Z. Jones, Illus.). Somerville, MA: Candlewick.

Booth, T. (2017). *Don't blink*. New York, NY: Feiwel and Friends.

Breen, S. (2013). *Pug & Doug*. New York, NY: Dial.

Brenner, T. (2017). *And then comes summer*. (J. Kim, Illus.). Somerville, MA: Candlewick.

Brett, J. (2015). *The turnip*. New York, NY: Putnam.

Brinckloe, J. (1985). *Fireflies*. New York, NY: Simon & Schuster.

Britt, P. (2017). *Why am I me?* (S. Qualls & S. Alko, Illus.). New York, NY: Scholastic.

Brosgol, V. (2016). *Leave me alone!* New York, NY: Roaring Brook.

Brown, M. (2011). *Marisol McDonald doesn't match/Marisol McDonald no combina*. (S. Palacios, Illus.). New York, NY: Lee & Low.

Brown, M. (2013). *Tito Puente, mambo king/Tito Puente, reydel mambo*. (R. López, Illus.). New York, NY: HarperCollins.

Brown, M. T. (1996). *Arthur writes a story*. New York, NY: Little, Brown.

Brown, M. W. (1954/1982). *I like bugs*. (G. B. Karas, Illus.). New York, NY: Random House.

Brown, P. (2009). *The curious garden*. New York, NY: Little, Brown.

Brown, P. (2011). *You will be my friend!* New York, NY: Little, Brown.

Bunting, E. (1991). *Fly away home*. (R. Himler, Illus.). New York, NY: Clarion.

Burleigh, R. (2015). *Trapped! A whale's rescue*. (W. Minor, Illus.). Watertown, MA: Charlesbridge.

Byrne, R. (2014). *This book just ate my dog!* New York, NY: Holt.

Byrne, R. (2015). *We're in the wrong book!* New York, NY: Holt.

Byrne, R. (2016). *This book is out of control!* New York, NY: Holt.

Byrne, R. (2017). *I want to go first!* New York, NY: Holt.

Campoy, F. I., & Howell, T. (2016). *Maybe something beautiful: How art transformed a neighborhood*. (R. López, Illus.). Boston, MA: Houghton Mifflin Harcourt.

Carle, E. (2014). *What's your favorite animal?* New York, NY: Holt.

Carle, E. (2017). *What's your favorite color?* New York, NY: Holt.

Carr, M. (2017). *Superbat*. New York, NY: Scholastic.

Casanova, M. (2003). *One-dog canoe*. (A. Hoyt, Illus.). New York, NY: Farrar Straus Giroux.

Casanova, M. (2013). *One-dog sleigh*. (A. Hoyt, Illus.). New York, NY: Farrar Straus Giroux.

Charlip, R. (1964). *Fortunately*. New York, NY: Simon & Schuster.

Cherry, L. (1990). *The great kapok tree: A tale of the Amazon Rain Forest*. Orlando, FL: Harcourt.

Chin, J. (2017). *Grand Canyon*. New York, NY: Roaring Brook.

Choi, Y. (2001). *The name jar*. New York, NY: Knopf.

Choldenko, G. (2017). *Dad and the dinosaur*. (D. Santat, Illus.). New York, NY: Penguin.

Chrustowski, R. (2015). *Bee dance*. New York, NY: Holt.

Chung, A. (2017). *OUT!* New York, NY: Holt.

Clement, R. (1997). *Grandpa's teeth*. New York, NY: HarperCollins.

Cline-Ransome, L. (2017). *Before she was Harriet*. (J. E. Ransome, Illus.). New York, NY: Holiday House.

Cocca-Leffler, M. (2015). *Janine*. Chicago, IL: Albert Whitman.

Collins, R. (2011). *Doodleday*. Chicago, IL: Albert Whitman.

Collins, R. (2015). *There's a bear on my chair*. Somerville, MA: Candlewick.

Cooper, F. (2017). *The ring bearer*. New York, NY: Philomel.

Cordell, M. (2012). *Hello! Hello!* New York, NY: Disney/Hyperion.

Cornwall, G. (2017). *Jabari jumps*. Somerville, MA: Candlewick.

Costa, M. S. (2016). *How to find a friend*. Boston, MA: Clarion.

Cottin, M. (2006/2008). *The black book of colors*. (R. Faría, Illus.). Toronto, Ontario: Publishers Group West.

Cox, L. (2014). *Elizabeth, Queen of the seas*. (B. Floca, Illus.). New York, NY: Schwartz & Wade.

Cummins, L. R. (2016). *A hungry lion or a dwindling assortment of animals*. New York, NY: Atheneum.

Czekaj, J. (2011). *Cat secrets*. New York, NY: HarperCollins.

Dale, P. (2015). *Dinosaur rocket!* Somerville, MA: Candlewick.

Danneberg, J. (2000). *First day jitters*. (J. Love, Illus.). Watertown, MA: Charlesbridge.

Davies, N. (2003). *Surprising sharks*. (J. Croft, Illus.). Somerville, MA: Candlewick.

Davies, N. (2011). *Dolphin baby!* (B. Granstrom, Illus.). Somerville, MA: Candlewick.

Davies, N. (2012). *Just ducks!* (S. Rubbino, Illus.). Somerville, MA: Candlewick.

Davies, N. (2013). *The promise*. (L. Carlin, Illus.). Somerville, MA: Candlewick.

Davies, N. (2017). *King of the sky*. (L. Carlin, Illus.). Somerville, MA: Candlewick.

Daywalt, D. (2017). *The legend of rock paper scissors*. (A. Rex, Illus.). New York, NY: HarperCollins.

de la Peña, M. (2015). *Last stop on Market Street*. (C. Robinson, Illus.). New York, NY: Putnam.

dePaola, T. (1975). *Strega Nona*. New York, NY: Simon & Schuster.

dePaola, T. (1988). *The legend of the Indian paintbrush*. New York, NY: Putnam.

Desmond, J. (2015). *The blue whale*. New York, NY: Enchanted Lion.

Desmond, J. (2016). *The polar bear*. New York, NY: Enchanted Lion.

Diesen, D. (2013). *Picture day perfection*. New York, NY: Abrams.

DiPucchio, K. (2014). *Dog days of school*. (B. Biggs, Illus.). New York, NY: Disney/Hyperion.

DiPucchio, K. (2017). *Antoinette*. (C. Robinson, Illus.). New York, NY: Simon & Schuster.

DiTerlizzi, A. (2014). *Some bugs*. (B. Wenzel, Illus.). New York, NY: Simon & Schuster.

DiTerlizzi, A. (2016). *Some pets*. (B. Wenzel, Illus.). New York, NY: Simon & Schuster.

Dominy, A. F., & Evans, N. (2017). *Cookiesaurus Rex*. (AG Ford, Illus.). New York, NY: Disney/Hyperion.

Donaldson, J. (1999). *The gruffalo*. (A. Scheffler, Illus.). New York, NY: Dial.

Dotlich, R. K. (2015). *One day, the end: Short, very short, shorter-than-ever stories*. (F. Koehler, Illus.). Honesdale, PA: Boyds Mills.

Dyckman, A. (2016). *Horrible bear!* (Z. OHora, Illus.). New York, NY: Little, Brown.

Ebbeler, J. (2015). *Click!* New York, NY: Holiday House.

Ellis, C. (2015). *Home*. Somerville, MA: Candlewick.

Emberley, R., Emberley, A., & Emberley, E. (2009). *There was an old monster!* New York, NY: Orchard.

Engle, M. (2015). *Drum dream girl: How one girl's courage changed music*. (R. López, Illus.). New York, NY: Houghton Mifflin Harcourt.

Engle, M. (2017). *All the way to Havana*. (M. Curato, Illus.). New York, NY: Holt.

Escoffier, M. (2014). *Take away the A*. (K. Di Giacomo, Illus.). New York, NY: Enchanted Lion.

Evans, S. W. (2012). *We march*. New York, NY: Roaring Brook.

Falwell, C. (1998). *The word wizard*. New York, NY: Houghton Mifflin.

Fan, T., & Fan, E. (2016). *The night gardener*. New York, NY: Simon & Schuster.

Farrar, S. (2012). *The year comes round: Haiku through the seasons*. (I. Plume, Illus.). Chicago, IL: Albert Whitman.

Federle, T. (2015). *Tommy can't stop*. (M. Fearing, Illus.). New York, NY: Disney/Hyperion.

Ferry, B. (2015). *Stick and stone*. (T. Lichtenheld, Illus.). New York, NY: Houghton Mifflin.

Ferry, B. (2017). *A small blue whale*. (L. Mundorff, Illus.). New York, NY: Knopf.

Fleming, C. (2002). *Muncha! Muncha! Muncha!* (G. B. Karas, Illus.). New York, NY: Atheneum.

Fleming, C. (2010). *Clever Jack takes the cake*. (G. B. Karas, Illus.). New York, NY: Schwartz & Wade.

Fleming, C. (2016). *Giant squid*. (E. Rohmann, Illus.). New York, NY: Roaring Brook.

Fleming, D. (1993). *In the small, small pond*. New York, NY: Holt.

Fleming, D. (1997). *Time to sleep*. New York, NY: Holt.

Fletcher, R. (1997). *Twilight comes twice*. (K. Kiesler, Illus.). New York, NY: Houghton Mifflin.

Floca, B. (2013). *Locomotive*. New York, NY: Simon & Schuster.

Fogliano, J. (2016). *When green becomes tomatoes: Poems for all seasons*. (J. Morstad, Illus.). New York, NY: Roaring Brook.

Foster, T., & Long, E. (2017). *Give me back my book!* San Francisco, CA: Chronicle.

Frazee, M. (2003). *Rollercoaster*. Orlando, FL: Harcourt.

French, V. (2004). *T. Rex*. (A. Bartlett, Illus.). Somerville, MA: Candlewick.

Friend, C. (2007). *The perfect nest*. (J. Manders, Illus.). Somerville, MA: Candlewick.

Frost, H. (2017). *Wake up!* (R. Lieder, Photographer). Somerville, MA: Candlewick.

Gehl, L. (2014). *One big pair of underwear*. (T. Lichtenheld, Illus.). New York, NY: Beach Lane.

Gianferrari, M. (2017). *Hello goodbye dog*. (P. Barton, Illus.). New York, NY: Roaring Brook.

Graegin, S. (2017). *Little fox in the forest*. New York, NY: Schwartz & Wade.

Graham, B. (2008). *How to heal a broken wing*. Boston, MA: Walker.

Gray, K. (2015). *Frog on a log?* (J. Field, Illus.). New York, NY: Scholastic.

Gray, K., & Gray, C. (2017). *Dog on a Frog?* (J. Field, Illus.). New York, NY: Scholastic.

Gray, R. (2010). *One big rain: Poems for every season*. (R. O'Rourke, Illus.). Watertown, MA: Charlesbridge.

Guiberson, B. Z. (2013). *The greatest dinosaur ever* (G. Spirin, Illus.). New York, NY: Holt.

Guiberson, B. Z. (2015). *The most amazing creature in the sea*. (G. Spirin, Illus.). New York, NY: Holt.

Guiberson, B. Z. (2016). *The deadliest creature in the world*. (G. Spirin, Illus.). New York, NY: Holt.

Hadfield, C., & Fillion, K. (2016). *The darkest dark*. (The Fan Brothers, Illus.). New York, NY: Little, Brown.

Hale, C. (2012). *Dreaming up: A celebration of building*. New York, NY: Lee & Low.

Halfmann, J. (2011). *Star of the sea: A day in the life of a starfish*. (J. Paley, Illus.). New York, NY: Holt.

Harkness, A. (2016). *Bug zoo*. New York, NY: Disney/Hyperion.

Harvey, J. W. (2017). *Maya Lin: Artist-architect of light and lines*. (D. Phumiruk, Illus.). New York, NY: Holt.

Hatke, B. (2014). *Julia's house of lost creatures*. New York, NY: Roaring Brook.

Helakoski, L. (2008). *Woolbur*. (L. Harper, Illus.). New York, NY: HarperCollins.

Heos, B. (2015). *I, Fly: The buzz about flies and how awesome they are*. (J. Plecas, Illus.). New York, NY: Holt.

Hester, D. L. (2005). *Grandma Lena's big ol' turnip*. (J. Urbanovic, Illus.). Chicago, IL: Albert Whitman.

Higgins, R. T. (2015). *Mother Bruce*. New York, NY: Disney/Hyperion.

Higgins, R. T. (2016). *Hotel Bruce*. New York, NY: Disney/Hyperion.

Higgins, R. T. (2017). *Be quiet!* New York, NY: Disney/Hyperion.

Higgins, R. T. (2017). *Bruce's big move*. New York, NY: Disney/Hyperion.

Higgins, R. T. (2018). *We don't eat our classmates*. New York, NY: Disney/Hyperion.

Hood, S. (2017). *Double take! A new look at opposites*. (J. Fleck, Illus.). Somerville, MA: Candlewick.

Hoppe, P. (2011). *The woods*. San Francisco, CA: Chronicle.

Huber, R. (2015). *The flight of the honey bee*. (B. Lovelock, Illus.). Somerville, MA: Candlewick.

Jackson, R. (2016). *In plain sight*. (J. Pinkney, Illus.). New York, NY: Roaring Brook.

Jarvis. (2016). *Alan's big, scary teeth*. Somerville, MA: Candlewick.

Jenkins, M. (2003). *Grandma elephant's in charge*. (I. Bates, Illus.). Somerville, MA: Candlewick.

Jenkins, S. (1997). *What do you do when something wants to eat you?* New York, NY: Houghton Mifflin.

Jenkins, S. (2014). *Eye to eye: How animals see the world*. New York, NY: Houghton Mifflin Harcourt.

Jenkins, S. (2016). *Animals by the numbers: A book of animal infographics*. Boston, MA: Houghton Mifflin Harcourt.

Jenkins, S. (2017). *Apex predators: The world's deadliest hunters, past and present*. New York, NY: Houghton Mifflin Harcourt.

Jenkins, S., & Page, R. (2003). *What do you do with a tail like this?* New York, NY: Houghton Mifflin.

Jenkins, S., & Page, R. (2014). *Creature features: 25 animals explain why they look the way they do*. Boston, MA: Houghton Mifflin.

Jocelyn, M., & Jocelyn, N. (2013). *Where do you look?* Plattsburgh, NY: Tundra.

John, J. (2016). *I love you already*. (B. Davis, Illus.). New York, NY: HarperCollins.

John, J. (2017). *The bad seed*. (P. Oswald, Illus.). New York, NY: HarperCollins.

Johnson, A. (2005). *A sweet smell of roses*. (E. Velazquez, Illus.). New York, NY: Simon & Schuster.

Johnston, T. (2016). *A small thing. . . but big*. (H. Hooper, Illus.). New York, NY: Roaring Brook.

Judge, L. (2014). *Born in the wild: Baby animals and their parents*. New York, NY: Roaring Brook.

Kaiser, L. (2017). *Rosa Parks*. (M. Antelo, Illus.). New York, NY: Frances Lincoln.

Kasza, K. (2003). *My lucky day*. New York, NY: Putnam.

Keating, J. (2016). *Pink is for blobfish: Discovering the world's perfectly pink animals*. (D. DeGrand, Illus.). New York, NY: Knopf.

Keating, J. (2017). *Shark lady: The true story of how Eugenie Clark became the ocean's most fearless scientist*. (M. Á. Miguéns, Illus.). Naperville, IL: Sourcebooks Jabberwocky.

Keely, C. (2017). *A Book of bridges: Here to there and me to you*. (C. Krampien, Illus.). Ann Arbor, MI: Sleeping Bear.

Keller, L. (2016). *We are growing*. New York, NY: Disney/Hyperion.

Kellogg, S. (1979). *Pinkerton, behave!* New York, NY: Dial.

Kellogg, S. (1991). *Jack and the beanstalk*. New York, NY: William Morrow.

Ko, S. (2015). *A dog wearing shoes*. New York, NY: Random House.

Kostecki-Shaw, J. S. (2015). *Luna and me: The true story of a girl who lived in a tree to save a forest*. New York, NY: Holt.

Kraegel, K. (2017). *Green pants*. Somerville, MA: Candlewick.

Krishnaswami, U. (2010). *Out of the way! Out of the way!* (U. Krishnaswamy, Illus.). Berkeley, CA: Groundwood.

Krosoczka, J. J. (2014). *Peanut Butter and Jellyfish*. New York, NY: Knopf.

Kuefler, J. (2017). *Rulers of the playground*. New York, NY: HarperCollins.

Lambert, J. (2016). *The great AAA-OOO!* Wilton, CT: Tiger Tales.

Laminack, L. (2004). *Saturdays and teacakes*. (C. Soentpiet, Illus.). Atlanta, GA: Peachtree.

Larsen, A. (2016). *A squiggly story*. (M. Lowery, Illus.). Tonawanda, NY: Kids Can.

Larsen, A. (2017). *Goodnight, hockey fans*. (J. Lee, Illus.). Toronto, Ontario: Kids Can.

Layton, N. (2016). *The tree*. Somerville, MA: Candlewick.

Lê, M. (2018). *Drawn together*. (D. Santat, Illus.). New York, NY: Disney/Hyperion.

Leannah, M. (2017). *Most people*. (J. E. Morris, Illus.). Thomaston, ME: Tilbury.

Lehrhaupt, A. (2016). *Chicken in space*. (S. Kober, Illus.). New York, NY: HarperCollins.

Lehrhaupt, A. (2017). *Chicken in school*. (S. Kober, Illus.). New York, NY: HarperCollins.

Levine, E. (2007). *Henry's freedom box*. (K. Nelson, Illus.). New York, NY: Scholastic.

Levis, C. (2017). *May I have a word?* (A. Rash, Illus.). New York, NY: Farrar, Straus and Giroux.

Lichtenheld, T. (2011). *Cloudette*. New York, NY: Holt.

Lichtenheld, T., & Fields-Meyer, E. (2011). *E-mergency*. San Francisco, CA: Chronicle.

Litwin, E. (2016). *Groovy Joe: Ice cream and dinosaurs*. (T. Lichtenheld, Illus.). New York, NY: Scholastic.

Litwin, E. (2017). *Groovy Joe: Dance party countdown*. (T. Lichtenheld, Illus.). New York, NY: Scholastic.

Lloyd, M. W. (2016). *Finding wild*. (A. Halpin, Illus.). New York, NY: Knopf.

Locker, T. (1997). *Water dance*. San Diego, CA: Harcourt.

Loggins, K. (2016). *Footloose*. (T. Bowers, Illus.). Lake Forest, CA: MoonDance.

London, J. (2015). *Hippos are HUGE!* (M. Trueman, Illus.). Somerville, MA: Candlewick.

Long, E. (2016). *Lion and Tiger and Bear: Tag! You're it!* New York, NY: Abrams.

Loy, J. (2015). *Weird and wild animal facts*. New York, NY: Holt.

Ludwig, T. (2013). *The invisible boy*. (P. Barton, Illus.). New York, NY: Knopf.

Luyken, C. (2017). *The book of mistakes*. New York, NY: Dial.

Lyon, G. E. (2011). *All the water in the world*. (K. Tillotson, Illus.). New York, NY: Simon & Schuster.

Mack, J. (2012). *Good news bad news*. San Francisco, CA: Chronicle.

Mack, J. (2013). *AH HA!* San Francisco, CA: Chronicle.

Mack, J. (2015). *Look!* New York, NY: Philomel.

MacLachlan, P. (2017). *Someone like me*. (C. Sheban, Illus.). New York, NY: Roaring Brook.

Magliaro, E. (2016). *Things to do*. (C. Chien, Illus.). San Francisco, CA: Chronicle.

Magruder, N. (2016). *How to find a fox*. New York, NY: Feiwel and Friends.

Manley, C. (2017). *Shawn loves sharks*. (T. Subisak, Illus.). New York, NY: Roaring Brook.

Mantchev, L. (2015). *Strictly no elephants*. (T. Yoo, Illus.). New York, NY: Simon & Schuster.

Martin, D. (2016). *Shh! Bears sleeping*. (S. Johnson & L. Fancher, Illus.). New York, NY: Penguin.

McDermott, G. (1974). *Arrow to the sun: A Pueblo Indian tale*. New York, NY: Penguin.

McDonnell, P. (2011.) *Me. . . Jane*. New York, NY: Little, Brown.

McDonnell, P. (2014). *A perfectly messed-up story*. New York, NY: Little, Brown.

McDonnell, P. (2016). *Tek: The modern cave boy*. New York, NY: Little, Brown.

McDonnell, P. (2017). *The little red cat who ran away and learned his ABC's (the hard way)*. New York, NY: Little, Brown.

McGhee, H. M. (2017). *Come with me*. (P. Lemaître, Illus). New York, NY: Putnam.

McGinty, A. B. (2013). *Gandhi: A march to the sea*. (T. Gonzalez, Illus.). Las Vegas, NV: Amazon.

Medina, M. (2015). *Mango, Abuela, and me*. (A. Dominguez, Illus.). Somerville, MA: Candlewick.

Meltzer, B. (2014). *I am Abraham Lincoln*. (C. Eliopoulos, Illus.). New York, NY: Dial.

Meltzer, B. (2014). *I am Amelia Earhart*. (C. Eliopoulos, Illus.). New York, NY: Dial.

Meltzer, B. (2016). *I am George Washington*. (C. Eliopoulos, Illus.). New York, NY: Dial.

Meltzer, B. (2016). *I am Jane Goodall*. (C. Eliopoulos, Illus.). New York, NY: Dial.

Messier, M. (2016). *The branch*. (P. Pratt, Illus.). Tonawanda, NY: Kids Can.

Messner, K. (2011). *Over and under the snow*. (C. S. Neal, Illus.). San Francisco, CA: Chronicle.

Messner, K. (2015). *How to read a story*. (M. Siegel, Illus.) San Francisco, CA: Chronicle.

Messner, K. (2015). *Tree of wonder: The many marvelous lives of a rainforest tree*. (S. Mulazzani, Illus.). San Francisco, CA: Chronicle.

Messner, K. (2015). *Up in the garden and down in the dirt* (C. S. Neal, Illus.). San Francisco, CA: Chronicle.

Messner, K. (2017). *Over and under the pond*. (C. S. Neal, Illus.). San Francisco, CA: Chronicle.

Miller, P. Z. (2018). *Be kind*. (J. Hill, Illus.). New York: Roaring Brook.

Morris, R. T. (2014). *This is the moose*. (T. Lichtenheld, Illus.). New York, NY: Little, Brown.

Murray, C. (2017). *Cricket in the thicket: Poems about bugs*. (M. Sweet, Illus.). New York, NY: Holt.

Murray, D. (2016). *City shapes*. (B. Collier, Illus.). New York, NY: Little, Brown.

Murray, D. (2017). *Doris the bookasaurus*. (Y. Chen, Illus.). New York, NY: Imprint.

Naberhaus, S. (2017). *Blue sky white stars*. (K. Nelson, Illus.). New York, NY: Dial.

Naylor, P. R. (1991). *King of the playground*. (N. L. Malone, Illus.). New York, NY: Simon & Schuster.

Nelson, K. (2015). *If you plant a seed*. New York, NY: HarperCollins.

Novak, B. J. (2014). *The book with no pictures*. New York, NY: Dial.

O'Malley, K. (2005). *Once upon a cool motorcycle dude*. (K. O'Malley, C. Heyer, & S. Goto, Illus.). New York, NY: Walker.

O'Malley, K. (2016). *The perfect dog*. New York, NY: Random House.

O'Neill, A. (2002). *The recess queen*. (L. Huliska-Beith, Illus.). New York, NY: Scholastic.

Orloff, K. K. (2004). *I wanna iguana*. (D. Catrow, Illus.). New York, NY: Putnam.

Otoshi, K. (2008). *One*. San Rafael, CA: KO Kids Books.

Pak, K. (2016). *Goodbye summer, hello autumn*. New York, NY: Holt.

Pak, K. (2017). *Goodbye autumn, hello winter*. New York, NY: Holt.

Palacio, R. J. (2012). *Wonder*. New York, NY: Knopf.

Palacio, R. J. (2017). *We're all wonders*. New York, NY: Knopf.

Palatini, M. (2000). *Bedhead*. (J. E. Davis, Illus.). New York, NY: Simon & Schuster.

Palatini, M. (2003). *The perfect pet*. (B. Whatley, Illus.). New York, NY: HarperCollins.

Parr, T. (2016). *Be who you are*. New York, NY: Little, Brown.

Parsley, E. (2015). *If you ever want to bring an alligator to school, don't!* New York, NY: Little, Brown.

Parsley, E. (2016). *If you ever want to bring a piano to the beach, don't!* New York, NY: Little, Brown.

Parsley, E. (2017). *If you ever want to bring a circus to the library, don't!* New York, NY: Little, Brown.

Paul, M. (2015). *One plastic bag: Isatou Ceesay and the recycling women of the Gambia*. (E. Zunon, Illus.). Minneapolis, MN: Millbrook.

Paul, M. (2015). *Water is water*. (J. Chin, Illus.). New York, NY: Roaring Brook.

Pett, M. (2016). *This is my book!* New York, NY: Knopf.

Petty, D. (2015). *I don't want to be a frog*. (M. Boldt, Illus.). New York, NY: Random House.

Petty, D. (2017). *Claymates*. (L. Eldridge, Illus.). New York, NY: Little, Brown.

Pinkney, J. (2006). *The little red hen*. New York, NY: Dial.

Pinkney, J. (2009). *The lion and the mouse*. New York, NY: Little, Brown.

Pinkney, J. (2017). *The three billy goats gruff*.

Plourde, L. (2016). *Bella's fall coat*. (S. Gal, Illus.). New York, NY: Disney/Hyperion.

Portis, A. (2017). *Now* ... Br...

Posada, M. (2014). *Who was here? Discovering wild animal tracks*. Minneapolis, MN: Lerner.

Prelutsky, J. (2006). *Behold the bold umbrellaphant and other poems*. (C. Berger, Illus.). New York, NY: Greenwillow.

Raczka, B. (2010). *Guyku: A year of haiku for boys*. (P. Reynolds, Illus.). New York, NY: Houghton Mifflin.

Rankin, L. (2007). *Ruthie and the (not so) teeny tiny lie*. New York, NY: Bloomsbury.

Raschka, C. (2013). *Everyone can learn to ride a bicycle*. New York, NY: Schwartz & Wade.

Rees, D. (2017). *Tyrannosaurus Rex vs. Edna the very first chicken*. (J. Henry, Illus.). New York, NY: Holt.

Reid, B. (2011). *Picture a tree*. Chicago, IL: Albert Whitman.

Rex, A. (2016). *School's first day of school*. (C. Robinson, Illus.). New York, NY: Roaring Brook.

Reynolds, A. (2012). *Creepy carrots*. (P. Brown, Illus.). New York, NY: Simon & Schuster.

Reynolds, A. (2015). *Nerdy Birdy*. (M. Davies, Illus.). New York, NY: Roaring Brook.

Reynolds, A. (2017). *Creepy pair of underwear!* (P. Brown, Illus.). New York, NY: Simon &Schuster.

Reynolds, P. (2003). *The dot*. Somerville, MA: Candlewick.

Reynolds, P. (2004). *Ish*. Somerville, MA: Candlewick.

Reynolds, P. (2017). *Happy dreamer*. New York, NY: Scholastic.

Reynolds, P., & Reynolds, P. (2014). *Going places*. New York, NY: Atheneum.

Rinker, S. D. (2017). *Mighty, mighty construction site*. (T. Lichtenheld, Illus.). San Francisco, CA: Chronicle.

Robbins, D. (2017). *Margaret and the moon: How Margaret Hamilton saved the first lunar landing*. (L. Knisley, Illus.). New York, NY: Knopf.

Robbins, J. (2009). *Two of a kind*. (M. Phelan, Illus.). New York, NY: Atheneum.

Roberts, J. (2014). *The smallest girl in the smallest grade*. (C. Robinson, Illus.). New York, NY: Putnam.

Robinson, M. (2013). *How to wash a woolly mammoth*. (K. Hindley, Illus.). New York, NY: Holt.

Robinson, M. (2014). *There's a lion in my cornflakes*. (J. Field, Illus.). New York, NY: Bl...

..., .. (2014). *Blizzard*. New York, NY: Disney/Hyperion.

Rodman, M. A. (2005). *My best friend*. (E. B. Lewis, Illus.). New York, NY: Penguin.

Rosenberg, L. (2015). *What James said*. (M. Myers, Illus.). New York, NY: Roaring Brook.

Rosenstock, B. (2014). *Ben Franklin's big splash: The mostly true story of his first invention*. (S.D. Schindler, Illus.). Honesdale, PA: Highlights.

Rosenthal, A. K. (2009). *Duck! Rabbit!* (T. Lichtenheld, Illus.). San Francisco, CA: Chronicle.

Rosenthal, A. K. (2009). *Yes day!* (T. Lichtenheld, Illus.). New York, NY: HarperCollins.

Rosenthal, A. K. (2013). *Exclamation mark*. (T. Lichtenheld, Illus.). New York, NY: Scholastic.

Rosenthal, A. K. (2015). *Friendshape*. (T. Lichtenheld, Illus.). New York, NY: Scholastic.

Roy, K. (2014). *Neighborhood sharks: Hunting with the Great Whites of California's Farallon Islands*. New York, NY: Roaring Brook.

Rubin, A. (2015). *Robo-sauce*. (D. Salmieri, Illus.). New York, NY: Dial.

Ryan, P. M. (2001). *Hello ocean*. (M. Astrella, Illus.). Watertown, MA: Charlesbridge.

Rylant, C. (2001). *Poppleton in winter*. (M. Teague, Illus.). New York, NY: Scholastic.

Rylant, C. (2017). *Life*. (B. Wenzel, Illus.). New York, NY: Simon & Schuster.

Salas, L. P. (2014). *Water can be*. (V. Dabija, Illus.). Minneapolis, MN: Lerner.

Salas, L. P. (2017). *If you were the moon*. (J. Kim, Illus.). Minneapolis, MN: Lerner.

Sanders, R. (2017). *Rodzilla*. (D. Santat, Illus.). New York, NY: Simon & Schuster.

Sanna, F. (2016). *The journey*. London, England: Flying Eye.

Santat, D. (2016). *Are we there yet?* New York, NY: Little, Brown.

Santat, D. (2017). *After the fall: How Humpty Dumpty got back up again.* New York, NY: Roaring Brook.

Sarah, L. (2014). *Big friends.* (B. Davis, Illus.). New York, NY: Holt.

Sayre, A. P. (2015). *Woodpecker wham!* (S. Jenkins, Illus.). New York, NY: Holt.

Sayre, A. P. (2016). *Squirrels leap, squirrels sleep.* (S. Jenkins, Illus.). New York, NY: Holt.

Schaefer, L. M., & Schaefer, A. (2016). *Because of an acorn.* (F. Preston-Gannon, Illus.). San Francisco, CA: Chronicle.

Seeger, L. V. (2007). *First the egg.* New York, NY: Roaring Brook.

Seeger, L. V. (2015). *I used to be afraid.* New York, NY: Roaring Brook.

Shaffer, J. J. (2018). *A chip off the old block.* (D. Miyares, Illus.). New York, NY: Penguin.

Shea, B. (2016). *The happiest book ever.* New York, NY: Disney/Hyperion.

Sheneman, D. (2017). *Nope! A tale of first flight.* New York, NY: Viking.

Silvestro, A. (2017). *Bunny's book club.* (T. Mai-Wyss, Illus.). New York, NY: Doubleday.

Sirotich, E. (2017). *Found dogs.* New York, NY: Dial.

Sis, P. (2017). *Robinson.* New York, NY: Scholastic.

Slade, S. (2010). *Climbing Lincoln's steps: The African American journey.* (C. Bootman, Illus.). Chicago, IL: Albert Whitman.

Smith, L. (2011). *Grandpa Green.* New York, NY: Roaring Brook.

Smith, L. (2017). *A perfect day.* New York, NY: Roaring Brook.

Spinelli, E. (2008). *The best story.* (A. Wilsdorf, Illus.). New York, NY: Dial.

Spires, A. (2014). *The most magnificent thing.* Tonawanda, NY: Kids Can.

Spires, A. (2017). *The thing Lou couldn't do.* Toronto, ON: Kids Can.

Staniszewski, A. (2017). *Dogosaurus Rex.* (K. Hawkes, Illus.). New York, NY: Holt.

Stanton, B., & Stanton, M. (2015). *This is a ball: Books that drive kids crazy.* New York, NY: Little, Brown.

Starr, R. (2014). *Octopus's garden.* (B. Cort, Illus.). New York, NY: Simon & Schuster.

Stead, P. C. (2012). *Bear has a story to tell.* (E. E. Stead, Illus.). New York, NY: Roaring Brook.

Stead, P. C. (2016). *Samson in the snow.* New York, NY: Roaring Brook.

Sterer, G. (2017). *Skyfishing.* (P. Bernatene, Illus.). New York, NY: Abrams.

Stevens, J. (1995). *Tops and bottoms.* Orlando, FL: Harcourt.

Stewart, M. (2014). *Feathers: Not just for flying.* (S. S. Brannen, Illus.). Watertown, MA: Charlesbridge.

Stone, T. L. (2013). *Who says women can't be doctors? The story of Elizabeth Blackwell.* New York, NY: Holt.

Sullivan, M. (2013). *Ball.* Boston, MA: Houghton Mifflin.

Swanson, M. (2017). *Everywhere, wonder.* (R. Behr, Illus.). New York, NY: Imprint.

Taback, S. (1997). *There was an old lady who swallowed a fly.* New York, NY: Penguin.

Tekiela, S. (2012). *Whose butt?* Cambridge, MN: Adventure.

Thomas, P. (2008). *Red sled.* (C. L. Demarest, Illus.) Honesdale, PA: Boyds Mills.

Tibo, G. (2016). *All the world a poem.* (M. Gauthier, Illus.). Ontario, CA: Pajama.

Tolstoy, A. (1998). *The gigantic turnip.* (N. Sharkey, Illus.). Cambridge, MA: Barefoot.

Torrey, R. (2015). *Ally-saurus and the first day of school.* New York, NY: Sterling.

Tullet, H. (2011). *Press here.* San Francisco, CA: Chronicle.

Twohy, M. (2016). *Oops pounce quick run! An alphabet caper.* New York, NY: HarperCollins.

Van Dusen, C. (2017). *Hattie and Hudson.* Somerville, MA: Candlewick.

Van Slyke, R. (2017). *Lexie the word wrangler.* (J. Hartland, Illus.). New York, NY: Penguin.

Wenzel, B. (2016). *They all saw a cat.* San Francisco, CA: Chronicle.

Wenzel, B. (2018). *Hello hello.* San Francisco, CA: Chronicle.

Whitcomb, M. E. (1998). *Odd Velvet* (T. C. King, Illus.). San Francisco, CA: Chronicle.

Willems, M. (2007). *My friend is sad.* New York, NY: Disney/Hyperion.

Willems, M. (2009). *Naked Mole Rat gets dressed.* New York: Disney/Hyperion.

Willems, M. (2010). *Can I play too?* New York, NY: Disney/Hyperion.

Willems, M. (2010). *We are in a book!* New York, NY: Disney/Hyperion.

Willems, M. (2011). *Should I share my ice cream?* New York, NY: Disney/Hyperion.

Willems, M. (2012). *Happy pig day!* New York, NY: Disney/Hyperion.

Willems, M. (2012). *Listen to my trumpet.* New York, NY: Disney/Hyperion.

Willems, M. (2013). *That is not a good idea!* New York, NY: HarperCollins.

Willems, M. (2015). *I will take a nap!* New York, NY: Disney/Hyperion.

Willems, M. (2016). *Nanette's baguette.* New York, NY: Disney/Hyperion.

Williams, L. (2017). *If sharks disappeared.* New York, NY: Roaring Brook.

Williams, L. E. (2010). *The can man.* (C. Orback, Illus.). New York, NY: Lee and Low.

Wilson, K. (2011). *Bear's loose tooth.* (J. Chapman, Illus.). New York, NY: Margaret K. McElderry.

Winter, J. (2010). *Biblioburro: A true story from Columbia.* New York, NY: Beach Lane/Simon & Schuster.

Winter, J. (2011). *The watcher: Jane Goodall's life with the chimps.* New York, NY: Schwartz & Wade.

Winter, J. (2017). *The world is not a rectangle: A portrait of architect Zaha Hadid.* New York, NY: Beach Lane.

Wyeth, S. D. (1998). *Something beautiful.* (C. K. Soentpiet, Illus.). New York, NY: Random House.

Wood, A. (1984). *The napping house.* (D. Wood, Illus.). Orlando, FL: Harcourt.

Woodson, J. (2012). *Each kindness.* (E. B. Lewis, Illus.). New York, NY: Penguin.

Woollard, E. (2015). *The giant of jum.* (B. Davis, Illus.). New York, NY: Holt.

Yaccarino, D. (2013). *Doug unplugged.* New York, NY: Knopf.

Yamada, K. (2013). *What do you do with an idea?* (M. Besom, Illus.). Seattle, WA: Compendium.

Yamada, K. (2016). *What do you do with a problem?* (M. Besom, Illus.). Seattle, WA: Compendium.

Yeh, K. (2016). *The friend ship.* (C. Groenink, Illus.). New York, NY: Disney/Hyperion.

Yolen, J. (1987). *Owl moon.* (J. Schoenherr, Illus.). New York, NY: Philomel.

Yolen, J. (2017). *How do dinosaurs choose their pets?* (M. Teague, Illus.). New York, NY: Scholastic.

Yolen, J. (2017). *Thunder underground.* (J. Masse, Illus.). Honesdale, PA: WordSong.

Yoon, S. (2016). *Be a friend.* New York, NY: Bloomsbury.

Young, E. (1992). *Seven blind mice.* New York, NY: Penguin.

Yousafzai, M. (2017). *Malala's magic pencil.* (Kerascoët, Illus.). New York, NY: Little, Brown.

Yum, H. (2016). *Puddle.* New York, NY: Farrar Straus Giroux.

Zolotow, C. (2017). *The seashore book.* (W. Minor, Illus.). Watertown, MA: Charlesbridge.

Index

A SAGE Publishing Company

CORWIN HAS ONE MISSION: to enhance education through intentional professional learning.

We build long-term relationships with our authors, educators, clients, and associations who partner with us to develop and continuously improve the best evidence-based practices that establish and support lifelong learning.

Because...

ALL TEACHERS ARE LEADERS

At Corwin Literacy we have put together a collection of just-in-time, classroom-tested, practical resources from trusted experts that allow you to quickly find the information you need when you need it.

PAMELA KOUTRAKOS

Word Study That Sticks and its resourceful companion deliver challenging, discovery-based word learning routines and planning frameworks you can implement across subject areas.

DOUGLAS FISHER, NANCY FREY, OLIVIA AMADOR, JOSEPH ASSOF

With cross-curricular examples, planning templates, professional learning questions, and a PLC guide, this is the most practical planner for designing and delivering highly effective instruction.

DOUGLAS FISHER, NANCY FREY, AND JOHN HATTIE

Ensure students demonstrate more than a year's worth of learning during a school year by implementing the right literacy practice at the right moment.

DOUGLAS FISHER, NANCY FREY, AND JOHN HATTIE

High-impact strategies to use for all you teach—all in one place. Deliver sustained, comprehensive literacy experiences to K-5 learners each day.